N
c2

THE WORLD'S
GREATEST ESCAPES

THE WORLD'S
GREATEST ESCAPES

by

IAN FELLOWES-GORDON

TAPLINGER PUBLISHING COMPANY
New York

First published in the United States, 1967

TAPLINGER PUBLISHING CO., INC.
29 East 10th Street
New York, New York, 10003

Library of Congress Catalogue Card Number: 67-19284

Printed in Great Britain

CONTENTS

CONTENTS

Illustrations

Facing page

Acknowledgements

The author would like to express his indebtedness to the following publishers for permission to quote extracts from books published by them as follows:

Secker and Warburg Ltd., *They Fought Alone* by John Keats and *Mao-Tse Tung, Emperor of the Blue Ants* by George Paloczi-Horvarth; Collins Ltd. and Mr. Eric Williams, *The Wooden Horse* by Eric Williams; The Bodley Head, *The Road to En-dor* by E. H. Jones.

INTRODUCTION

To Escape, the dictionary tells us, is to Get Free. A word with overtones, deriving from the Latin for "cloak". Furtive, hidden, in disguise.

And probably, of all the kinds of adventure which can befall men and women, the one which most catches at the imagination, sticks in the memory, is the escape. The escape from death, from disaster, from fate itself.

It is a fascination with escape which makes us watch, open-mouthed, as the trapeze artist does his stunt a hundred feet above our heads. The skill, the timing, is lost on us, we watch to see whether he escapes from the broken neck which seems so inevitable. We hold our breath.

One of the most notable men of his day was Houdini, who devoted a whole life to escaping—from ropes, chains, handcuffs. He was buried alive, trussed like a chicken and flung into ponds, locked into cells. Somehow he managed to escape.

But these pages are of real escapes—unstaged, earnest, desperate ones—which I believe to be the greatest on record. Here and there a personal preference may shine through, with the omission of one, the inclusion of another, less well-known—but the assessing of escapes seems to me a less subjective business than making a list, say, of one's heroes.

An escape, I feel, should be measured against two sorts of yardstick. First: what is its significance; what happened as a result? Second: how remarkable was it at the time?

By this measurement we exclude a few of the old favourites. Prisoner-of-war escapes are often exciting—but few of them made a difference to the outcome of the battle. There are a number of POW escapes in these pages, escapes whose excitement outweighs their lack of significance. The disappearance of three young Englishmen from Stalag-Luft III made little difference to the outcome of the Second World War, but the extraordinary method of their exit makes the story a "must" for any collection of escapes.

A great escape by both yardsticks, and probably my own favourite, is that of submariners Donald Cameron and Godfrey Place, against fantastic odds, after crippling the German *Tirpitz* in her almost impregnable Norwegian fiord. Mussolini's escape from captivity in Italy is one of the war's strangest adventures—yet Mussolini's adventure was historically almost meaningless—a postponement of fate. But the story is here, just because it is extraordinary. Napoleon's—his escape from Elba—is included even though the details of his passage from the island to the coast of France are less than gripping—because Napoleon's escape set half the world on fire.

Douglas Macarthur's, from the Philippines, was as significant in its way as Napoleon's—but Macarthur made an even less troubled exit by sea, with luggage, family and Filipino *amah*. There is another American escape from the Japanese which is exciting as well as significant, and Macarthur has had to make room for it—for gallant "General" Fertig and his mobile—very mobile—HQ.

In doing research for this book, I came up against an interesting fact: there are far more escapes and attempted escapes by the British, particularly British prisoners-of-war, than by any other nationality.

Why should the British have this greater urge to get home, back to their damp little island; a greater urge than, say, the Americans?

I think a part of the reason lies in that love of adventure which has characterized the British, from Elizabethan times, through the Empire-building years, to the present day.

Perhaps the other part is less flattering.

We British are conscious of what our friends think of us—more so, perhaps, than any other people in the world. The Scots sociologist, Professor Tom Patterson, once noted that a working man in Britain cares far less about his wages than about the good opinion of his mates.

And whereas American, German or French prisoners-of-war might reasonably decide their chances of getting home were slender, that a return home would make no difference to the war, that they were in fact mortgaging a chance of getting there in one piece by attempting to escape—the British approach to the matter is different.

Shortly after the war, I had an opportunity to consider this at first hand. As an army officer attached to the R.A.F., I accidentally flew an aeroplane over the border between West and East Germany in a storm, and ignominiously crash-landed. The Russians who arrested me were firm but courteous; I was well treated, and after I had shown them that stupidity and not espionage had been my crime they were even friendly, while politely refusing, "till orders received", to let me go. (So courteous were they that I even wrote gleaming, field-booted little Colonel Komyekov a bread-and-butter letter when I got back on my side of the border: it seemed unthinkable not to.)

But by the end of the first week I had worked out the basis of an involved plan of escape, via Berlin. Had I put it into effect I would probably have ended up with a bullet in the back of my head.

Why did I consider escape? Did I feel the Army Needed Me?

Not on your life. I made my plan because, as the days crept by, I wondered, with increasing unease, just what the rest of my unit would think of me, staying here. *Dared* I stay here indefinitely, a well-fed prisoner of the Russians? What would the unit, the chaps in the mess and the rest of it, think when I got back?

(It never occurred to me that I might *never* get back, that the Russians might keep me forever, or chop off my head—and I cannot claim that as a reason for planning to leave.)

I was released a day later. And when I sat down to think of my "escape plan", I realized that, far from its being daring or courageous, it was an expedient to which I was driven by sheer moral cowardice.

And that sobering fact has been just another of the points for the author to bear in mind in assessing them—"The World's Greatest Escapes".

IAN FELLOWES-GORDON

July, 1966

Chapter 1

MOSES AND THE ISRAELITES
ESCAPE FROM EGYPT

THE Old Testament abounds in tales of adventure, even if some of them are more remarkable for colour than accuracy. One of the best authenticated stories is that of the Israelites' escape from their long captivity in Egypt.

Both in the colourful Exodus version and in what historians believe to have been the facts of the case, the escape must rank as one of the world's greatest. It was a mass escape on a scale seldom attempted, before or since: it was made necessary by an almost unbelievable repression; and it was furthered by a long and fascinating series of what we may call, if we wish, Acts of God.

It was in the city of Ur in Chaldea, on the Persian Gulf, that the Patriarch Abraham decided to take his family with him to a more fertile land. He had, the Book of Genesis tells us, received a call from God—the One True God his people believed in. The Lord had said unto Abraham: "Get thee out of thy country, and from thy kindred, and from thy father's house, unto a land that I will show thee: and I will make of thee a great nation, and I will bless thee and make thy name great; and thou shalt be a blessing: and I will bless them that bless thee, and curse him that curseth thee; and in thee shall all families of the earth be blessed. So Abraham departed as the Lord had spoken unto him."

We can place this historical fact at somewhere between 2000 and 1700 B.C.

The land Abraham and his descendants moved to was called Canaan or "The Low Lands"—the coastline of Palestine. It was everything they had been led to believe: the land was fertile, the rainfall regular and adequate; crops and beasts flourished, as did the descendants of Abraham, who grew mightily in numbers.

It was later, in the time of Jacob, that the name Israel or "God Fighteth" came into being. The Lord had spoken to Jacob, much as he had spoken with Jacob's ancestor Abraham, had taken him aside, given him certain advice. The advice had concluded: "Thy name shall be called no more Jacob, but Israel: for as a prince hast thou power with God and with men and hast prevailed."

And so the people of Jacob began to style themselves the Children of Israel.

Disaster struck: the rainfall in Canaan, which had been so regular, generous and gentle, now failed altogether; the crops and flocks withered and died. Jacob received further advice from his Lord, and ordered a new migration, to Egypt. The Children of Israel, a far larger band than had entered Canaan in the time of Abraham, departed, moved on to Egypt. There were practical reasons for choosing Egypt: the fertility of Palestine depended entirely on rainfall, whereas the Egyptian water supply derived from the River Nile and could be relied on, year after year, to produce fine crops of corn. Indeed, the Children of Israel—or Israelites, as we can now call them—had already sent men into Egypt to buy corn and bring it back.

And so they travelled into this new land.

At first they were welcomed by the people, and the Pharaoh who ruled them. Pharaoh addressed Joseph, Jacob's son, who had been living in Egypt for a number of years. "Thy father and

14

thy brethren are come unto thee: The land of Egypt is before thee—in the best of the land make thy father and brethren to dwell."

The Israelites settled eagerly into this new land, yet with an intention at the back of their minds, much like that of so many nineteenth-century immigrants into Australia and America, to return, some day, to "home".

And, rather before they had intended, this vague intent became real and urgent. The Pharaoh who had welcomed them into his land died, and his successor, Rameses II, began to feel quite differently about having alien tribes multiplying within his borders. "The Children of Israel were fruitful, and increased abundantly and multiplied and waxed exceeding mighty; and the land was filled with them."

And the new Pharaoh viewed this with alarm. He said to his people: "Behold, the people of the Children of Israel are more and mightier than we: Come on, let us deal wisely with them; lest they multiply, and it come to pass, that when there falleth out any war, they join also unto our enemies and fight against us."

So the Israelites were put to hard labour. No longer were they allowed to graze flocks, grow corn: from now on, they would be servants of the Egyptian people. They were set to work building new cities, like Pithom and Raamses, and temples all over Egypt: and if they faltered or dropped in the course of the work they were whipped by overseers until they either got on with the work or died.

But still they multiplied. The Egyptians grew steadily more alarmed, took greater and greater measures of repression: every menial task throughout the kingdom was allotted the Israelites, to keep them in subjection, so they should not unite as a people and rise against their masters. To stop them multiplying, orders were given that midwives would kill every male child born to an Israelite mother.

One woman who had a boy child at this time was Jochebed. She hid him for three months, but eventually, the risk of discovery being too great, she had to part with him. She placed him carefully in a little basket of bulrushes and let him drift away among the reed beds along the bank of the Nile, hoping some kind soul might discover and take pity on him.

Her wish was granted: the little ark was spotted by one of Pharaoh's daughters who was washing at the water's edge when it came by. She scooped the child out of it, saw instantly that it was of Hebrew birth, but gathered it gently into her arms and took it away.

The little boy was lodged with a wet nurse, who, through the good offices of a royal maidservant, was in fact his own mother.

The child came back, after weaning, to Pharaoh's daughter, who adopted him as her own and called him Moses, "because I drew him out of the water". He grew to manhood and then, because of royal favour, not having to do manual labour like other Hebrews, he set out one day to see how they were faring. What he saw distressed him greatly: he watched in sorrow as men and women struggled to make bricks under the lash of the overseer.

Then, in the distance, he saw an Egyptian brutally beating an Israelite.

Quickly he made his way up to the two men, glanced rapidly round to see no one else had noticed, and struck the Egyptian, who fell down dead.

But he had been seen, and a few days later he was forced to leave the country. He took himself far away, to the land of Midian, north of the Gulf of Akaba, where he settled down and soon married a Midian chief's daughter, Zipporah. He began to lead the life of a shepherd.

But, all the while, he thought and grieved over the fate of his own oppressed people in Egypt, wondering how he could get back and help them.

One day, as he was tending his sheep, he had a vision. A large bush burnt with a bright gold flame: but the burning continued and the bush was not consumed; it remained as large, as green, as ever.

And from the centre of this strange, non-burning flame there appeared the angel of the Lord. Through this angel, God himself delivered a message to Moses: "I have surely seen the affliction of my people which are in Egypt, and have heard their cry by reason of their taskmasters: for I know their sorrows. And I am come down to deliver them out of that land unto a good land, unto a land flowing with milk and honey; unto the place of the Canaanites, and the Hittites, and the Amorites, and the Perrizites, and the Hivites, and the Jebusites.

"Now therefore, behold, the cry of the children of Israel is come unto me: and I have also seen the oppression wherewith the Egyptians oppress them.

"Come now therefore, and I will send thee unto Pharaoh, that thou mayest bring forth my people, the Children of Israel, out of Egypt."

Moses obeyed and went straightway to Egypt. He crossed the border quite openly, for years had passed and those who had wanted to kill him were now dead themselves. He went to the elders of Israel with a new message from the Lord, ordering them out into the wilderness—three days' march—to perform a sacrifice. To do this, they had to ask Pharaoh's permission.

This he firmly refused to give. The Israelites were a subject people, they had work to do, and no time could be spared, even for their elders. "Who is the Lord, that I should obey his voice to let Israel go? I know not the Lord, neither will I let Israel go.

"And they said, the God of the Hebrews hath met with us: let us go, we pray thee, three days' journey into the desert, and sacrifice unto the Lord our God, lest he fall upon us with pestilence, or with the sword."

But still Pharaoh refused, and added for good measure: "Ye are idle, ye are idle: therefore ye say, Let us go and do sacrifice to the Lord. Go therefore now, and work: for there shall no straw be given you, yet shall ye deliver the tale of bricks." His anger—which he was soon to regret—had made him order them to make a full daily quota of bricks, but without straw being provided. They would have to go and fossick in the fields for stubble and grass, anything to bind the clay.

And if they dropped by as much as one brick from their daily quota, they would be severely punished.

Hardly surprising, therefore, that the elders, when they left this unpleasant meeting, were extremely angry with Moses. He was a meddlesome fool; he had succeeded in making their lives a thousand times worse.

And hardly surprising that Moses should be abashed and should demand an explanation of his Lord. God, the Old Testament tells us, sent him back to Pharaoh to impress the Egyptian ruler with sorcery. The stout stick he carried could be made at will into a serpent, and changed back when the trick was over. As a piece of conjuring this was fine: the stick became a serpent. But Pharaoh, not to be outdone, produced his own sorcerers, who proceeded to do exactly the same trick with their own cudgels.

And the performance ended quite disastrously for Moses, when his serpent gobbled up the others and crawled to its master, swollen and content, to be translated into a walking-stick.

This strange and rather ridiculous episode has been explained by modern scholars as a variant of the well-known snake-charmer's trick, in which a cobra is made rigid, like a stick, until its hypnosis is over.

Whatever the trick, whatever its reason, it enraged Pharaoh. He tightened still further his restrictions on the Israelites. What they must now have felt about Moses one can only guess.

But his triumph was to come. The Lord instructed him to threaten Pharaoh with a series of plagues—only one at a time so that the unfortunate king would have no idea what came next—if he refused to grant permission for the Israelites to leave. He was threatened with a sudden fouling of all river water, so that it "turned to blood", killing all the fish and becoming quite unpalatable for humans: he was adamant, the plague duly came and lasted for seven days when it seemed Pharaoh might relent, but he did not. Moses then threatened a plague of frogs which would come out of the water in their slimy millions and die in heaps all over Egypt. The prospect failed to daunt Pharaoh and the plague of frogs duly took place, and was followed in hideous procession by plagues of lice and flies. At which point Pharaoh relented sufficiently to permit the Israelite elders to go into the wilderness and sacrifice, but still refused permission for the people to leave.

Any physical explanation of these plagues on the Egyptians is lost in obscurity, but something of the sort happened. And, as Moses had promised to his people, they, though forced to live in Egypt, were not affected.

He next threatened and brought about the death of most of the Egyptian cattle; then an epidemic of boils. Throughout all these natural disasters Pharaoh's own sorcerers, smarting perhaps from the loss of their trained serpents, were busily trying to countermand each disaster or do something as spectacular themselves. Sadly, when it came to boils, or so Exodus tells us: "The magicians could not stand before Moses because of the boils."

Boils were followed by hail, locusts, a total eclipse of the sun.

This was too much for Pharaoh. He ordered that the Israelites go, and go quickly. There was but one condition: they would leave their sheep and cattle behind.

But Moses, having now found himself capable of visiting every sort of disaster upon the Egyptians, was having none of it: "Our cattle also shall go with us, there shall not an hoof be left behind."

Foolishly, Pharaoh objected. And almost before he knew it, the worst plague of all descended upon him.

From this last plague, and the steps taken by the Israelites to avoid its impact on themselves, stems one of the most hallowed observances of the Jewish people, the Passover. They had been spared each plague as it came, without conscious effort on their own part. Now, to avoid the final one, they were instructed to take a certain action.

Each household would sacrifice a lamb. "And they shall take of the blood, and strike it on the two side-posts and on the upper door-post of the houses, wherein they shall eat it." An elaborate ceremonial was laid down for the manner in which the meat was to be cooked and eaten. It would be roasted and eaten with unleavened bread and bitter herbs; eaten by men and women with: "Your loins girded, your shoes on your feet, and your staff in your hand: and ye shall eat it in haste; it is the Lord's passover.

"For I will pass through the land of Egypt this night, and will smite all the first-born in the land of Egypt, both man and beast; and against all the gods of Egypt, I will execute judgement. I am the Lord."

And it happened.

"It came to pass that at midnight the Lord smote all the first-born in the land of Egypt, from the first-born of Pharaoh that sat on his throne unto the first-born of the captive that was in the dungeon; and all the first-born of cattle. And Pharaoh rose up in the night, he and all his servants, and all the Egyptians: and there was a great cry in Egypt, for there was not a house where there was not one dead."

Pharaoh tells them to go, take their flocks with them. And in order to speed the departure, the panic-stricken, grief-stricken Egyptians give them "jewels of silver and jewels of gold, and raiment". And so fast do the Israelites go that they seize up the bread they are making, even before it is leavened, and carry it away.

And so at last, in about the year 1280 B.C., the Israelites left the hateful land of their captivity: a land which had seemed so fertile and so joyous when they had arrived, all those generations ago, which was now but a prison. There were 600,000 children of Israel, and they marched with light heart and step, out of the country, towards the east.

Their troubles were not over. No sooner had they left Egypt than Pharaoh, who must have been one of history's least likeable rulers, even making allowance for the frogs and boils that assailed him, decided to pursue them. "Why have we done this, that we have let Israel go from serving us? And he made ready his chariot, and took his people with him."

Off he sets in hot pursuit. The Israelites have been told to go via the marshy land at the north of the Red Sea, and it is as they are encamped here, rather south of their intended crossing point—the sea here is still wide and impassable—that they make out the dust of Pharaoh's chariots in the distance.

Once again, they turn on Moses. Why has he led them out of Egypt only to be slaughtered by Egyptians? "For it had been better for us to serve the Egyptians than that we should die in the wilderness."

But God, through the agency of Moses, has one last trick to play. Moses stretches out a hand towards the sea, "and the Lord caused the sea to go back by a strong east wind all that night, and made the sea dry land, and the waters were divided.

"And the children of Israel went into the midst of the sea upon the dry ground: and the waters were a wall unto them on their right hand and on their left."

The Egyptians are not so favoured. They hurtle on in pursuit, across the desert, along the baking, salt-white sand at the edge

20

of the sea, whipping on their chariots, to wheel dramatically into the pathway which seems to have been cleared for them through the sea, and along which the Israelites are scurrying. God and the east wind wait until the entire Egyptian Army is within the embrace of the Red Sea, with waters piled high on either side; then the waters thunder back over the chariots, wiping out every man and every horse.

Meanwhile the Israelites have got dry to the farther shore. But there are more privations and dangers ahead. Soon they are in the desert of Sinai, where there is no water and men die of thirst. The sun burns down with a malice they have never before encountered and once again there are those who curse Moses for having led them into this hell. Surely, no man will get out alive?

But—so the Old Testament tells us—God is good to his children and after testing them always provides an answer. Moses is able to make the waters of a bitter lake drinkable with the branches of a certain tree, and a little farther on they come to an oasis where the water is pure and plentiful, and at which quail alight. Many of these are killed for food, and then, when the supply appears to be running out—as well it might, with an army of 600,000 to be fed—there is "manna" on the ground. This is believed to drop from Heaven—but no matter whence it comes, it is good to eat.

The Israelites remained in the Sinai desert, kept alive by such Acts of God, for a number of years. The reason for this lengthy, unpleasant and apparently unnecessary sojourn in the wilderness was the warlike presence in Canaan—or Palestine—of just those tribes of which the Lord had advised them before they set out: "The Canaanites, and the Hittites, and the Amorites, and the Perrizites, and the Hivites and the Jebusites." Understandably, none of these tribes wants to share its territory with newcomers —however ancient their claim on it.

A situation which, of course, has been exactly duplicated in our present century, some three thousand years later.

These hostile tribes kept the children of Israel out of Palestine for a number of years, but eventually they were able to work a way eastward, south of the country, and attack it from that quarter. They were able to enter their Promised Land from the east, and Moses, just before they did so, was taken up on a hill by the Lord, to see it. After this, his work done, he died.

There was more hard fighting ahead, but the Israelites had reached their goal. They had fought and bled, and were back in what they held to be their own land. Gratefully, they set about building a temple in their city of Jerusalem to the One True God, who had led them in their escape. They selected from among themselves a first King of the Jews, a wise, upstanding man and a brilliant general, named Saul.

And though the fight back into their Promised Land was long and bloody, it is the escape from cruel Egyptian masters, that breathless dash with bread still unleavened, and the miracle of the opening of the waters, which is remembered in Jewish history.

For though there was hardship ahead, the Jewish people were free.

Chapter 2

MOHAMMED'S DASH ACROSS
THE DESERT

W E have many, many reasons for remembering it. One of
the more bizarre is this:

$$\text{A.H.} - \frac{3\text{AH}}{100} + 621 = \text{A.D.}$$

This is the formula converting a Moslem date into one of our
own, "A.D." being our own "Anno Domini" and "A.H." repre-
senting the bastardized Romano-Arabic of "Anno Hejira", or
the Arabic date, counted as it is from the year of Mohammed's
flight, or "Hejirah", from Mecca to Medina. It was the Caliph
Umar, in the middle of the seventh century A.D., one of the
successors to Mohammed as religious head of the Arab world,
who instituted this method of keeping the date. It would commemorate the Hejirah, keeping the ancient Arabic lunar months,
but making the new era begin with the first month of the year
in which Mohammed's great flight took place.

Or, in our calendar, 16 July, 622.

The great flight took place in September of that year. To glimpse its huge significance we must look first at the man Mohammed and the time in which he lived.

His parents, of the Hashim clan in Arabia, were poor. He was born in Mecca, towards the west of that desert land, in about A.D. 570, and very soon after that he was orphaned. His grandfather looked after him for a while, then his uncle, Abu Talib, a strong and upright man who was to live many years and remain an influence in the boy's, then the man's, life.

We are told that Mohammed was taller than his tribe, that he grew into a fine-looking man with large and lustrous eyes and a mane of black hair. Like everyone else in his community and the countless wandering communities of the desert, he was an animist, believing that sticks and stones and sun and moon and stars had souls and minds and motives, and had to be placated or fought, according to circumstance. The animist religion still flourishes in many parts of the world—the north of Burma, for example—but it was Mohammed who replaced it in Arabia, and thence a large part of the world, by a totally different code of belief and behaviour, an aggressive international freemasonry which would inspire its adherents to go out and conquer the world.

Mecca, even in those days, was a religious centre—the name comes from the Arabic word for "temple"—and pilgrimages were made from it to the nearby holy mountain of Arafat. It was also a thriving commercial centre and a staging point on the caravan route from Syria to South Arabia. Without a strict and shared religion to bind them—with each tribe worshipping its own choice of gods—there was almost constant petty warfare. Three times a year a truce had to be proclaimed, to allow the Mecca caravans to pass.

Young Mohammed was involved with these caravans, for he had been put into apprenticeship with a widow, Khadijah, who was trying hard to keep up the trading business left by her late husband. Mohammed did much to get this business thriving and his work gave him opportunity to travel with the caravans and observe the way men and women lived in other parts of Arabia.

He was twenty when his employer, fifteen years his senior, but still a woman of beauty, agreed to become his wife. Soon, thanks

24

to this alliance, he was a man of importance in Mecca, a prosperous merchant who also travelled widely. During these travels he had begun to notice the change in religious climate; the old animism was beginning to battle against the incursion of new beliefs: Judaism and Christianity. There was also among some people in the Arabian peninsula, an awareness of an omniscient, single, God, an "Allah".

It was this last belief that seized Mohammed. He thought long and hard about the existence of God, sometimes going alone to the summit of Mount Hira to meditate; and one of the thoughts that began to occupy his mind was the vagueness of any concept of that "Allah". The Being existed, but had given very little sign of existence. He had given no orders, as had the God of the Jews or of the Christians, for the conduct of life.

At last, a vision came to Mohammed, a vision which he later described as the angel Gabriel. The angel told him that he, Mohammed, was the prophet of the one true God.

The vision went, and Mohammed thought. Then he went to his wife and told her what he had seen. She believed him—and straightway became his first disciple. She had been tolerant for years of her husband's ascetic and sometimes strange behaviour, for she knew he was utterly sincere in everything he did and said.

Khadijah's belief was further confirmed by the utterances of her husband during the strange fits that now seized him. During these he was insensible of what went on around him, spoke in a strange voice about "The Word of Allah".

It has been suggested, as it has of Christ, that Mohammed was an epileptic. Quite possibly this is true. But there were plenty of soothsayers and wise men in Mecca who went into trances and made pronouncements, and at first Mohammed was regarded by his neighbours as no different from these. He went on, though, preaching his belief in a single, universal God. Soon his adherents numbered not only his wife but his daughters and many more. Some became disciples, travelling with him as he preached, others simply converts who threw away their animist beliefs, became believers in Allah and followers of his prophet Mohammed, but went about their normal daily tasks. Most of these were poor men, for the code of behaviour which Mohammed had received from his God had begun to appear less than attractive to the rich. For a start, it forbade the eating of pork, the drinking of wine.

He had begun to call his new faith "Islam", or Submission to the Will of God. It was similar in many ways to the beliefs of both Christians and Jews, but different in its observances. Christ, Mohammed said, had indeed existed, but there was nothing Divine about him: he was one of no less than twenty-eight prophets since the dawn of time, beginning with Adam.

But the only prophet to whom God's truth had been confided, in full, was Mohammed.

The whole of this truth, in the form of utterances by Mohammed, was being collected by his disciples. Some twenty years after his death it was assembled into a great and holy book, the Koran—which has almost certainly been more widely read than any other book in history.

But there was much on the way for Mohammed before the appearance of any such book. His unpopularity mounted steadily among the rich merchants of Mecca, who questioned the overthrow of old beliefs and at the same time resented the ascetic way of life this mad visionary preached. What was the point in being rich and successful if one couldn't eat and drink what one wanted? How wrong that it should now be considered pagan and a sin to possess paintings or carvings of the human face or figure! And who, among the busy merchants of Mecca, had time to kneel down and pray to Allah as often as Mohammed demanded, or to fast as often in the year?

One of the few concessions, if we may style it thus, which Mohammed allowed was a plurality of wives, and he himself possessed a dozen or more. (But only one, Khadijah, during her lifetime.) This, though, made little difference to the rich men of Mecca: the new faith would have to be stamped out. The only way of doing this would be to capture and kill Mohammed.

Easier said than done. The tall man with the strange and lustrous eyes was now surrounded at every minute of every day by a host of disciples. He was also under the protection of his powerful and well-regarded uncle, Abu Talib. Any man who sought to lay hands on Mohammed would have been torn limb from limb within seconds. But it was easy and psychologically rewarding to set upon isolated bands of his followers and kill or torture them. Some of these now began to flee, taking their beliefs with them to other parts of Arabia, like the town of Medina. Mohammed encouraged them. Some entered Africa: one party of eighty sought sanctuary in Abyssinia.

The community of followers that remained behind in Mecca was soon embattled, and while Mohammed counselled as many as were able to go abroad for safety and to spread the word of the True God, he himself resolved to stay and defend his beliefs.

Now came a sudden convert to Islam—a change of heart almost as surprising and far-reaching in its results as that of St. Paul, half a millennium before. A very rich and powerful man of Mecca, who had ardently persecuted all followers of Mohammed, joined them. He, too, had seen a vision, which told him Allah was unquestionably God, the only God, and that Mohammed was his chosen prophet. Umar ibn-al-Khattab was a powerful addition to the ranks. Many who had wavered, frightened of declaring their conversion, now rushed to be known as followers of Mohammed (Mohammedans, or Muslims, or Moslems, or any of many other names, according to dialect).

But though the adherence of Umar greatly increased the number of converts, it strengthened the resolve of the Meccan magnates to crush this hateful faith which was subverting even wise and good men like Umar. Fate played into their hands: this rise in their determination to get rid of Mohammed coincided with the death of his wife Khadijah and of his uncle Abu Talib, who had become a good disciple and remained a powerful protector. Now opposition to Mohammed grew more open, and when he tried to recruit followers at the great Mecca fair he was greeted with shouts of abuse, and with stones, so that he had to seek refuge. At one point he had to flee Mecca and hide with a kinsman in the town of Taif, a few miles to the east. But soon he was back again, preaching the word of Allah.

It was at one of these great fairs of pilgrims, in Mecca, that the cause of Islam was greatly furthered: within a few years, thanks to this happy accident, the word of Allah as related by Mohammed would have spread many hundreds of miles and its adherents would be numbered in tens of thousands and be ever growing. A group of tribesmen from distant Yathrib were at the fair. They were sophisticated men who had heard the word

27

of the Jews and of the Christians during their travels; they recognized similarities in this new faith, and they listened carefully to what the young man was saying.

There was the usual mutter of discontent while he spoke, but one of the men from Yathrib got up, fingered a knife. The muttering stopped.

The tribesmen went back to Yathrib, and so profoundly had they been moved by what they heard that every one of them became an active evangelist. Some returned to Mecca in the following year bringing their own converts, and Mohammed instructed these further in the beliefs and laws of Islam.

But though the word of Allah was spreading like smoke in all directions, it was still a forbidden word in the home of its first appearance. The rich men of Mecca, and poorer ones who sought to curry favour with them, still persecuted the followers of Islam. One by one, these left and made a perilous way, two hundred and fifty miles north, to Medina. This city, by such immigration, and by a slow change of heart among its inhabitants, was becoming a centre of the new faith.

But a centre without a head, without a leader.

Soon, only Mohammed and a few disciples remained behind in Mecca, but as those who had fled did so in secrecy, the fact was not generally known. Had his enemies known Mohammed was all but unprotected they would have killed him then and there.

So the new faith flourished in Medina—and its leader was virtually a prisoner in Mecca. It was an army without a general. With other, less aggressive, faiths this might have made little difference. But one of the teachings put forward by Mohammed had been the necessity of making converts, at the point of the sword if necessary. The growing army of Islam in Medina wanted their general to join them, lead them.

Mohammed was a prisoner. He was allowed to walk about the streets of Mecca, but his every move was studied. The men of Mecca had no need for Mohammed in their city, but they were determined not to let him escape and set up a "holy city" of his own, a centre for converts to the new faith. He was followed everywhere he went, yet no one dared attack him openly: no one knew how many disciples and followers would spring up, like dragons' teeth, to avenge him.

But Mohammed, with his last close friend and disciple, Abu Bakr, was planning an escape. Carefully leaving all his possessions in his own house, he moved in with his friend to make the final preparations for what would begin as a moonlit dash from the city. If it was discovered that the two were alone and preparing to leave they would be captured and killed, but they stayed hidden in Abu Bakr's house and at first no one seemed to notice their absence.

At last, the night they had waited for arrived, with its bright full moon, and the two men slipped off, out of the house, along the deserted streets of Mecca and to the desert. Here they mounted camels.

They headed north and at first they made good speed. It was a cold but pleasant night, with the stars splashed wide and brilliant over the sky, and an easy matter to head in the right direction, keep moving along it.

When their first dawn came, and the baking sun rose in the sky, they hid themselves behind some dunes and scanned the horizon for sign of pursuers. There were none to be seen, and they set off again, with the sun beating down on their backs and the two camels rolling like ships as they spurred them on. By now a pursuit would have started, and they must make all possible speed.

At last they reached a mountainous land, with caves dotted through it like holes in cheese, and into one of these the two men rode. Already the rising pillar of white sand to the south, a swirling, twisting pillar which advanced towards them at a terrifying rate, told they were being followed by an army.

And, indeed, there was a real and angry army which had swarmed out into the desert after Mohammed. The killing of the prophet had now become almost an article of faith in Mecca, and thousands of men pursued him, on horse and camel, and bearing arms; the long Arab lances decorated with horsetail; the vicious, curving swords.

A wind got up as the pursuers drew near, obliterating the camels' tracks; but the Meccans searched the hills thoroughly, and began to enter caves. At night, with the job incomplete, they camped outside the very cave in which Mohammed and Abu Bakr were hiding. Abu had begun to fear discovery; the men outside were, all of them, skilled trackers, able to follow any desert animal, however small, and kill it in its lair: men able to read the signs both of nature and of man. But Mohammed had no fear: Allah had already caused the wind to wipe away their tracks; Allah would protect.

At dawn the next morning it began to look as if Allah had forgotten. Men stood outside the very mouth of the cave, and from a cold, damp spot in the shadows the two fugitives could see bodies passing in silhouette against the rose-pink of the eastern sky. The voices grew louder.

But Allah protected.

As they watched, a dove lit at the very mouth of the cave, and they saw that the bird had a nest already made, among a pile of small white stones like quartz. Surely the nest had not been there when they entered? And no bird would be likely to come and settle in a nest as close to humans as this. For, though the Meccans had not yet sensed their quarry, there was no question but that a wild mountain bird would do so.

Yet the bird nested, exactly in the centre of the cave entrance. And as it sat, a large black spider appeared from out of the darkness, drew its web across the cave mouth.

The hunters came up, looked at the cave. One made a move to enter.

"But look," said another. "There can be no man within— there is a dove, nesting on the very floor."

"And see," said another. "A spider's web."

It was a thick, coarse web. The spider had done its work, miraculously, in minutes.

"Yes." A man laughed. "That great web has been there since before Mohammed was born. No man can be inside the cave, for the web covers the whole entrance."

They left. And this is perhaps the only miracle in the Moslem faith, pointing the moral that all nature conspires to protect the Beloved of God.

The pursuers—having, so tradition tells us, relieved themselves against the rocks at the mouth of the cave—rode off to continue their search elsewhere. When it seemed safe, the two fugitives left their cave and pressed on, over the desert.

On the 20th September of the year 622 in our calendar, the

prophet and Abu Bakr arrived at the outskirts of Medina. It had been a long, hazardous journey over deserts which baked like ovens during the day and were ice cold at night. They had been able to carry hardly any provisions and they were tired and sick and starving when they arrived. But Mohammed's followers streamed out from Medina to meet them. The prophet had come, the word of Allah was with them: each man tried to lead the prophet to his own part of the city.

Mohammed refused these offers of assistance. Dropping the reins of his camel, he let the beast wander into the town till it halted. He dismounted. This would be his home: the flight was over.

A simple tale, this "Hejira", and one of the most important in world history. As we have seen, it is the point from which the Moslem calendar begins. From now on, Islam ceased to be a furtive, hole-in-corner religion and Mohammed grew less of a preacher, more of a leader and politician. He made a sudden call to arms, declared a Holy War against unbelievers. Islam has never been a pacifist creed and now, operating from Medina, it became a warlike, even a cruel, one. Some of that spirit has survived to today.

Mohammed announced his intention of bringing Mecca into subjection and converting its inhabitants, those "hypocrites" to whom the Koran so often refers, those men of Mecca who, while not actively working for Mohammed's death while he lived there, put their own interests before that of the new religion. His followers began to raid caravans bound for Mecca, and one of these raids led to the battle of Badr in which Mohammed's followers defeated the Meccans. But Mohammed was unable to invest the town at the time, having lost many of his own men, and it was not until 628 that he led a huge army against it, an army which undoubtedly would have destroyed Mecca had not the inhabitants offered peace terms and promised that Mohammed could come in peace to the annual pilgrim's fair.

It gives us some insight into the nature of Islam to learn that Mohammed, now a great general as well as spiritual leader, hated to disappoint his followers in their hopes for loot. To compensate them for the loss of spoil from Mecca he attacked and sacked the Jewish town of Khaipar.

31

The Meccan pilgrims' fair, dating back to the furthest days of antiquity, had been a pagan affair, though other religious ideas were blended with simple animism, and men came from hundreds of miles to indulge in a number of different observances. But when Mohammed re-entered Mecca, the days of paganism were numbered. By the force of his personality, rather more than the sharpness of his sword, he succeeded in wiping out the last vestiges of the old pagan belief.

To Mohammed, who was absolutely sincere in a belief that he was the mouthpiece of God, the capture of men's minds and bodies within the ancient city of Mecca had been a lifetime obsession, from the moment he saw his first vision: it had stayed with him through all the years of evangelism within Mecca itself, and during and after the flight. Perhaps the secret of his success was that he kept this single and simple objective in mind throughout his life. Some verses in the Koran sound almost as if he had set his heart on world domination, but the universe Mohammed coveted for Allah was bounded by the borders of Arabia.

It was only when Mohammed died, in A.D. 632, that the army and the people he left behind set out to spread his doctrine over as much of the world as they could reach. The homeland of the religion remained Arabia, with Mecca as spiritual centre, but the word of Allah was carried by fire and sword into Palestine, Syria, Persia, and along the coast of North Africa. Soon it had been carried across the straits of Gibraltar into Europe, and it was only in 732, exactly a hundred years after his death, that the Arab armies received a first check, were beaten in France by the Frankish leader Charles Martel.

But the Arab world expanded further after this setback, striking fear into the hearts of men as far afield as England, and giving rise to the Crusades—after which what Christians held to be the "Infidel Menace of Islam" began to recede.

And all this springs—and a calendar too—from a wild dash across the desert, and a miracle in a cave.

Chapter 3

LORD EDWARD FLEES FROM
HEREFORD CASTLE

KING JOHN is probably the most unpopular monarch in English history—but he was hardly the worst. When he died, in 1219, his heir Henry III was a boy of nine. The kingdom was taken over by a Regency and they, bearing in mind the recent unpleasantness at Runnymede, ruled in the spirit of the Magna Carta John had been forced to sign.

But Henry, foolish Henry, elected, on coming of age, to behave as if Magna Carta had never been. He ignored his barons, chose advisers from French relatives of his mother. Not only this, but he acted unwisely on the advice he got: the early years of his reign were a series of diplomatic disasters.

At the battle of Lewes, in May, 1264, the barons under Simon de Montfort, Earl of Leicester, defeated the King and his son, Edward, taking them both prisoner.

This weighed heavily on twenty-five-year-old Edward, "The Lord Edward". For it was he who, with hot-headedness, impetuosity, had been responsible for this disastrous defeat.

I like to think of him, this thoughtful young prisoner in Hereford Castle, pondering the battle of Lewes, making plans to avenge the defeat and restore himself in the estimation of his father.

Some day—and he knew it—he would inflict a terrible revenge on de Montfort; but here on the ramparts of Hereford Castle, the last of the several prisons in which he had been incarcerated, he could only hope. He was a lonely young man, hating captivity and devoting time each day to prayers that it might soon be ended, with revenge for his father and himself. The two had been a long time separated in their captivity and Edward had at first had little idea where his father was taken. Now, with his father's pitiful, impotent, "Court" brought to this very Castle of Hereford, they were near each other again. And this—when he looked into his father's anguished, helpless eyes—only made it worse.

The sky above was clear, but below him, with dawn slipping over the town, the mist was dank and chilly. He looked long into it, then went slowly to his devotions in the chapel. Here, deep in the hard stone heart of the castle, there was a different chill, warmed slightly—at least to the eye—by the oily flicker of candles. The chaplain was there, arranging the altar, and Edward knelt, fingered his rosary.

Somehow, his mind seemed to wander. It travelled, with a mingled sense of triumph and despair, back to Lewes: what a fool one had been! His own and his father's armies far exceeded those of de Montfort and the barons, and so it had been tempting to throw one's might against the barons' east flank, manned by the despicable Londoners who had come out in their support. The line of Londoners had broken and Edward's force was in among them, hacking and stabbing, grinding underfoot. Those not butchered in the first minute fled, and with a whoop of joy Edward spurred his steed, ordered his men in pursuit.

The wonderful chase had lasted four hours, down the valley, across the river, and beyond. When at last he called it off, there was scarce a Londoner left. Flushed with success—this would show townspeople how to treat a king—he trotted back to the battle.

But here disaster struck. The King, deprived of so much

cavalry, hemmed in on all sides, had fought gallantly but suffered grievous losses. When Edward arrived, saw with horror what his own stupidity had wrought, he charged into a pack of de Montfort's soldiery, slashing and cursing, killing a score before he, too, was surrounded, his own force cut down.

Father and son—Henry III of England and the Lord Edward —were prisoners of Simon de Montfort, Earl of Leicester, and his rebellious barons.

And what made it worse was that his father had so little reproach for him. It is God's will, Edward. And by God's will we shall have our revenge.

They had been separated, then re-united. A year later, having been moved to Dover, then Kenilworth, he was in this most impregnable of fortresses, with his father and his father's "Court". There was more freedom here than in earlier incarcerations. He had been put under two escorts—Henry de Montfort, the hated Simon's son, who regarded him with suspicion and dislike, and Thomas of Clare, the Duke of Gloucester's younger brother. This friendly, high-spirited youth, not forgetting his rôle of unobtrusive gaoler, had yet done much to lighten the distress of captivity. With his pair of escorts, Edward hunted in the woods for deer and wild boar. When the hunting was poor, they raced each other on their steeds.

It was pleasing—but miserable, for there was no hope of escape. Wherever he rode, however fast, however difficult the terrain, one or other of the two was always a few yards away.

He rose from his prayers, went to take breakfast. This, as he was not hungry, occupied little time, and he strolled to the window, stared out of a narrow slit at the spring sunshine touching the fields with gold. It was May again: a whole year had crept by since Lewes.

He felt a presence behind and spun round. It was Thomas.

"Good day," he said.

"Good day, my lord." Edward noticed that his cloak was damp. He must have been out: perhaps it came from the river mist, which even with sun mounting in the sky lay like gruel upon the water.

"Where have you been, so early?"

Thomas looked round him, smiled. "Be of good cheer, my lord. I can say nothing now——" His voice sank to a whisper and Edward frowned: normally the man played his part of jovial gaoler to perfection.

"I see. May we then speak elsewhere?"

"Yes, my lord. We must hunt together, my lord—and I shall speak."

They arranged to hunt and made a point of asking Henry de Montfort to join them. The sun was at its zenith when they entered the forest, but it had dropped to a handsbreadth above the horizon before de Montfort was able to make his kill. It was a fine stag and he dismounted, as was the custom, to commence his own butchery.

The other two moved slightly away on their horses.

"You know, my lord, that my brother, Richard, Duke of Gloucester, has fallen out with the de Montforts?"

"I hear tell. But why?"

"Even his strong stomach could not tolerate any longer this de Montfort rabble, the exaltation of a whole family like a second royal house—like this young pup here, with the skinning knife——"

Edward smiled. "I see."

"And the continued captivity of your father the King—there is no need for him to be kept in captivity. The state of things in England, under the 'House of de Montfort', is as bad as ever it has been."

"Have your thoughts only now changed—today?"

Thomas had the grace to look embarrassed. "I have only now been talking to my brother—and only now my eyes are opened."

Three rode back to the castle and the plan took shape in the minds of two.

That plan was already in the mind of Gilbert, Duke of Gloucester, Thomas's elder brother.

On Thursday, 28 May, the Prince rode out again with Thomas and Henry. Their grooms were with them, for this was a day in which the merits of steeds would be discussed, tested and proved. The three seemed in high spirits, though it might be discerned that two were slightly nervous and Thomas in mounting caught his foot in the stirrup and fell.

"How now, Master Clare!" shouted de Montfort. "Are you frightened of a gallop?"

"Not I," said the young man, though his face had paled.

"And you, my lord?"

Edward grinned. "Not I."

"Good, then. Let us go." Without further ado, he spurred his great chestnut stallion to a gallop and was gone. Thomas, seated on his own bay mare, looked at Edward on his roan, and smiled.

"Yes?"

"Not now. The game must be played with skill—and caution —or it be lost."

He spurred his own horse and it thundered into the wood. The Prince did the same.

They all trotted back to the grooms.

"I will try Titus," said de Montfort to his man. "This beast is sluggish today."

"Is it?" asked Edward. "It seemed to move like the wind——"

"Ha," said de Montfort. "I am used to moving like the wind. Next I will take the white mare. But, on *any* of my horses, I will challenge any man in Christendom."

They changed mounts, had another gallop, changed again. Thomas drew close to Edward, tapped him on the arm and pointed to de Montfort's great chestnut, all of sixteen hands. It was rested now.

"Master Henry——"

"My *lord*?" There was the note of sarcasm in the voice which always made Edward bite his lip, but he forced a smile.

"I will try your mount. Perhaps you will take mine."

There was a pause: then pride got the better of prudence. De Montfort smiled. "Yes, my lord. And methinks you never will find another with such a turn of speed. Yet I am prepared to try yours."

Edward mounted the great chestnut, with its fine sloping shoulder, and he could feel, even as he sat it, the power trembling up through his seat and his fingers.

The temptation was almost overwhelming; but one must be cautious. Play the game, Thomas said, with skill and caution. Thomas had changed horses, and now Edward spurred his beast and it leapt forward with the strength of two. He galloped a hundred paces and came back.

"A wonderful beast," he said, and de Montfort smiled his usual odious smile. "Indeed he is, my lord. But I will put this nag of yours through its paces. Perhaps he will move faster than before." Another quick smile, he spurred Edward's horse and galloped away.

"Now!" said Thomas. They wheeled horses and set off like the wind in the opposite direction.

It was like flying, like being on the back of some huge bird. Within seconds Edward was three lengths ahead of his companion and drawing further ahead. The hooves of the chestnut stallion thudded into the damp of the forest like a salvo of distant guns and he began to wonder if ever he would be able to stop him. On and on they went, across a great clearing half a mile in extent, which shot behind them like a narrow paddock. He looked back, saw Thomas urging on his mare, three hundred yards behind. As yet, no sign of de Montfort.

At the edge of the forest they turned, skirted it for three furlongs, cut back in again. He had discussed this with Thomas, rehearsed it for the past week. Now the stallion seemed to guess what he was thinking, to anticipate his every move.

They were out in the open now. Seeing Thomas drop still farther behind, and no sign of de Montfort—perhaps they had given him the slip after all—he slowed, let the other man gain on him.

Thomas drew level and at that moment they saw the signal.

A lone horseman, arm raised, half a mile ahead. As they drew nearer, the man waved, turned his horse about and galloped off. They followed him.

This, then, was the way to Wigmore, twenty miles away from Hereford, the hateful Hereford Castle which, God willing, neither would ever see again. When it was certain they had shaken off pursuit, they dropped into a trot. Then the silent, nameless horseman spurred again and they were off at a gallop.

They reached Wigmore just as the sun was setting and here the wife of loyal Roger Mortimer saw their horses changed and gave them meat and beer. From Wigmore they galloped on to Ludlow, the castle of Geoffrey de Genevill. Roger Mortimer and the Earl of Gloucester, whose plan it had been, greeted them.

All over England the news was out: the Lord Edward, gallant fighter, noble prince—rebel-killer—had escaped. Men flocked to join him.

Simon de Montfort meanwhile panicked. He sent out frantic appeals for help, the people of England must not be mistaken about what was happening, Edward had not been a prisoner at all, he had willingly given himself up at Lewes as a hostage; he had been treated with great kindness and yet now he had deserted his broken-hearted old father and was spreading a pack of lies. He must not be believed.

But it was of no avail: the people rose in their thousands in support of Edward and on 6 August, at Evesham, he inflicted a crushing defeat on de Montfort. Ironically enough, he used the same strategy which had brought about his own downfall at Lewes, by encouraging a part of de Montfort's force to pursue his retreating flank, and then closing in on a bend of the River Avon to annihilate those left behind. Simon was killed, as he would have wished, in battle. In the eyes not only of Edward and his father, but of many others beside, he was a traitor, and his body was accordingly dismembered on the field and sent to the four corners of the kingdom.

And Edward, when the excitement of his escape and victory had worn off, became a good ruler. He was not, for another seven years, the King of his country, but his wise influence over his father grew each month. By 1270 the country was so peaceful, so prosperous, so content, that he was able, still as heir-apparent, to set off on a Crusade. On his return to Europe two years later he learnt of his father's death, and though he spent another two years in France settling affairs, the young Lord Edward was peacefully crowned king in 1274.

Chapter 4

CORTES EVADES
THE MEXICANS

To understand the audacity—and the breathless panic—of Cortes's departure from the island city of Mexico we must look for a moment at the strange significance of his being there in the first place.

For Cortes's entry into Mexico with a handful of Spaniards, his progress from the coast to the fabulous inland island city, is one of the most extraordinary tales in history.

Cortes, to the Mexicans, was a god.

The exact date and manner of his coming, his exact appearance and behaviour, had been foretold. There could be no question of resisting him, even though his arrival, this second coming, presented all manner of problems. How would the other, jealous, gods react? Would they punish the Mexican people for letting him return? Would the great god Quetzalcoatl (for that was his name, however much he might, playfully, style himself Cortes), would the returning god wreak havoc in the land in order to avenge himself on the other god, Tezcatlipoca, who had exiled him, and on the people who had allowed that to happen?

All this and more raced through the mind of the Emperor Montezuma when news came from the coast that Quetzalcoatl had landed. In a despairing move to get advice from other gods, he sacrificed an enormous number of human victims with his own hands, tearing their beating hearts out on his own private altar, splashing himself and the attendant priests with their blood, hoping for a word of assurance. None came.

He sent emissaries to the coast where the god and his attendants were encamped, wishing Quetzalcoatl well, welcoming him back to his ancient land. The emissaries took fruits, turkeys and tender little chihuahua dogs for the god to eat. They also brought a message, which must have startled Cortes, that they themselves were his for the eating. If the god required but the blood of a single human, a single set of arms and legs to eat, then their fat colleague Cuitlapitoc was his man.

If, on the other hand, Quetzalcoatl required more in the way of human nourishment, all the messengers were his. To a man.

One wonders what Cortes made of this offer.

And with it—surely as grand a gesture as man can make—came a suggestion. The road, those hundreds of mountainous miles from the coast to the city of Mexico, was dangerous, long and tiring. If the god would only stay encamped by the sea, Montezuma would send him all the gold he could carry, all the jewels of Mexico. And then, perhaps, when the god had rested after his long sea trip from the rising sun, he would re-embark, go back whence he had come. Laden, of course, with riches.

Cortes refused.

He had made his first mistake.

This story is about Cortes's escape; but it is important to see how it came to pass that a Spanish adventurer should be greeted as a god. Had he not been a god, he and his followers would have been wiped out, to a man, the moment they set foot on dry land.

They were not wiped out. Mexican scripture had prophesied that the exiled god, Quetzalcoatl, would return by sea in a boat, from the East, on his own personal name day, 20 April, and in a "One-Reed Year". One-Reed Years, like our Leap Years, were based on astronomy, though they recurred only at intervals of a great many years: 1363 had been a One-Reed Year; so had 1467. Quetzalcoatl had not come. 1519 would be a One-Reed Year. And the god, if he chose to come this time, would be, as always depicted, white-faced, bearded and dressed in black. He would not look like a brown-skinned, beardless, gaudily-dressed Mexican.

On 20 April, 1519, Cortes, having sailed in from the East, from Cuba, landed. It was Good Friday, and he was therefore dressed in black. His black beard was neatly combed, his black eyes shone in a pale face.

There could be no doubt of it: he was Quetzalcoatl. And the god, on disembarking, built a temple or two on the coast and then, as Montezuma had feared, headed straight for the capital. The journey ahead of Cortes was two hundred and fifty miles, but after adventures and battles with small, non-Mexican tribes, his small force arrived, two and a half months later, within sight of Mexico City.

It was a sudden, thrilling vision. They had just rounded the volcano Popacatapetl, which had started to smoke in their honour, after many years of quiescence, when suddenly, twenty miles in front and five thousand feet below, they saw the city in the centre of its fifty-mile-long lake. It was joined to the mainland by three causeways, and while they looked and wondered the snow came down and they lost it.

The Spaniards descended slowly to lake level, seven thousand feet above the sea. Soon they had reached the southern causeway, and now, with an escort of Mexican nobles, they marched on to it. Five miles ahead was the beautiful city itself, all palaces and temples, and in half these temples, did they but know it, human sacrifices were being made by the hundred to propitiate their "divine" leader. As one of the Spaniards wrote later: "Some of our soldiers asked whether what we saw were not a dream. I do not know how to describe it all, for we were looking at what had never been heard of or seen before, nor even dreamed about. . . ."

On, on they marched: four bearded Spanish riders at the head of a column, then an ensign with a banner, then soldiers with shield and sword. More riders, with lances, bells tinkling on their bridles: more foot-soldiers with crossbows: then more cavalry, and finally foot-soldiers with muskets. A force, tiny in comparison with the Mexican army, which could yet take care of itself.

So Cortes thought.

Halfway along the causeway they met the great Montezuma. Cortes was to write: "I dismounted, was about to embrace him, but the two lords in attendance prevented me, with their hands. I could not touch him."

Montezuma, slim and straight under a canopy of feathers and embroidery, was in fine cloth and wearing sandals of gold. And, despite the caution of his lords, he and Cortes were able to greet each other, with every sign of friendship—though the Mexican trembled as he spoke: "Oh Lord, our Lord, with what trouble, what fatigue, have you journeyed to reach us, have arrived in this land, your land, your own City of Mexico. . . ."

The Mexican girl, "Dona Maria", given to Cortes *en route*, translated the speech for him. He made fitting reply.

They marched together along the last mile of the causeway to the city, while curious crowds of Mexicans stared from each side and from hundreds of canoes which kept pace with the procession.

Cortes had made a mistake in pressing on to Mexico, with all its wealth his for the asking. But he had high hopes of being made viceroy if he added that unknown, fabulous territory to the realms of King Charles of Spain. And what now puzzled, upset and frightened him when he settled in the palace which had been prepared for him was that Montezuma, despite constant protestations of humility, still obviously regarded himself as absolute ruler. (As well he might, for gods rule in heaven and emperors on earth.) And it was now that Cortes made his second, greater mistake. He imprisoned Montezuma—in the greatest luxury in his own, Cortes's, palace—with court, wives and children.

This precipitate action was hastened by a report that Cortes's rearguard on the coast had been attacked. The report was true, but though Mexicans had made the attack, it had been a mistake, and Montezuma, shocked at the information, was not in any way responsible. But Mexican prisoners taken in the skirmish were now, on Cortes's instruction, rushed to the city and there, with Montezuma to witness the deed, burnt at the stake.

No doubt this hideous act seemed as nothing to Cortes, compared with the daily ritual of human sacrifice in the capital. A few days later, having tried to persuade the Mexicans to give up the practice, he insisted on placing a cross on one of the sacrificial pyramids and an image of the Virgin Mary inside one of the temples.

Rebellion was mounting. For Cortes, by taking and keeping Montezuma a prisoner, was destroying him as a ruler. A ruler who believed, unquestioningly, that Cortes was a god. There were other Mexicans, and the number was growing, who doubted it. And others who, while believing him a god, thought other gods would win in the end.

A dash back to the coast to deal with a landing of Spaniards sent by Velasquez, the Governor of Cuba. Cortes had sailed thence, with the Governor's blessing and financial aid, but had now ignored Velasquez completely and was corresponding direct with Charles V in Spain, in the hope of being promoted to Velasquez's level. Now a large party—far larger than the one with Cortes—had landed with instructions to capture him, bring him back to justice.

Cortes, learning that his base was attacked from this unexpected quarter, went back. By now, Montezuma had handed over sufficient gold and jewels for him to bribe the whole of the newly arrived Spanish force: and this is exactly what Cortes did. Soon the entire force had joined with his own, was heading for the island city.

When they got there, things were quite out of hand. One of his lieutenants had fired, in an access of panic, at a party of Mexican dancers. Brightly costumed, they were making a great deal of noise, and advancing, or so it seemed, on the palace where the Spaniards and Montezuma were living. The Spaniards rushed out, opened fire and killed several, and the enraged Mexicans drove them back into their palace and confined them.

Cortes, arriving there, found a strange, unpleasing stillness in the city. Yet he and his forces were allowed in and entered their palace. Montezuma had already harangued his own people from the battlements and calmed them, and now he greeted him with affection. Cortes, pleased with his success in dealing with a far larger Spanish force, but angered by a notable lack of ceremony over his return, rebuffed the Emperor.

A week later, more than half of Cortes's men would be dead, many of them sacrificed on the sacred stone. Montezuma, to whom he owed success and life itself, would be dead with them.

It was soon apparent, even to Cortes, that rebellion was mounting fast. At first he was unruffled: the garrison had been eighty strong; now it numbered a thousand, thanks to the Cuban "punitive expedition" which had so meekly joined him.

All this, of course, had taken many months: it was now June of 1520. On the twenty-fifth, a Spanish soldier was sent along one of the causeways on an errand from Cortes. He carried out the errand, on the mainland at Tacuba, but on the way back was attacked and only escaped with his life to report to Cortes that the Mexicans had begun to destroy bridges on all three causeways.

Cut off from the mainland, the Spanish would not be able to hold out. Cortes dispatched a fighting patrol and it was cut to pieces by Mexican soldiers.

Rebellion had become war.

Events succeeded each other at terrifying speed. The next day Montezuma himself was killed, standing on the battlements, trying to calm his frenzied people. He had been forced up there after saying: "No, I beseech you, for I cannot get them to stop fighting—they are resolved you shall not leave the city alive." He extended his arms in a gesture of peace, there was a volley of stones from the square below, and the Emperor was dead.

Cortes, who in his strange way had loved Montezuma, arranged to hand his body over to the besiegers. "But soon afterwards they fell on us in greater force and fury, with loud yells and whistles and showers of missiles, shouting, 'Now, for certain, you will pay for his death.'"

Now Cortes knew he had to fight his way out.

The causeways, as we have seen, had been sabotaged. Of these, that leading westward to Tacuba was shortest, only two miles in length, and this he now selected as an escape route. It had contained three bridges and now all were down, but the

Spaniard, several hundred years ahead of his time, improvised a lightweight and portable assault bridge.

As darkness fell on 30 June, Cortes and his garrison made ready to escape. Two hand-picked generals would lead the vanguard, a third bring up the rear. Cortes himself would command the centre.

The escape began at midnight. Rain was falling and it was dark. The vanguard led the way up to the end of the causeway, apparently undetected, then started to put the portable bridge in position over the first gap.

Suddenly, trumpets and whistles sounded and what had been utter silence became bedlam. Within moments half the Mexican army seemed to have appeared from the darkness and be attacking them. Canoes full of soldiers swept furiously past and landed further down the causeway to cut them off.

So far, so good. The Mexican army would be unable to inflict many casualties from its bobbing, sinkable canoes. The Spaniards would negotiate the first gap, then the remaining seven, with their portable bridge, losing a few men here and there, but inflicting terrible casualties with far greater armament.

But somehow—within seconds it seemed—the Mexicans destroyed the all-important portable bridge. The vanguard and part of the main body, including Cortes himself, had crossed when this disaster struck, and Cortes was faced with an immediate, agonizing decision: to stay and try to get the remainder, who numbered half his force, over a non-existent bridge, or to press on down the causeway to safety before it was too late.

He took the only possible decision. There were another seven gaps to ford, and he charged them, one by one, using his armoured cavalry like a battering ram, driving Mexicans before him like chaff and swimming, or leaping, the gaps.

Eventually he got to the mainland, with five hundred men. He immediately turned back and went with a small party to see what had happened to those he had been forced to leave behind.

In five minutes he had learnt the worst. A badly wounded officer, staggering down the causeway towards him, announced that all on the far side had been killed or captured, with all the Spanish artillery and all the booty which—foolishly, perhaps—

they had been trying to bring with them. The wounded officer had only escaped by climbing over the bodies of dead men and horses which filled the gap.

More than half of Cortes's army had gone: and he had only regained the mainland—there were two hundred and fifty miles ahead of him, to the coast. Bereft of half an army and almost all its armament, facing an enormously greater force, Cortes stood no chance at all of making it.

But he did.

Simply because the Mexicans were too busy sacrificing to God—another god, needless to say, not Quetzalcoatl—sacrificing the eight hundred Spaniards they had captured. Before the break-out, a Mexican chief had shouted up at them: "We will sacrifice your hearts and blood to our gods, and there will be enough of you to glut their appetites. We will feast on your arms and legs, we will throw your bodies to the serpents."

So closely was life in Montezuma's Mexico bound up with religion, so subservient was it to religion, that this un-military delay (which allowed Cortes to escape, against all odds) was in fact an essential part of the pursuit. For by sacrificing the enemy, cutting out its hearts on a dozen altars, letting the blood gush down the stone pyramids, and banqueting on the limbs, the Mexican people would not only be made, kept, strong: they would propitiate the one and only God; and would be sure to win any battle, any war.

For Quetzalcoatl was already a discredited god. It was Tezcatlipoca, his age-old enemy, who was on the winning side; all Mexico resolved to stay on that side.

But in doing so the victorious Mexican army lost its war. For Cortes, though halved in numbers, was able to regroup and resist a major attack, a few days later. He was able to assure his men that if they killed only the Mexican leaders, who would be distinguished by their "gorgeous accoutrements, plumes, banners which were attached to their backs, mantles with devices, face-jewels and head-dresses in the form of serpents and ocelots", they would demoralize and destroy the Mexican army.

The Spaniards did just this. The Mexicans, just as Cortes had foretold, broke ranks and fled.

And now Cortes had become a supernatural being in the eyes

of both sides. Few Spaniards had expected to survive the battle, but they had; the enemy, in an incredible way, had fled, leaving not a trace behind. As for the Mexicans, when their leaders fell, they realized, suddenly and to a man, that Montezuma had been right: it was folly to fight a god, particularly Quetzalcoatl. They had lost, not just a battle, but the war. Perhaps life itself—for if a victorious, angry Quetzalcoatl felt like it, the sun would cease to shine, the crops to grow. Life, for Mexico, would be over.

From all indications, life was already over. The Mexican army dispersed miserably to its homes, and awaited the end.

But Cortes, whose thousand-odd men had once been defeated by these same Mexicans, was now down to four hundred and forty, all of them wounded, and with no gunpowder. A glimmer of commonsense on the part of their Mexican opponents, and they would have been wiped out in half an hour—but that was not to be. The Spaniards made their way *en route* to the coast, to the territory of the Tlaxcalans, a nervously anti-Mexican tribe. These noted with surprise that the powerful Mexican army was still in headlong retreat over the horizon and decided to offer sanctuary.

And it was in the land of the Tlaxcalans that Cortes, recovering from the grievous wounds which had been inflicted on his pride as to his body, decided not to press on to the coast, but to regroup, bribing allies if possible, and go back to destroy Mexico.

He was helped in the plan by shipments of Spaniards, sent, in those days of slow communication, to reinforce the expedition which had set out, moons ago, to capture Cortes. Half at least of that expedition had been killed or sacrificed by the Mexicans, the remainder were loyal soldiers of the man they had been sent to destroy. The subsequent shipments from Cuba were seized by Cortes's rearguard, subverted, and sent forward to join him in Tlaxcala. Within a few months, Cortes's army and armament were up to their original strength.

We are not concerned here with Cortes's re-conquest of Mexico. He succeeded beyond his own expectations. The Tlaxcalans rallied to him, some ten thousand of them, and with their help he was able to make large vessels such as the Mexicans had never dared consider, to attack their flimsy canoes in open naval warfare on their lake. He and his allied army carried these sloops in sections to the lake, assembled them, and defeated Mexico.

The utter defeat of Mexico might have resulted in anarchy, but Cortes, when he judged his victory complete, demanded each tribe recognize as their sovereign lord Charles V of Spain. He then organized the territory wisely, using the Mexican nobility to help him rule the country, and treating them courteously as equals. He imported cattle, pigs, poultry. While forcing the Roman Catholic religion upon the people, he still allowed the old religion to exist—but without the human sacrifice he had so abhorred. Today there are still temples to Cortes (or "Quetzalcoatl"), side by side with Christian churches, all over Mexico. That land, with its own unique and extraordinary culture, flourishes as an honoured member of the community of nations.

But if Cortes—foolish, lucky Cortes—had not entered this forbidden empire by the happy accident of being a god, and then been fortunate enough to escape, where would Mexico stand today? For Mexican geography, Mexican pride, are such that, even today, the world might be kept at bay.

Only a god could sell the pass.

Chapter 5

A YOUTH LEADS MARY QUEEN OF SCOTS
FROM LOCH LEVEN

THE tale of Mary Queen of Scots is one of the most pitiful
in our possession, but it is neatly bisected halfway through
her tragic life by an incident which has all the beauty, the pathos
and the thrill of fiction by a master hand. In assembling this
collection of escapes one has now and then thought: This must
be included—but if *only* one could change the facts a little. . . .
If only one could be allowed the fiction writer's privilege of
tampering. If only, for example, Napoleon had slithered down
a rope of knotted sheets from Elba and not calmly embarked
without let or hindrance in a boat of his own navy; if only Prince
Edward had ridden away with a squadron of cavalry at his heels;
if only Benito Mussolini had been a man for whom one could
feel real sympathy; if only . . .

The facts about Mary need no treatment.

She was Queen of Scotland before she was a week old, but
they sent her to France and she was educated there. In 1561,
when she was nineteen, a great beauty and already widowed

once (she had been married to the dauphin of France), she returned to Scotland as its rightful queen. She found that the Protestant Reformation was law, the demagogue John Knox dominated the country and her Catholic faith was now anathema to most of her subjects.

So feebly do we cling to our beliefs, when it becomes convenient to change them.

From now, with the brief bright interval of her escape from Loch Leven, it was tragedy all the way. She made an unfortunate second marriage with her cousin Darnley, who disappointed and disgusted her by his intrigues with other women and the obvious fact that he cared nothing for her, everything for her crown. He grew jealous of her chief minister, the Italian Rizzio, and succeeded in a conspiracy to murder him. A little later a son, who would soon be James VI of Scotland, was born to them, but this was not sufficient to keep the marriage a going concern: Mary had begun to suspect that Darnley planned to murder her too. There was complete separation—and, in February of 1567, Darnley's house at Kirk o' Field was mysteriously blown up and he was killed. Unfortunately for Mary's reputation, it was proved that Bothwell, her new favourite, was involved in the plot. He was tried, he was acquitted—but the taint clung to the Queen.

But Bothwell, like Darnley, was most interested in the throne of Scotland and he took the remarkable step of kidnapping his Queen and taking her to Dunbar Castle. Then, on 6 May, he dragged her off to Edinburgh, allowed nobody to speak with her, and on the fifteenth forcibly married her.

Most of her countrymen, egged on by John Knox, ranting from his pulpit, allowed themselves to be convinced Mary had gone freely with Bothwell and married him of her own free will. The belief is current today—but facts do not bear it out. If Mary had wished to marry Bothwell she could have done so with ease, for the nobles of Scotland had already expressed the desire that she should (in the so-called "Ainslie Bond" signed in Edinburgh's Ainslie Tavern), but nothing seems to have been further from her mind. And as a Catholic she would certainly not have allowed herself to be wed in the rites of the Protestant Church, as she was.

51

She was dressed in full mourning for the ceremony—mourning she had worn since Darnley's death—and she looked utterly crushed. One comment at the time was: "The opinion of divers is that the Queen is the most changed woman in fact that in so little time, without extremity of sickness, they have seen." The French Ambassador, Du Croc, refused to attend the hateful ceremony, but did manage to have a few words with the Queen the following day. Shocked by her appearance, he reported the Queen's words that: "He must not be surprised that he saw her sorrowful for she could not rejoice, nor ever should again. All she desired was death."

The lords of Scotland were, as ever, divided among themselves, but there were many aware of the injury done to their Queen, and a group gathered with their forces at Stirling to rescue her. Bothwell hastily retreated from Edinburgh, taking Mary with him to Borthwick Castle, twelve miles away. It was from here that Mary made a first, unsuccessful attempt at escape, dressed as a soldier and riding off alone at midnight on a stolen horse: she was recaptured by Bothwell's men at dawn.

The lords occupied Edinburgh and, with a certain confusion of motive, pressed on to "revenge the death of Darnley" and "rescue the Queen". Bothwell, for his part, raised an army in the Queen's name to defend himself and his marriage to the throne of Scotland, and at Edinburgh it was defeated. He fled from the field of battle and from the pages of history, to die, years later, in Denmark.

Mary surrendered herself to the lords and now discovered the truth that many of those who had fought to rescue her believed her the murderer of Darnley: it was these who arranged she be lodged in a grim Edinburgh mansion called the Black Turnpike, often used as a temporary prison. She was shut up in this place shortly before midnight, having had no food or rest all day. When she was seen the next morning at the window, she appeared to have gone out of her mind with grief. She had torn her clothes to shreds, her long copper hair was down over her naked bosom. Many of the Edinburgh crowd who saw her were grieved at what had been done in their name.

The imprisonment was all things to all men and one of its muddled intentions had been that she would now agree to divorce Bothwell, the murderer. This she refused to do, for, to add to her other worries, she now believed herself pregnant by him. However much she despised the man, she would not have her child born illegitimate.

By now there was mounting popular feeling in favour of the Queen and the Lords began to fear an insurrection with the object of restoring her to freedom. On the other hand, while John Knox thundered threats from his pulpit about "burn the hoor", there was danger that a Protestant mob might seize her for their own reasons. It was decided to imprison her where she could not escape and where no man could reach her.

The place chosen was the Castle of Loch Leven, built on one of four small islands in a loch which, in those days, was fifteen miles in circumference. It was in fact a royal castle and had been used for generations of Scottish kings for hawking and fishing. The governor of the castle was Sir William Douglas, laird of Loch Leven and the surrounding country. Upon him would fall the responsibility of guarding his Queen.

At midnight she was roused from an exhausted sleep, wrapped, while still in her night-clothes, into a cloak-and-hood of coarse brown cloth, and dragged from her room by soldiers. They got her into the street, mounted her on a horse and took her at a fast trot to the port of Leith. Here she was put on a boat and ferried to the north shore of the Forth.

There she was made to mount another horse and ride, under heavy escort, to the shore of Loch Leven, where she was pushed into a boat and rowed out to the castle. The boat grounded on the island just as the first rays of dawn came over the hills.

She was unlucky in the timing of the move. Had the party reached Loch Leven ten minutes later they would have met and been overpowered by Lord Seton with a rescue force—but the loyal lord arrived too late, with the sun, and saw his Queen being dragged from her boat and into the castle.

For her first fifteen days, we are told, "she remained in her room without eating, drinking or conversing with the inmates of the house". No doubt an exaggeration, but all reports agree that she was a heartbroken and very sick girl when she arrived. She fainted frequently—so much so, it was believed she had epilepsy—she had some painful stomach complaint, probably a gastric ulcer; and she was pregnant.

Sir William and Lady Douglas were soon won over by her charm and by pity for her misfortunes. Gradually, through the kindness and nursing of Lady Douglas, she grew stronger.

No sooner was she able to walk about and try to enjoy the summer weather than she had a miscarriage.

It was at this point, 24 July, that a majority of Scottish lords vowed she must abdicate and make way for her infant son, James. They sent a delegation to the castle and, while she lay there grievously ill, forced her on pain of death to sign the instrument of abdication. One angered lord even struck her. Weeping, she made her signature, gave back the paper.

Her health recovered again and she learnt, some months later, in January of 1568, that three of the conspirators who had been at Kirk o' Field the night Darnley was murdered had been hanged and quartered. They had each, even on the gallows steps, repeated that the Queen was completely innocent of the affair. They then had begun to name others *not* innocent and the executions were rushed through in haste.

Out in the middle of Loch Leven, this was cold comfort. The little Queen busied herself with embroidery in her tower room. Her charm had won over all the Douglas family and their servants, and the laird himself now often took her out, when the winter weather was clement, in a boat on the loch. His younger brother, George Douglas, became helplessly infatuated with the beautiful prisoner, so much so that it was necessary to banish him from the castle. Someone equally infatuated was a young boy, Willie Douglas, who, while sharing the family names, was but a page. He had been brought to the island as a foundling, though there is some evidence that he was the laird's illegitimate son. Be that as it may, he spent as much time with her, cheering her up, as his duties would permit. She called him "my little friend".

She spent much time by herself, working on a tapestry which was to tell the story of her life and her misfortunes. (The unfinished work, just as she left it, can be seen still.)

It is unfinished because she escaped. But a first attempt which failed very nearly made a second impossible. This first attempt was made with the connivance of a laundress visiting the castle. Throughout her life, Mary was able to get ordinary folk to help her; she was, for example, permitted no writing materials during her captivity, but she wrote a stream of letters to the mainland, using materials brought to her by devoted castle servants, who then smuggled the letters ashore. In this case, the laundress agreed to change clothes with her, knowing the severest penalty would befall her if the ruse failed.

Disguised as the laundry woman, wearing a veil, Mary succeeded in leaving the castle and getting into a boat. Here the plot was foiled. One of the oarsmen accidentally bumped her and she threw up her hand to stop the veil from coming off. The beautiful, cared-for hand was obviously not that of a laundress and the boatmen stopped, rested on their oars.

Mary knew what they were thinking and she tried to command them. "Yes—I am your Queen. The Queen of Scotland. And I command that ye take me to the shore."

For a moment it seemed they would. Then fear of punishment made them hesitate and at last, with obvious reluctance, they rowed her back to the castle.

Mary must have been almost in despair at this point, for vigilance at Loch Leven Castle was redoubled. But she had not reckoned with the devotion of little Willie Douglas.

On Sunday, 2 May, he came into her room. She looked up from the tapestry and smiled.

"How now, my little friend?"

"Ma'am?"

"Yes, Willie?"

"Make ready to leave. Today, Ma'am——"

"Today, Willie? But how can I, a poor prisoner on an island, prepare to leave? Where would I go, Willie? And how?"

"I will take you, Ma'am. Tonight. I will be back at eight."

And the lad was gone.

She thought for a while, looking out from her tower room in the south-east of the castle at the broad gold pathway of the sun across the water. A pathway to freedom. It was spring, and summer not far behind. She got up.

At eight o'clock, just as he had promised, Willie was back.

With him was the Queen's ten-year-old serving maid, dressed roughly as a peasant child, and at first Mary failed to recognize her.

The girl handed her a cloak-and-hood and silently Mary slipped it on.

Twenty-six-year-old Queen, ten-year-old serving maid, looking like peasant woman and daughter, followed sixteen-year-old Willie down the long stone passage. The light came in every few yards, a dagger blade in the darkness through slitted windows, as they reached the end of the passage, started down the spiral stone stairs.

A moment later they were out in the evening sunshine.

Sir William and his wife would be having their evening meal, and Willie led his two ladies round the other way so they should not be observed from that window.

But, thought Mary, how would he get them out of the castle yard? The gate was kept locked, only opened, and for very good reason, by the laird himself. There was but one key and this Sir William carried day and night.

To her amazement, as they approached the massive portal, Willie took out a linen napkin from inside his shirt, unfolded it and took out the key. She watched, heart in mouth, as he put it in the lock, turned it and leant his small frame against the door.

Slowly, terribly slowly, it opened.

Half running, half walking, they made their way to the line of boats which was always chained to stakes at the water's edge, got into the nearest one. Willie slipped its chain off the stake, settled himself amidships, began to row.

As they pulled away from the island, Mary saw the chains of the other boats had been tangled and knotted: it would take half an hour to get any one of them free.

"But Willie, my little friend, how did you get the key?"

Willie was too hard at work with the oars to answer. Then, with a grin, he gasped: "Dropped the napkin on it at table, Ma'am. Always puts it beside his plate, Ma'am. . . ."

Halfway to the mainland, Willie stopped rowing for an instant, took out the key and hurled it into the loch. (In the nineteenth century, when the loch was dry as the result of a drought, it was found by a fisherman: half eaten with rust, it still fitted the castle door.)

In the distance she could make out the form of George Douglas on the shore, waving frantically. She took off her veil, waved back. Willie rowed the faster.

The boat grounded on the shore and George Douglas lifted her from it.

She was happier, perhaps, than she had been in all her life. Happier than she would be ever again. She was free. She mounted the horse George had brought for her, and refused to move until the exhausted Willie was helped on to his and they could start off together.

She saw now that it had been George Douglas's plan. He had chosen the date, warned the loyal lords, sent messages to Willie. They rode on into the gathering darkness and entered a wood. A mile farther on they were hailed loudly and the Queen gasped with alarm. But it was Lord Seton, to whose castle they were travelling. He thanked God the plan had been successfully carried out and joined them with a troop of cavalry.

At Seton's castle, in Long Niddry, the party rested two hours while the Queen wrote letters. Then they rode on to Hamilton Castle, reaching it a little after sunrise.

The news had preceded them and a large and enthusiastic army was beginning to gather from all over Scotland. It would be a few days before it assembled, and Mary was urged, in the meantime, to move into the impregnable stronghold of Lord Fleming at Dumbarton. From here, if something went wrong, she could make a retreat to France, or stay within its walls for as long as she wished.

Mary failed to take the advice.

That morning, Monday, 3 May, a messenger rode up to Moray, Regent of Scotland, who was to rule during the minority of the child James VI, and informed him the Queen had escaped the night before from Loch Leven.

For Moray, there was no time to lose. Mary could easily rally a large part of Scotland to her cause and assume the throne. After all, an instrument of abdication signed under duress by a grievously ill woman would hardly stand in a court of law. He rushed to assemble an army.

The two forces, Moray's and Mary's, met at the village of Langside, in Renfrewshire, and Mary, who should have been safe in Dumbarton Castle, was allowed to watch it from a high hill.

The battle, Mary's battle, was lost. Stricken by this new disaster, just when it seemed that most of her people were behind her at last, she tried frantically to reach the safety of Dumbarton Castle. She was too late and Moray's force cut her off. With a handful of followers she rode off to the south-west.

She managed to elude her pursuers and, in great distress, sent a message to Queen Elizabeth of England placing herself under the older woman's protection.

But Elizabeth was in a quandary. Though she strongly disapproved of rebellion against any monarch, and had supported Mary from a distance throughout her troubles, she was aware that Mary was her greatest rival. And Mary, when she reached the north of England, found herself a prisoner.

She remained one for the rest of her life. Nineteen years later, "being involved in a conspiracy", she was led off to the scaffold. On that day, 8 February, 1587, a tragic life ended.

A pitiful story. But it was brightened, as a sudden burst of sunshine lights a storm, by that brief span of ten days between Willie Douglas's stealing of her prison key and the battle of Langside.

Chapter 6

KING CHARLES II'S FLIGHT AFTER THE
BATTLE OF WORCESTER

> King Charles
> Walked and talked
> Two days after
> His head was chopped off

—as every schoolboy knows. And the missing full stop at the end of the second line makes it into a macabre little puzzle.

When this unfortunate monarch, Charles I, had paid the penalty in 1649, his son, though banished to France, was immediately proclaimed King Charles II by his Scottish subjects. A bit more than a year later, Charles II landed in Scotland. On 1 January, 1651, he was crowned in Scone.

Nine months after that, on a fateful first Wednesday of September—3 September—his forces, having penetrated as far south into England as Worcester, were utterly defeated by those of Oliver Cromwell. Charles displayed the greatest bravery throughout a battle which raged from midday till evening, but after his army had been routed there was nothing for it but to make his escape as best he could and hope to get back to France. From here he might perhaps be able to organize another expedition. And the next time, he swore, he would succeed.

And so began a frantic flight and pursuit lasting six weeks which has some of the elements of French bedroom farce, but which shows the young Charles—he was twenty-one—in favourable light as man of courage, humour and humility. Qualities very different to those he subsequently exhibited when the English people, tired of Puritan repression, demanded his return.

But all that was a decade ahead. The problem for Charles on the evening of Wednesday, 3 September, was to save his own neck.

The country folk of Wales were royalist and, as their land was reasonably near, he set off with a few trusted supporters in its direction—knowing full well that every hazard and inconvenience would lie between. The first hazard was the River Severn, and, as this was seen to be closely guarded, the party changed direction north, into the county of Shropshire. Charles had divested himself of his armour and was wearing the cavalier's laced coat, linen doublet, grey breeches and brown gloves. He had managed to get hold of a fresh horse at the end of the battle and now, thick with dust and blood, but smiling, he led his party at the gallop along the road to Kidderminster.

They passed through newly harvested fields to the east of it, galloped on through Stourbridge, stopped for a few minutes for refreshment, then rode on through the night. The party included, as well as the Duke of Buckingham, Lord Derby, Lord Wilmot and Lord Shrewsbury, a number of lesser mortals, including Mr. Charles Giffard. Shortly before dawn on the fourth they came as planned to Mr. Giffard's large half-timbered manor-house of Whiteladies. The bailiff, George Penderel, flung open the massive door and the King rode straight into the hall.

The door, with a monstrous clang, shut behind him.

Half an hour later it opened and a stranger emerged. He was wearing leathern doublet and breeches of coarse green cloth. His hair was cut short, his face was grubby (as, indeed, it had been half an hour previously), and he answered with an oddly familiar crooked grin to the name of Will Jones. He carried, a little awkwardly, a vicious billhook.

The party now dispersed. Sadly, within a few hours, many of them, including Mr. Giffard, had been captured, and a number put to death. Will Jones, though, had been led by the bailiff's brother, Dick Penderel (whose clothes he was wearing), out into a wood at the back of the house, called The Spring Coppice. He was given food and blankets and his loyal subject apologized for the fact that it had started to rain. Then, with the sun beginning to climb into a damp grey sky, the King found himself alone.

This worried him not at all, and he slept through the day, rolled up in sodden blankets under a tree. When Penderel sloshed back over the marshy ground to rouse him, Charles was so stiff he could hardly move, but he laughed at his decrepitude, hobbled into the house by the back door and wolfed a plate of bacon.

Penderel's plan was to guide the King across country, on foot, a distance of nine miles to the Severn. Here he had a royalist friend living in a house on the bank. The friend would hide his Sovereign and then, when time was ripe, get him across the river into Wales.

But those nine miles were peculiarly horrible. The two walkers were straightway soaked to the skin; the King's borrowed shoes hurt his feet so much that, had he been forced to run, he would have fallen on his face in agony; and they were a dozen times frightened half out of their wits by villagers who appeared suddenly out of bushes and darkness to ask them their business. Each time, as they told a different story, they were sure the game was up—and each time the villager, mumbling, walked off into the rain.

But eventually they reached the house. Charles hid himself under a hedge while Penderel went in, and a hideous night was made still more memorable by his immediate reappearance with the news that every crossing-place, up and down the length of the Severn, was guarded by Cromwell's troops. Furthermore, the house itself was being watched.

There was no question of the King hiding there—and even Wales had begun to seem an impossible refuge. He would have to hide for a few hours, rest his blistered feet, in the barn across the way.

Twenty-four hours were thus wasted: for by the end of the following night Penderel and his King were back in the manor-house of Whiteladies. Charles made light of it, saying the eighteen miles had toughened him—and his feet—for the exertions which must lie ahead. He was steadily perfecting his disguise, had now adopted a shambling, rustic gait, and dyed his face and hands with berries and nuts, so that he seemed more gypsy than King.

Another supporter, Colonel Careless, who had been acting as rearguard since Worcester, now arrived at Whiteladies and he urged his Sovereign not to stay another day under the trees, but to climb up into one of them, where he stood less chance of being discovered. Charles cheerfully agreed; they hammered together a small wooden platform among the branches of a large oak, and both went up and made themselves as comfortable as possible on it.

This particular incident in Charles's escape is perhaps the most famous, lending itself to much embroidery. Half the trees in the neighbourhood have been whittled to pieces for "souvenirs" of the day; vivid tales abound of Cromwellian soldiers wandering about underneath, sitting at the foot, eating meals, singing hymns and even considering sawing it down for firewood—but we have little evidence for any of this. We know only that Charles and Colonel Careless were up the tree from dawn to dusk, very uncomfortable indeed, and very glad to descend.

News at ground level was bad: a cordon had surrounded the neighbourhood, was rapidly closing in. A reward of £1,000 had been put on the King's head. Charles seemed to think this amusing, and he settled down inside the house to a huge meal. A little later he was asleep. It was the first night he had slept indoors since the battle.

The following evening, Sunday the seventh, the cordon had been withdrawn and he was able to set off with Colonel Careless and the three faithful Penderels towards the manor house of Moseley, belonging to the royalist Mr. Whitegreave. The trip was uneventful; he was greeted by Father Huddleston and Colonel Lane as well as his host, and the Penderels set off home to resume the less exacting tenor of their normal lives. The priest was startled by the King's appearance. We learn that "he had on his head a long white steeple-crowned hat, without any other lining than grease, both sides of the brim so doubled with handling that they looked like two spouts; a leathern doublet full of holes and half black with grease; an old green coat, threadbare and patched, with a pair of breeches of the same cloth and in the same condition, the flaps hanging down loose to the middle of his legs; hose and shoes of different parishes. The hose were grey, much darned and clouted, especially about the knees, under which he had a pair of flannel riding-stockings of his own with the tops cut off. His shoes had been cobbled with leather patches and so slashed, to adapt them to his feet, that they could no longer defend him either from water or dirt. This exotic and deformed dress, added to his short hair by the ears, his face coloured brown and a rough crooked thorn stick in his hand, had so metamorphosed him that it became scarcely discernible who he was, even to those that had been before acquainted with his person."

This apparition stayed at Moseley through the Monday and Tuesday, eating, sleeping and planning his next move. On the Tuesday afternoon he was very nearly captured by a band of soldiers who burst in to search the house. He was hastily stuffed into a nook behind the panelling, where he crouched for an hour while soldiers shouted and barked orders, inches from his head. Eventually they withdrew, and after a discreet interval the King set off again.

The plan, as now developed, appealed to him. Colonel Lane had a sister who lived a little way away, and a permit had been obtained for this lady to enter the town of Bristol and reside there, if need be, "with a servant".

The servant, of course, would be Charles. But in order to play this new rôle, the King pointed out, he would have to dress more respectably. No lady would dream of employing him now.

The gallant Colonel agreed, produced a grey suit, and led him off to meet the lady.

Twenty-four hours later the King was riding at the front of a party heading for Bristol. Headed by this well-scrubbed yeoman in the grey suit and cloak, whose name was now Will

Jackson, the party consisted of Miss Jane Lane and three others. A glance at the map will show us the extraordinary route they adopted, heading in every direction but the right one, a necessary —and successful—attempt to put Cromwell's troops off the scent.

They went first to the little village of Bromsgrove, where Will Jackson's horse, having lost a shoe, needed attention from the blacksmith. Charles, throughout this long chase, seems to have been able to put himself into whichever rôle he chose, and he soon struck up a voluble friendship as the smith hammered in his nails. "So you say the King has fled to Scotland?"

"Nay—he'll stand no chance in that direction," said the smith. "You mark my words, he'll be lurking round these parts."

"Indeed. And where would he be, this King?"

The blacksmith roared with laughter. "I know not—but I wish I did. For I would be richer by a thousand pounds."

Charles found this sort of discussion entertaining and indulged in it at every opportunity. Eventually the smith shook hands with him, wished him and the rest of his party god-speed, and they went on.

The next day they were at Stratford-on-Avon, where they galloped straight into a mounted troop of soldiers. Their disguise was effective, and the men let them pass, courteously returning their salute, and the fugitives cantered on to the village of Long Marston. Here they spent the night in lodgings, and the King, determined to play his rôle of servant to the full, made a way to the kitchen. He then brought disapproval on his head by a strange unfamiliarity with items of equipment, such as a roasting jack, which he was unable to work. But the royal ignorance seems to have been forgotten, for they were not questioned, nor were they followed when they left.

It was Thursday, 11 September, when the little party reached the Cotswold hills. The day was cool and crisp, a first harbinger of that icy winter which would soon descend, with at first not a cloud in the sky, but a soggy grey blanket above by the time they arrived. They had made greater progress than before, covering almost forty miles before sunset, and arriving for the night at the Crown Inn in Cirencester.

The next day took them through Chipping Sodbury to Bristol —where Miss Jane's letter allowed her to enter with her

With the co-operation of the Lord, Moses has caused the waters of the Red Sea to open, leaving dry land between (*above*). The Israelites, fleeing from an Egyptian army with horses and chariots, have got safe across and the Egyptians, drawing nearer each minute, have entered the valley between the waters. Suddenly, as Moses looks back, the waters return in a flood, seizing the Egyptians and their horses, drowning them all. (*Right*) Cortes has made his breathless escape from the island city of Mexico, has defeated the Mexicans for the time being and arrived, here, in the friendly city of Tlaxcala. He will soon regroup his Spanish survivors and then, with Tlaxcalans as his allies, go back to deal Mexico its final, crushing defeat.

The Earl of Nithsdale, sentenced to death for his part in the Jacobite rising of 1715, was flung into the Tower of London. Here, with stubborn dignity, he refused to make efforts to escape. Eventually, but with reluctance, he agreed to a scheme devised by his young wife, by which he would dress in clothes she smuggled in. After a complicated chain of mistaken identities, he got free (*right*) and went to France, where his wife joined him. Mary, Queen of Scots (*below*) so endeared herself to the staff of Loch Leven Castle that more than one attempt was made to help her escape. In this rather fanciful representation of the successful one, she is being helped into the boat which takes her to the mainland.

"servant". There had been a faint hope that a ship would be available immediately and the King might be loaded into it with the minimum of ceremony, but even before the party reached the gates of the city the hope had vanished. Miss Jane and her servant went in one gate and out another—there was no point in lingering to risk detection in such a populated centre—and put up for the night in the neighbouring manor house of Abbots Leigh. This was perched high on the downs, overlooking the wide expanse of the Severn estuary.

A Norton family owned the house, and as it was necessary for the whole party (which was here reunited) to stop a few days, Jane Lane announced that her servant Will Jackson was ill of a fever and would have to rest a few days. He was given a room to himself and there, sniffling and groaning, he put on a superb performance as well-meaning but not-too-courageous servant. Miss Jane, for her part, complained constantly about him. "That wretched, wretched boy," she called him; and certainly Charles, having lost a deal of weight about the face, and being only twenty-one, looked the part of seedy, surly youth to perfection.

Mrs. Norton was about to be delivered of a child, and she greatly welcomed the presence of Miss Jane—a situation which would soon cause them alarm. But a still more alarming situation arose when the Nortons' butler, who had been at the battle of Worcester, suddenly asked "Will Jackson" if he were King.

"King, you say? I?"

"Aye—King. Be you King, sire?"

There was a long pause.

"Yes," said Charles. "I am."

"God bless you then, sire. God bless you—and bring you to us as our rightful King."

Charles was a good judge of his fellow-men and he trusted this one immediately. The next day the butler was dispatched into Bristol to find out whether, after all, there might not be a ship in a day or two.

The news was as discouraging as before. No vessels were sailing for at least a week, and, when they did, it would be well-nigh impossible to smuggle a man on board. Every approach to the waterfront was blocked, every jetty guarded.

This was a numbing blow. The whole escape, so far, had

depended on getting a ship near Bristol, or if necessary from the coast of Wales. Now there was nothing for it but to journey, at even greater risk, right across the country to the south coast. Here there were more ports, and more opportunity of finding a fishing smack which might be hired to take a man out of England.

A few days, and the plans had been concerted, so Will Jackson was able to recover from his indisposition, and the party set off south into Dorset, leaving behind an angry and upset Mrs. Norton, who had wanted Miss Lane's help at her confinement. On the seventeenth, Jane Lane parted from her "servant", kissing his hand before riding away. She had played her part well, and, though they had failed to find a ship in Bristol and seemed no nearer safety, Will Jackson never forgot her. One of the more attractive aspects of his subsequent reign was the way in which every single person who had helped him in his troubles was remembered and rewarded. Jane Lane, who went on to marry a Warwickshire squire, was showered with jewels by her grateful monarch and granted a royal pension. The family coat of arms was augmented by the words, "Garde le Roi".

All this, of course, was a number of years in the future. The first incident of note after Charles's parting from the young lady was a wild celebration in Trent: church bells were being rung hysterically, hour after hour. When they inquired, they were told it was to celebrate the King's death. The man who claimed to have killed Charles was a common soldier, and now he strutted backwards and forwards in the square, wearing an ill-cut coat which he assured one and all had been the King's own. So much the better, thought Charles: if I am dead, there is little cause for me to remain hidden; and his four days in Trent were comparatively relaxed ones, staying with Colonel Wyndham and his wife, who knew his identity but treated him in public as a servant. He enjoyed playing the part, even wandered forth, to his host's considerable alarm, to discuss details of his own death with those who professed to know them.

Colonel Wyndham had set himself to finding, somewhere along the south coast, a vessel suitable for their purpose. After much reconnaissance and bargaining, the master of a coasting vessel at Charmouth, near Lyme (soon to be Lyme Regis), agreed to

66

take two men to France. It had been agreed that Lord Wilmot would accompany his King.

At Charmouth another drama was played out, much to Charles's liking. The lady in charge of the Queen's Arms had been carefully informed of a great nobleman, remaining anonymous, who had fallen in love with a maid and was eloping with her. The landlady was delighted by this romantic tale and eagerly prepared a decorous pair of rooms for the lovers. A highly suitable young lady had been found—Colonel Wyndham's young cousin, Juliana Coningsby—and the landlady was overjoyed as the couple trotted in at dead of night—sharing one horse—and were made welcome and sent to their separate rooms. Colonel Wyndham, who had arrived at the same time, went out again to find the captain of the vessel and fix up details.

He was out for the rest of the night, and the young couple, who might have been expected to have other things on their mind, grew worried. Wyndham came in, a little after dawn, and stated that he had found no trace of man or vessel.

Then the truth came out. Someone had decided that Charles was not dead after all and a hasty proclamation had been made warning that anyone aiding the King was liable to the death penalty. Anyone apprehending him would receive a reward of £1,000. The captain had had his suspicions of the identity of his intended passengers: now he discreetly vanished from the scene.

They must ride westward along the coast, to Bridport. One of the horses in the party had to be shod first, and the sharp-eyed smith noted a number of peculiarities, from the type of nails to the condition of the beasts. He said nothing till the job was done and payment made, then dashed off to confide in the ostler, who, in turn, went to the parson. This worthy man refused to be consulted until he had finished his devotions: by the time he arrived at the inn with the ostler the King had flown with all his party. Piecing together the evidence, the parson decided it must indeed be the King. Being a staunch Cromwellian, he rushed to the local military. A troop of horse was dispatched, in the wrong direction.

The town of Bridport was packed with soldiers preparing to embark for an expedition to Jersey. This was not a place to stop for the night, and after a hurried meal the fugitives set off again for Trent.

The alarm was now out. They had just left after their meal when there was a thunder of hooves and a band of soldiers galloped past in pursuit, towards Dorchester. In fact, utter confusion now reigned. The romantic landlady from Charmouth, sadly disillusioned on hearing that Charles had invaded her premises in disguise, now convinced herself that it was the "young lady" who had been the King. Now that she recalled "her" face, she was certain of it. And of course, as she pointed out to the neighbours, if the King had been dressed as a man, him with his features so distinctive like, he would have been recognized by everyone. Whereas, in that bonnet . . .

So the whole of southern England was soon in hot, rushed pursuit of a damsel, convinced she was the King. All along the coast, pretty girls were being apprehended and forced to reveal sex and identity.

Time, too, had begun to rush—with the chase growing ever wilder. The whole south coast was watched and guarded and there could be no question of moving along it to a port. The King would have to retire inland until the certainty of a boat, then dash to the coast and board it by night. He was taken to Heale House, near Salisbury, on Monday, 6 October, and here young Juliana Coningsby left him, having played her romantic part to perfection. Under the circumstances, it is amazing she should have reached her home without being molested as fugitive King, but she did so.

Throughout this nerve-racking period, the King seems to have been cheerful and unperturbed. From his new quarters outside Salisbury he calmly went out and admired the various sights he had long wanted to visit, notably Stonehenge. He was unable to do anything further to assist his own escape: he might as well use each day as profitably as possible, for the widening of a King's experience.

It was Lord Wilmot now who learnt of a vessel. A small coal brig had docked at Brighthelmstone (now Brighton), and the master, Nicholas Tattersal, agreed for the sum of £60 to ferry to France two young men who had been "involved in a duel" and wished to flee the country.

On Monday, 13 October, they set off at two in the morning from Salisbury. At first it was only Charles and a Colonel Phelips, but a little after dawn they were met by Wilmot and a Colonel Gounter, who pretended to be coursing hares and to be surprised that these two friends should discover them at it. They rode on together, spent the next night in an inn, and Charles, feeling himself at last in sight of his goal, entered more fully than ever into his part. The landlord dropped a tankard and swore, and the King, now more Puritan than Cromwell himself, flung up hands in horror. "Oh, dear brother—I beseech thee, do not swear! No, never swear, dear brother!" He had by now acquired a black hat, and the landlord, ashamed of himself, apologized profusely.

Their last day's ride was Wednesday, 15 October. The flight had lasted exactly six weeks, and this day was as hazardous as any. Passing Arundel Castle, they had to hide from the Governor himself, going out to hunt. Near the village of Bramber, they were hotly pursued by Cromwellian soldiers and began to fear that, having come so far, they had lost everything in the last few miles. Hideous thoughts chased each other through their minds. Their horses were tired and all the time the thunder of hooves was getting closer behind them. Looking over his shoulder, Charles saw soldiers fifty yards behind, then thirty yards, then ten.

Then the pursuers were so close the leading horses could be felt breathing down their necks.

But the troop rode straight on through them, at full gallop. A minute later and they were out of sight.

At Brighthelmstone they stopped at the George Inn. The captain of the vessel joined them after supper, and the landlord, who now recognized his royal visitor, knelt suddenly and kissed the royal hand.

At midnight, Charles and Lord Wilmot were led to the brig *Surprise*. Here they embarked, down a ladder, and hid themselves. The vessel sailed at seven the next morning, heading, to disarm suspicion, for the Isle of Wight.

It was late in the afternoon before Captain Tattersal altered course for France, and early the following morning that the *Surprise* anchored two miles off Fécamp. From here Wilmot and

Charles rowed ashore and the ship turned round and returned to Brighthelmstone—via a brief but obvious call at the Isle of Wight.

Charles's exile was not entirely happy. The French, while at first making him welcome, required him to leave the country in 1654. He spent the next six years in wandering from one European country to another. Cromwell died in 1658 and the people of England, heartily fed up with Puritanism and austerity, were ready to have a king again, but the formalities took time and it was not until May, 1660, that King Charles II landed at Dover.

He was not a good king. But he was generous, as we have seen, to all those who had helped him become one. Even the dirty little coal brig had its name changed to *Royal Escape*, and remained for many years a proud, painted exhibit in the Thames.

But perhaps, for Charles, the finest hours had been those between the Battle of Worcester and the coast of France.

Chapter 7

ROBERT KNOX TRADES HIS
WAY TO FREEDOM

"A ND so we were passed from Town to Town, until we arrived at the Fort called Arrepa: it being about four of the clock on Saturday afternoon, October the eighteenth MDCLXXIX. Which day God grant us grace that we may never forget, when he was pleased to give us so great a deliverance from such a long Captivity, of nineteen years, and six Months, and odd days, being taken Prisoner when I was nineteen years old, and continued upon the Mountains among the Heathen till I attained to Eight and Thirty."

And so—but not quite—ends one of the strangest adventure stories in history: a true story which greatly influenced Daniel Defoe in the writing of *Robinson Crusoe,* Dean Swift in *Gulliver's Travels,* and a host of lesser writers in their work.

Robert Knox, who wrote those words, had been captured by the Sinhalese in 1659 and kept captive by them in the hill kingdom of Kandy for all but twenty years, until he and another Englishman managed to make their escape in 1679.

His book, *An Historical Relation of Ceylon,* was published in London in 1681. He was only forty, but he had crammed half a dozen lifetimes into those years, and ended his enforced sojourn in the island of Ceylon by an escape which would be hair-raising enough today but which in those days of ignorance and superstition must have been almost beyond the bounds of imagination.

He was a sailor by trade, son of another. His father, Robert Knox, Senior, was a prosperous sea captain, and in the year 1655 had a vessel built for himself and named her *Ann.* His son was now fourteen and eager to crew on her. This the elder Knox viewed without enthusiasm, having up to now insisted the boy go to boarding school at Roehampton, near the family home in Wimbledon.

But the boy had his way and accompanied his father on the *Ann*'s first voyage to India in December, 1655, returning in the middle of 1657. They had called in at Fort St. George (Madras), gone on to Bengal, and come back with a fine cargo, which they sold for a profit.

Accordingly they prepared to set sail again for India, as a private vessel. But just as they were about to leave, Oliver Cromwell revived the old, almost defunct, East India Company, and the *Ann* was forced to sail in her employ.

It was 21 January, 1658. Her commission stated she would trade a twelvemonth on the Coromandel Coast and along the shores of the Bay of Bengal. At the end of that year she would go to the Persian Gulf before returning home.

The *Ann* did her year and went to the Gulf. Here, though, she found very little trade, and Captain Knox, in order to arrive home with a full cargo, was forced to turn round and head back to India.

The ship reached the Bay of Bengal—and it was while crossing it that she was struck by a terrible hurricane. For hours it seemed she would go down with all hands, while the crew hacked feverishly at the mainmast, to get it down before she turned turtle.

Ann weathered the storm and put in at Kottiar, on the island of Ceylon, to set another mast.

The island, as those who have been there know, is one of the most beautiful in the world, with a likeable, cheerful people. The sailors who now went on shore to get provisions and wood for repairs had no reason to question this. The natives showered them with gifts: cows, buffaloes, antelopes, chickens, all sorts of fruit; and refused all payment. While repairs to the mast were being slowly carried out, parties from the *Ann* went ashore each day. To the coastal dwellers these light-skinned men from Europe were nothing out of the ordinary: the Dutch and Portuguese had been calling at the island for many years, and more recently the English; and though first the Portuguese, then the Dutch, had fought battles with the Sinhalese and annexed territories, there was little ill feeling remaining. A number of English vessels had called at Kottiar and most had reported a friendly reception. It was true that a few sailors over the years had been abducted by the Sinhalese, but no doubt they had misbehaved themselves in some way: this was hardly likely to happen to Captain Knox's well-disciplined crew.

Unfortunately for Captain Knox and his son, and fourteen others, this estimate of the Sinhalese was quite inaccurate. They knew nothing about the King.

Rajasinha II dwelt in his impregnable capital of Kandy, high in the mountains. He had met Europeans, had defeated Portuguese armies, had entered into alliance, briefly, with the Dutch. He liked some Europeans he met, disliked others, but there was much, he realized, that these people from distant lands could teach his own people.

He had a peculiar whim. He maintained a menagerie of European prisoners.

There were almost five hundred of these, all of them well treated and most of them allowed to wander about, to engage in trade or agriculture and to take unto themselves Sinhalese wives. Some might even enter the King's employ—but, as young Knox was soon to report, this honour, bringing with it all sorts of immediate advantage, had a serious drawback: when the King tired of a man's service, he was not permitted merely to take up normal life again. He was put to death, like the unfortunate maidens of the *Arabian Nights*.

When he learnt of the arrival of the *Ann*, Rajasinha sent a messenger down to the coast to ask what the Englishmen were

doing and how long they intended to stay. The message was
duly conveyed to Captain Knox on board his ship in the harbour.
He, suspecting nothing, sent his son and another officer to meet
the messenger a dozen miles inland.

The two Englishmen exchanged greetings with this messenger,
who seemed to them to be some high court official. Then they
became suspicious.

Knox dispatched a letter to his father, via Sinhalese runners,
warning him on no account to disembark, but to sit tight on
board and await further news.

The runners never delivered the message. Instead, they conveyed to the captain that his son wished him on shore. He,
"mistrusting nothing, came up with his boat into a small River
and being come on shore, sat down under a Tamarind tree."

A moment later, he and the seven men with him had been
surrounded by Sinhalese soldiers, taken prisoner.

Father and son were now reunited and Captain Knox realized
that neither they nor their men would be released. He got a
message back to the ship, ordering her to sail away to safety,
which she did.

Young Knox's account of what now befell them is one of the
frankest travel documents we possess, hardly touched by any
sort of prejudice. He seems, while obviously involved in what
happens, to be at the same time an impartial observer somewhere
on a cloud, considering the motives and behaviour of all parties
in every situation. He generously blames their capture on the
fact that the *Ann* had been in the harbour for several months
and "our Neglect, viz. in not sending a letter and Present to the
King at our first coming. Who, looking upon himself as a great
Monarch, as he is indeed, requires to be treated with suitable
state."

Knox soon learnt there were other captives in the Kingdom
and he began to ponder the reasons Rajasinha might have had
for detaining them. "It cannot be out of hope of Profit or
Advantage, for they are so far from bringing him any that they
are a very great charge, being all maintained either by him or
his People. Neither is it in the power of Money to redeem
anyone, for that, he neither needs or values. Which makes me
conclude, it is not out of Profit, nor Envy, nor ill will, but out

of Love and Favour, that he keeps them there, delighting in their company and having them ready at his command. For he is very ambitious of the service of these men."

On the way up into the hills, they were treated with great courtesy. "We still expected they would plunder us of our clothes, having nothing else to be plundered of: but the Chingulay Captain told us that the King had given order that none should take the value of a thread from us: which indeed they did not. As they brought us up they were very tender of us, as not to tyre us with Travelling, bidding us go no faster than we would ourselves. The way was plain and easie to Travail through great Woods, so that we walked as in an Arbour, but desolate of inhabitants. So that for four or five nights we lay on the Ground, with Boughs of Trees only over our heads. And of Victuals twice a day they gave us as much as we could eat, that is of Rice, Salt Fish, Dryed Flesh: And sometimes they would shoot Deer and find Hony in the Trees, good part of which they always brought unto us."

But when they got near the City of Kandy, a new order came from the King. The party would be split up in twos and threes and scattered over the kingdom, being quartered in towns whose inhabitants would be charged with looking after them.

Knox is as disappointed as anyone at being cut off from his friends, but he is philosophical. He explains that it is hard for the prisoners, but it is obviously "for the convenience of getting Food, being quartered upon the Countrey, at their Charge."

He and his father are placed in a town thirty miles north of Kandy, a day's march and more from the rest of the Englishmen, but as they are the captain and his son they get better treatment. They are given their choice of a house, and all their meals are brought to them. The others, while provided with food, have to cook it.

A little later, they are ill with fever. Young Knox recovers slowly, over many months, but his father gets steadily weaker and eventually dies.

He is now alone, and greatly alarmed when a message arrives from the King, demanding to know how the Captain died, and what he has left. The poor man had left only a gold ring, a few coins and his old clothes: "God knows but very little, yet it scared me, fearing they would take it away from me, and my want being so great: but they had no such order nor intent. The chief occasion of their coming was to renew the former order unto the People of that Town, that they should be kind to me and give me good victuals, lest I might dye also as my Father had done."

He has nothing to read until an old villager sells him a book he took from Colombo when the Portuguese were driven from that town. Miraculously, it is in English, and a bible. Knox is overjoyed: he opens it up and the first words are: "What shall I do to be saved? And he answered saying, Believe in the Lord Jesus Christ, and thou shalt be saved and thine house."

He is a devout man and needs no reminder to believe. But he can hardly have realized that the salvation for which he most yearned would be delayed for twenty years.

Well treated, lacking for nothing in the way of food and kindness, Knox yet sets himself to earn a little money. He starts to knit cotton caps. The yarn can be purchased locally for about threepence English money, and the caps sold for ninepence. He also begins to rear pigs and poultry and soon becomes a prosperous and envied member of the community. He begins to be allowed to travel, and is able to visit a number of his compatriots.

The months grow into years and, though Knox never gives up hoping to return to his own land, he lives a full life in the one to which fate has banished him. Unlike most of his fellow captives, he refuses to take a wife, but most of the joys of life are there: the lot of a well-to-do man in seventeenth-century Ceylon is in many ways more luxurious than that of one in England, and this Knox is ready to admit.

But still there is the nagging urge to return to England, and in 1664 there seems suddenly to be a chance. The English Governor of Fort St. George gets a message through to the Kandyan Kingdom, asking that the captives be released. At the same time, the Dutch send another, courteously asking for the release of their own men, and the King looks favourably on both requests. He orders the captives to Kandy, where it seems likely he will release them.

But suddenly, and without warning, there is revolt among the

Sinhalese against their King. Rajasinha flees his capital at dead of night and for a while there is anarchy.

Five days later the royalists overthrow the rebels and the King is back on his throne. At first he is suspicious that the captives have worked for his downfall, but eventually he is convinced they have not. But now he will not countenance their release.

Knox moves to another town, Eledatta, gets the locals to build him a large and handsome house, and invites three other bachelors to share it with him: Ralph Knight, Roger Gold and Stephen Rutland. As the captain's son, Knox still takes a paternal interest in his crew: he also seems to have become a misogynist. These two aspects of character are neatly set out in his statement that after he became rich he celebrated Christian festivals like Easter and Christmas by inviting "all the English men and their wives, & children, to my house, where I feasted them for two or three days together, with goates, hogs and hens, and the reason I invited their wives was to dress the victuals".

Yet Knox had a tender heart, and in the second half of his long captivity he adopted a little girl. He christened her Lucea and taught her the English language and the Christian religion. One of his few regrets on making his escape was that he had to leave her behind. He remembered her to the end of his life—and he lived for forty years after his escape—and he sent gifts and a portrait of himself via other prisoners, to "the Girl I brought up, Lucea, and you know I loved the child". He had also, before his escape, made a will leaving her everything he possessed in the island.

Having got a reasonable return from agriculture and an excellent one from the lending of grain against next season's harvest, for which he charged no less than fifty per cent interest, Knox began to look round for something else to do, which might further his escape. Caps, though they had been profitable, soon glutted the market and "Trading grew dead, so that we could not sell them at the former price: which brought several of our Nation to great want". But some other form of trading might help. Two of his three companions in the house had left to get married and he now began to concert plans for an escape with the remaining bachelor, Stephen Rutland. They had both learnt the "Chingulay" language fluently and were permitted to wander over most of the kingdom. They decided to provide themselves with a few more caps, despite the drop in value, and with other things, like "Tobacco, Pepper, Garlick, Combs, and all sorts of Iron Ware, &c.", and see how far they could travel from the city of Kandy, doing trade with these articles, before being stopped. The route of escape would be northward to the low country and the coast.

They leave—but have not reckoned on one obstacle. They get fairly far down towards the lower country, but this "being much subject to dry weather and having no springs, we were fain to drink of Ponds of Rain Water, wherein the Cattel lie and tumble, which would be so thick and muddey that the very filth would hang in our beards when we drank. This did not agree with our Bodies, being used to drink pure Spring Water only."

They become very ill on this first expedition and learn that the mountain Sinhalese suffer likewise, which is why they hardly ever visit the low country. Ill though they are, Knox and Rutland realize that this reluctance on the part of their captors to visit the low country may stand them in good stead.

And eventually, after some ten "trading expeditions" which, with the assembling of goods, travelling, trading and recovery from illness, occupy a number of years, they discover an antidote for the foul water. "It is only a dry leaf: they call it in Portugueze, Banga, beaten to powder with some of the country Jaggory: and this we eat Morning and Evening upon an empty Stomach."

But now an extraordinary drought holds them back: the low country is "almost starved for want of Rain: all of which time they never tilled the Ground. The Wells also were almost all dry; so that in the Towns we could scarcely get Water to drink, or Victuals to eat. Which affrighted us at those times from running into the Woods, lest we might perish from Thirst. All this, while upon the Mountains, where our dwelling was, there was no want of Rain."

They must often have wondered whether they would ever succeed in a plan, so carefully thought and exhaustively prepared, which was yet at the mercy of the weather.

But at last they judge the weather, their health and their preparations suitable for a final, all-out, attempt. It is 1679:

"On the two and twentieth of September, furnished with such Arms as we could well carry with safety and secrecy, which were Knives and small Axes; we carried also several sorts of Ware to sell as formerly: the moon being seven and twenty days old. Which we had so contrived, that we might have a light Moon, to see the better to run away by."

Thus provided, they set out boldly, soon reaching "the town of Bonder Cooswat, where my Father dyed", after which towns become less frequent. They are craftily selling caps and things on credit, the sums to be paid them on their "return". Soon, between the towns, the jungles are full of wild elephants, tigers and bears, and they are very frightened. They manage to survive this part of the trip and now head for Anuradhapura, "the lowest place inhabited belonging to the King of Cande: where there is a watch always kept. And nearer than twelve or fourteen miles of this Town as yet we never had been." They have carefully done the minimum of trading so far, in order to have a good supply as "a pretence to have an occasion to go further". But now a new hazard: the only possible route goes through a military headquarters, under command of the local Governor. They decide to go boldly up to his house and convince him, before he asks them, that they have permission to travel.

Neither of them can have been very happy about this desperate bluff, but they surprise themselves by pulling it off. They present the great man with tobacco and tell him they have come to take back dried meat to the hill country. This is a commodity found only in the plains. They hope he can help them.

The Governor thanks them for their gift and apologizes for the dry weather: only this has prevented his people from killing deer. Just as soon as rain comes, he will make it his business to load the two traders up with all the meat they can carry. In the meantime, he urges them to go from town to town, trying to find some.

"This answer of his pleased us wondrous well, both because by this we saw he suspected us not, and because he told us there was no dryed Flesh to be got. For it was one of our greatest fears that we should get our Lading too soon: for then, we could not have had an excuse to go further. And as yet we could not possibly fly: having still six miles further to the Northward

to go before we could attempt it, that is to Anarodgburro."
While they bide their time before the next stage to
Anuradhapura, they are alarmed when a body of troops arrives
from Kandy, with orders to tighten up all border posts. The
reason, they learn, is that some Sinhalese nobles have fallen
into disgrace and this is to prevent their escape. The soldiers
are genial and no attempt is made to apprehend the two
Englishmen.

The next morning they make their departure, ostensibly to
look for dried meat. Knox gives the Governor a present of a
little gunpowder, subtly suggesting that he may be able to shoot
some deer before their return. "In the meantime, according as
we had before layd the business, came Stephen with the bundle
of Goods, desiring to leave them in his house till we came back.
Which he was very ready to grant us leave to do. And seeing us
leave such a parcel of Goods, tho, God knowes, but of little
account in themselves, yet of considerable value in that Land,
he could not but suppose that we were intended to return again.
Thus we took our leave and immediately departed, not giving
him time to consider with himself, or consult with others
about us."

With unseemly haste, which they try to keep in check, they
plunge blindly into dense jungle and manage to emerge at more
or less the right point. Soon they have arrived at Anuradhapura,
some eighty miles north of Kandy, set in a wide, fertile plain,
and the people of the town are amazed by their coming. An
official asks them how they got leave to travel this far and now,
hardened liars both, they tell a fantastic tale and are believed.

They stay three days in Anuradhapura, pretending to look for
dried flesh, but stealthily acquiring necessities for their impending flight. Up till now, they have purchased provisions on the
way: this will no longer be possible. They buy rice, a brass pot
to boil it in, a deerskin to make shoes. They also spy out the
north road to the ports which are in Dutch hands.

They explain they are going back to Colliwella, the place
where they gave gunpowder to the Governor, for doubtless by
now he will have got some meat with it: the people believe this.

It is 12 October, 1679, and they set off, with loud farewells,
for Colliwella, which they have no intention of reaching. Soon

they will be off the main paths and they are beginning to fear the wild animals they will meet. "Tiger and Bear; and as for Elephants, there is no standing against them, but the best defence is to flee." The instant they take themselves into the jungle they come face to face with an elephant. They are unable to scare it away, so light a fire and wait until morning, when the beast has gone.

Soon they run into an unexpected town, but before they are spotted they manage to leap into an old hollow tree, where they stay several stiff and miserable hours. When they emerge from it, they are grateful to the elephants which follow them, for no man will be able to approach from that direction.

They are almost at sea level now; it is baking hot and they stagger exhausted along the dried-up bed of a river. In places there are pools and these are full of alligators, so that, what with avoiding these when they need water to drink, and dodging the other large and dangerous animals which the dry weather has brought in their thousands to the river bank, their journey is hazardous and unpleasant.

They are fairly sure they have left the King's realm, for they come to a community of "Malabars", speaking an Indian tongue. Here they buy meat, wrap it up in a hide and take it with them into the house where they have been given sleeping space. The meat is inches away from Stephen's head when they go to sleep, and there are two fires burning.

"Yet a Tiger came in the night and carried Deer and Hide and all away." They can scarcely believe this, but find the beast's footprints and pieces of the meat which it has dropped.

The next day, confident they have left the King's domain, their hearts are light as they move along the river bank. They meet more Malabars, who tell them in sign language that they are only a few hours' march from the Dutch fort, but make no effort to help them find it. The Malabars go their own way. Night falls and again they are terrified by elephants and have to save themselves by hurling firebrands at them.

The next day they meet a man who speaks a little Sinhalese and is willing to direct them to the fort. An hour later, filthy and exhausted, they stumble in.

"The Hollanders much wondered at our arrival, it being so

strange that any should escape from Cande; and entertained us very kindly that night: and the next Morning being Sunday, sent a Corporal with us to Manaar, and a Black Man to carry our few things."

(Already, as soon as they are back among Europeans, they have started to think again in terms of Black men and White.)

The rest of their triumphant return, via Colombo and Batavia, to England, need not concern us. It was September, 1680, when they reached England, after an absence of over twenty years. Knox was none the worse for his experiences (he had already written his account on the return from Batavia to England) and soon he was captaining his own vessel, the *Tonqueen Merchant*, and journeying to every corner of the globe.

But never again to Ceylon.

His *Historical Relation* was published in 1681. It is a remarkable book, divided into four parts, only the last of which deals with his own adventures. The other three deal in the greatest detail and accuracy with the Island itself, the King, and the People.

He soon became known as a literary man and was persuaded to write his autobiography, which was bound into the same volume as the *Historical Relation*. A few generations after his death, when men had become more blasé about travel and adventure, the volume was lost sight of, and only appeared by accident in the Bodleian Library of Oxford, where it was discovered in 1910.

Chapter 8

THE EARL OF NITHSDALE WALKS OUT
OF THE TOWER OF LONDON

QUEEN ANNE died in 1714. We know that the demise of this rather unromantic figure set in train the first of the two great Jacobite rebellions. "The Old Pretender", James, who had reason to hope he might be named Anne's successor—but was not—came over from France trying to take the throne by force. A number of people felt Anne might have stipulated that he succeed her, for, after all, though he was Catholic, he was her half-brother: the anti-royalist sentiment which had spawned Oliver Cromwell and chopped the head off James's ancestor, Charles I, was a thing of the past.

But the Scottish Catholics reckoned without the stolidly malevolent George I. He it was who had been invited to succeed Anne and had done so. He was now firm—if inarticulate, for he spoke only German—on the English throne. He dispatched a large force to deal with the Jacobites and thrashed them at Preston.

And, as had happened before, would happen again, cartloads

of the highest in the land were taken to the Tower of London to await the sovereign's pleasure.

There was no argument about George's pleasure. He wanted the death, and the sooner the better, of the lot of them. They included, in this full house, the Scottish Earls of Carnwath, Wintoun and Nithsdale, as well as an English Earl, of Derwentwater. There were cells full of less-exalted personages, all awaiting their fate.

Everyone was "tried": most were found guilty and among these was the Earl of Nithsdale. After various pleas for clemency, his death warrant was signed, on 23 February, 1716, sentencing him to the scaffold in two days' time.

But when the guards came to take him to that scaffold, Nithsdale had vanished.

Somehow or other the noble Earl had succeeded in escaping from the Tower of London. It was a long time before the full details came out, and then, to give fat George his due, he was highly amused. He laughed till the tears cascaded down his puffy, powdered cheeks. "Mein Gott!" he roared. "For a man in such an unpleasant situation, young Nithsdale did well——"

But Nithsdale, upright and dull, owed everything to his beautiful, energetic and imaginative wife, Winifred, who was just twenty-six. While Nithsdale was repeating a pious resolve never to lower himself in his own estimation by begging a pardon or leaving the Tower in any way but through the strength of his sword, Winifred was taking action. He had only just been incarcerated when she set out from their home in Scotland and galloped to Newcastle. Here she caught the stage-coach, which soon came to a halt in a snow drift. While the rest of the passengers cringed and shivered within, the young Countess of Nithsdale leapt out, found a man prepared to hire her a horse, galloped on through the snow.

Eventually, she reached London. Here she discovered what she had feared, that her husband had been sentenced to death. She went straight to the Prime Minister, Robert Walpole. Was there any hope of pardon?

There was not.

Could she go, then, and visit him in his cell?

Only if she were prepared to stay there till the end, remain

84

with Nithsdale until they took him out and hacked his head off. There would be no visiting, no smuggling in of tools, no furtive, shared plans for an escape. Nithsdale would die, and that was all there was to it.

But Winifred Nithsdale had no intention of taking no for an answer, least of all from this corrupt minister of a usurping foreign monarch. She turned on her heel, left the man's presence and went back to her lodgings.

She and her maid Evans, with Miss Hilton and Mrs Mills, both ladies of Jacobite persuasion, had taken lodgings in Drury Lane—which was as near as they were able to get to the Tower without arousing suspicion. Evans, like her mistress, was a very pretty girl and she had already found out from the soldiers who came carousing into Fleet Street exactly where Lord Nithsdale was imprisoned. He was occupying an apartment of two rooms, high up in what was known as the Lord Lieutenant's Tower.

The next day Winifred Nithsdale made her way to the Tower and used her own beauty—and her considerable wealth—to get past the warders and actually into her husband's apartment. As she had expected, he showed no interest in any subterfuge, but she went on talking brightly—and loudly—as she studied the layout of his prison. There was one halberdier on duty outside the heavy door, listening to every word they spoke, and two more sentries a little farther down, at the foot of the winding stone stairway.

It was obvious as she looked about her that no amount of force, of physical ingenuity, could effect an escape. There was only one window, high in the wall and heavily barred. Through this, out on Water Lane, she could see yet another sentry. As for the interior of the Tower, that was alive with soldiers.

No, any escape from this dungeon would have to be by subterfuge. Even bribery and persuasion, of which she was rapidly becoming a master, would serve no purpose. No sentry would dare allow a man like Lord Nithsdale to escape, however huge the reward. And there would be a dozen or more sentries to deal with.

She was slowly working out a plan in her head, but in response to her husband's suggestion she agreed to go to St. James's Palace and crave audience of the King. This was as far as

Nithsdale was prepared for his wife to go: he would not be attracted by other, shameful, methods of release, but "for the children's sake" his wife could go and petition the King.

George, though she waylaid him in his palace and flung herself on her knees before him, refused even to see the petition she was carrying.

Her mind was made up.

First—though she knew full well it would avail them nothing at all—she would go from one great man to another, seeking pardon for her husband. She would go, too, to the House of Lords, and be seen to be going. Then, and only then, would she put her plan into operation.

Two evenings later, having presented her petition to the House of Lords, she was seen by the sentries at the Tower to get out of her carriage and approach them. For the first time, there was a happy smile on her face.

"Share my joy."

"Your joy, my lady?" said the puzzled sentry.

"Yes, my good man—my joy. The House of Lords has heard my petition and looked on it with favour. It is now only a matter of days—a few days—before His Majesty grants us a pardon."

She went in, told this tale to other warders and sentries, and they, kind men all, agreed this was a fine, fine thing. Gratefully, they accepted the Countess of Nithsdale's money to drink the Earl's health.

"And that of His Majesty King George I, who is doing this for us."

"Aye, aye, your ladyship. And the King——"

A day later she propounded the details of her scheme to Evans, to Miss Hilton and to Mrs Mills.

"You," she said to Evans, "remain Evans—my faithful Evans——"

"Yes, my lady," said the puzzled girl.

"And you, Miss Hilton, are now—for a space—'Mrs Catherine'."

"I understand."

"And you, dear Mrs Mills, are 'Mrs Betty'."

It was the Friday—day before the execution.

"You must do everything I tell you. Now listen, very carefully. . . ."

She explained.

A little later all four of them drove to the Tower. The maid Evans remained outside, while the other three went together to the sentries, who smiled at Lady Nithsdale and let them all through.

As Winifred Nithsdale had anticipated, there were a number of middle-aged women who had managed to gain entry to the Tower and were now standing ghoulishly about, waiting to see her pass on what they believed would be the last occasion she saw her husband. These, without knowing it, were part of the plan. She strode on through the crowd, and the other two, Miss Hilton and Mrs Mills, lingered behind, scarcely noticed in the fading light of a winter afternoon, coming through barred windows.

She went on to her husband's apartment and stood outside the door for a moment, giving Miss Hilton time to catch up with her and be greeted loudly as a new arrival. "My dear Mrs Catherine, how kind of you to come. . . ."

Miss Hilton, a slim girl, was wearing extra clothes under a cloak, clothes which in fact included another cloak belonging to Mrs Mills. Once inside the ante-chamber of the Earl's apartment, she shed the extra clothes and went out again. Lady Nithsdale accompanied her to the top of the stairs and called after her, "Pray send my maid to me at once. It is late, and I must be dressed at once, or I shall be late."

Mrs Mills, as "Mrs Betty", now came up the winding stairs, a fat woman holding a handkerchief to her face and obviously in great distress. "Oh, but do come in, Mrs Betty——"

Once inside the apartment Mrs Mills, also wearing extra clothes, which included a riding-hood large enough to fit the Earl, divested herself of these, put on those which had been left for her by Miss Hilton, and went out again, a slimmer, smiling figure. "Goodbye, my dear Mrs Catherine. And, pray, do not omit to send my maid."

It was now almost dark. Any minute the candles would be lit, and the added illumination might easily sabotage the whole plan. Frantically, Winifred Nithsdale began to dress her protesting husband in petticoats: some of her own, some of Mrs Mills's. He was dirty and unshaven, so she wound a scarf round the lower half of his face, tied false ringlets on the upper. A dab of rouge, and the big riding-hood went on.

She opened the door and urged her husband ahead of her, staying close behind him so no one should remark on his strange, and strangely unfeminine, gait. All the while she kept up a stream of conversation, addressing him as "Mrs Betty" but never allowing him time to reply. The poor man, hopelessly confused by now, might easily have made some gruff comment and been unmasked, but he was never given a chance.

She got him into the courtyard. There the faithful Evans was waiting to take "Mrs Betty" by the arm, lead "her" across the yard, out into the street.

A moment later, the Earl of Nithsdale and his wife's maid had vanished into the darkness of the evening.

Winifred Nithsdale went back to her husband's empty cell. Much still depended on her ability to distract the guards and give her husband a chance to make good his escape before the whole garrison went off in pursuit. She began a loud conversation, making replies for him in a gruff bass voice and walking heavily up and down the apartment, as if the two of them were striding up and down in great agitation.

Eventually she decided Nithsdale must have reached safety. She took a deep breath, opened the door.

Before shutting it, she turned round and said, "Good night, dear heart. Something very strange must have kept my maid Evans, for she has never been late before. I must go home to change—but I must hurry, I shall probably be late. I will be back later to see you, dear husband——"

The guards, saddened by this exchange between a brave—and generous—woman trying to keep up her husband's spirits, and the condemned man himself, sunk in some deep depression, saluted as she went out.

Her last words in the Tower were: "I pray you—do not disturb my lord. He is at his prayers."

She left and made haste towards Drury Lane, for there was still much to do. For a start, she could no longer remain in these lodgings: soon the soldiers would be out after her. She prepared to leave, and although she badly wanted to join her husband in the attic room a mile away to which Evans, she knew, was taking him, there was too much risk involved.

Mrs Mills—no longer either fat "Mrs Betty" or thin "Mrs Catherine", had long had a friend who was servant to the Venetian ambassador. By a long and complicated ruse for which we have no space, she arranged that the Ambassador himself, all unsuspecting, get Lord Nithsdale, dressed in Venetian livery, to Dover. Soon he was on his way to France.

He reached there, still scarce able to believe his luck, and was joyously welcomed and looked after by Jacobite friends. A few weeks later he made his way to Rome, where James, the Old Pretender, held court. A frustrated and unhappy man, James was about to send for his fiancée, Clementina, of whom more in another chapter.

For brave Lady Nithsdale there was much to be done before she could join her husband. She had a young son still in Scotland, and as soon as she had seen the Earl safely on board his vessel —watching from a safe distance—she travelled north to hide the boy and put her family affairs in order. This involved more romantic dealings than are customary, for she had carefully buried her papers and her jewels in the garden at Nithsdale.

Having hidden and then taken her young son—for all she knew, the hateful George might seize him as hostage for his father—she came south again and crossed to France. She was soon an honoured member of the Jacobite Court-in-Exile. When the Pretender, after frustrations which were considerable but scarcely equalled those of the Nithsdale family, married his little Clementina, Winifred became a close companion and help to the Polish princess.

When James and Clementina produced children, she became their governess. Of the Earl of Nithsdale himself we know little after his escape—but of his brave and resourceful wife we know much. She lived to a great and honoured age, and had the distinction of being governess and guide to the much-loved "Bonnie Prince Charlie".

Chapter 9

PRINCESS CLEMENTINA'S RIDE
TO ROMANCE

THE tale of the little Polish princess has always seemed to me one of the most "romantic" escapes in history, and indeed it was seized upon by A. E. W. Mason as the basis for his romance *Clementina*. There is little apart from polish and marshalling that Mason was able to add to the actual facts, for the real-life details of the girl's flight are as thrilling as we could wish them to be.

And here, as far as little Clementina is concerned, are the facts. They are closely interwoven with the problems of the exiled Stewarts, but so many of the most gripping escapes have been that I make no apology for including a fistful in this book.

Prince James of Scotland, whom many had hoped to crown as King James III of England and VIII of Scotland after the death of Queen Anne in 1714, had failed notably in his attempt to gain that throne. Anne had died without recognizing him as a successor—he was her half-brother—and he had been encouraged by supporters in England and Scotland to come over and take the succession for himself. There would be a rising, they assured him, and James III would soon be on his rightful throne.

But the risings were futile: the Scottish invasion of England was utterly defeated at Preston, and things went rapidly from bad to worse. Soon James, as "The Old Pretender", had returned in haste and despair to the Continent. He settled himself in Rome.

He was still a young man and, partly in order to cheer him up, and more realistically to produce an heir who might carry on the struggle when James had grown too old or dispirited to do so himself, his advisers urged him to get married. Not, of course, to just any well-born lady who took his fancy, but to one of royal blood, fit to sit on the throne of England and Scotland.

James agreed to the scheme; agreed, too, that one of his advisers travel round Europe, paying calls on royal houses and considering, from the brief he had been given, which royal lady, by appearance, manner or other aspects of suitability, might be the right one.

Charles Wogan took his job seriously, scanning pedigrees, descending suddenly—but charmingly—on royal houses. And when he had completed his reconnaissance, there was no question but that one young lady far outshone the rest. She was the grand-daughter of the great John Sobiesky who had been elected King of Poland in 1674, who nine years later had routed the Turks when they attacked Vienna, and for good reason had been styled "The Saviour of Christendom". As for his granddaughter, the Princess Clementina, she was exceedingly beautiful, with "the agreeableness of seventeen and the solidity of thirty, happy in all the charms, both of mind and body, her sex can boast of." She spoke six languages.

She was sixteen.

But many pitfalls lay between proposal and consummation. the chief being the attitude of that ponderous German, the King of England. George I could hardly be blamed for looking askance at an alliance which was clearly aimed at supplanting him. He made no secret of his feelings and in fact threatened so loudly that he would upset the peace of Europe if this monstrous betrothal took place, that the unfortunate little princess was

91

arrested and kept under an armed guard in Innsbruck, until such time as all danger of the alliance had ended. No doubt James, refused his little Pole, would turn to some other lady: when that happened, Clementina could be released.

What now? James and his advisers had no intention of giving up so easily—but hundreds of miles separated the lovers: one in constant danger of his life, the other in prison.

Charles Wogan was sent for again.

A little later we find him in Innsbruck, plausibly disguised as a merchant. He is allowed to see the princess and her mother and reveals his true identity. He has come to arrange an elopement.

Clementina claps her hands with delight.

But father, the dour Prince Sobiesky, does nothing of the sort. Told of the scheme, he dismisses it as utter nonsense. Worse still, he refuses to countenance it.

But Wogan, old soldier of fortune, is used to waiting. "I quite understand," he says to the Prince, and accepts with grace an offer of a few weeks' entertainment. The Prince, like Clementina, finds him utterly charming, and on New Year's Day, 1719, Sobiesky gives his house guest, as a memento, a handsome jewelled snuffbox.

"Sire," says Wogan. "I am overwhelmed by gratitude. But I could not possibly accept it when my master, for whom I came here, languishes for love of your daughter. I could not go to him with a gift for myself—and nothing for him."

So moved is Prince Sobiesky by this gem of Irish blarney that he relents, gives his blessing to the elopement.

Wogan sets off (with the snuffbox) to pass the good news to James in Rome.

But before he gets there, a message from Sobiesky. He has thought it over and changed his mind again: it is far too risky an undertaking for his wife and daughter.

Wogan passes this news on to James, who replies that they must press on with the scheme, ignoring Sobiesky completely.

Wogan's plan goes into operation. He gets in touch with three relatives, all, like himself, Irish Catholics, and passionately behind James's cause. He outlines it to them.

The party of conspirators sets out across Europe to Innsbruck:

Wogan, Major Gaydon, Captain Misset and Captain O'Toole, with Mrs Misset and her personal maid Jeanneton.

The plan was a fairly straightforward one, by the customs of that period: somebody would change clothes with the Princess and let her escape in disguise. The someone was the maid, Jeanneton. But it was now that Wogan may well have wondered whether women as a sex were worth all this risk and trouble. In order to capture the interest of Jeanneton, who must not be told the whole truth, he gave her a fanciful tale about the burly Captain O'Toole having fallen head over heels in love with a young heiress, whose father refused to grant his daughter's hand.

Jeanneton, told of the part she was expected to play, was unenthusiastic. Wogan waxed more lyrical and at last she agreed.

But then, almost at the last minute, she refused to wear the low-heeled shoes which would bring her down to the little "heiress's" height. She had always worn high-heeled shoes—like these, see—and no heiress in the world, no love-sick Irish goat of a suitor, would make her change the habit now.

But at last—and history does not relate just how—the girl was persuaded, and the party completed their journey by carriage to Innsbruck.

At an inn, not far from the castle where Clementina was confined, there was a hurried meeting with yet another conspirator whom Wogan had managed to enlist. He was Monsieur Chateaudoux, gentleman-usher to Clementina's mother, and, after some argument and deliberation, he and Jeanneton, now in low heels, set forth through the rain to carry out their part in the plot.

There was no time to lose, the night was slipping by, and the party, with their Princess, would have to be out of Innsbruck before the sun arose, to stand any chance of success.

Chateaudoux was of course well known to the guards and he had no trouble in getting into the castle and bringing a young lady with him. The two made their echoing way along the cold stone passages to the wing in which Clementina was quartered, were let through by another guard, and found themselves in the little ante-room adjoining the Princess's bedchamber.

Her mother greeted them and pointed out that Clementina—still, in the eyes of Jeanneton, an heiress, who was somehow rich and important enough to be surrounded by soldiers and live in a castle—was pretending to be unwell. She had retired to bed the day before with "stabbing pains in the head".

Jeanneton was taken into the bedchamber; Monsieur Chateaudoux sat down in the ante-room. He had begun to feel nervous about the whole thing, and he hoped the Princess and Jeanneton would complete their change of identity with the utmost speed.

But this was not to be. The minutes ticked past and Chateaudoux, looking out again and again to see the first rosy signs of dawn, grew frantic. He had just got up to bang angrily on the Princess's door when she came out. One smile and he was her slave again, even if at first he had hardly recognized her in the maid's rain-soaked clothes.

"Pray forgive me, sir. I was saying adieu to my mother——"

"Of course. But we must make haste. Great haste."

A minute later, the two of them were out in the rain. By now a real storm had broken and the wind was screeching. Wogan and O'Toole, who had been standing at a corner of the road, now ran up to them and took them off to yet another inn, where hot drinks and a change of clothes were waiting.

Dawn was breaking when the carriage at last pulled out of Innsbruck, but with luck they would be several miles away before it was light. If Jeanneton continued to play her part in the Princess's bedchamber, they might be well on the way to safety before the elopement was discovered.

But suddenly the little Princess burst into tears.

What was wrong? Did she regret what she was doing?

No, no, not at all. But the parcel which held all her jewels, and which she thought she had smuggled out to Wogan earlier in the day, was not with them.

The horses were stopped and a hurried consultation revealed that her mother's page, who had been instructed to deliver them to the inn, had panicked and thrown them behind a door before running back to the castle as fast as his short legs would carry him.

Clementina was heartbroken. She was young and innocent and modest—and she could not believe that a man would accept her without her dowry, her jewels. She would not go on if they could not be found. If they were lost, then she would go back to her imprisonment.

This was too awful to contemplate and now it was O'Toole's turn to take action. Unharnessing one of the carriage horses, he galloped back into Innsbruck, tied the animal up some distance from the inn and made his way to it by stealth. He entered, made his way to the door behind which the jewels were believed to be hidden, found it locked.

Sweating with anxiety, he struggled to take the door off its hinges, found the parcel and got out into the square with it while the landlord still slumbered. Once on his horse, it was only minutes before he reached the carriage, but by now the sun was high in the sky.

They drove madly all day and by evening everyone but Clementina was exhausted. She was plying Wogan with questions about the weird customs of the English, and his adventures in Scotland with the man she was now to marry; and he, poor man, was forcing himself awake with huge doses of snuff.

During the next day they were shocked to find themselves trotting a few hundred yards behind the Princess of Baden's coach, containing the lady herself and her son, whom Clementina had recently refused to marry. They slowed down, allowed it to pull away from them, only to discover next that their own coachman was dead drunk. They had started careering all over the road and nearly crashed over a precipice before the man was relieved of his post by Misset and put in with the dismayed passengers to sober up.

They now reached the frontier of the Venetian States, and O'Toole leapt out to intercept any messengers from Innsbruck and to safeguard, if necessary, their retreat. Sure enough, he waylaid a rider bearing documents telling of the elopement and requesting that the Princess Clementina be arrested by anyone discovering her, and sent back post-haste to Innsbruck.

The poor fellow was swiftly dealt with by O'Toole and a little later, having decided there would be no need of retreat, he galloped up and joined the coach.

At Trent there were more difficulties. No horses were available to replace those which had been pulling the coach and were now winded, and while search was made for several hours by the other members of the party, Clementina lay at the bottom of the coach in the main square of the town.

And this was a town where the Duchess of Baden, who seemed determined to share their route, day after day, had stopped. She and her son walked by the Princess's hiding place, stopped and spoke, while she pressed herself flat against the floor and prayed. Then, still chatting, they strolled on.

Eventually, new horses came, the aching Clementina was allowed to sit up, and they trotted off.

A mile outside Trent the back axle broke.

Somehow it was repaired and the weary little party went on. They were safely over the frontier of the Venetian States, but the Baden family seemed destined to stay with them. Clementina dared to stick her head out of the window and at that moment the Duchess's coach caught up and passed them. The girl dropped like a stone to the bottom of the coach, and the other one trotted away in front, its occupants apparently unaware of the significance of the dusty, damaged vehicle they had just passed.

They reached Verona and now the flight was nearly over. The Princess was even able to have her hair dressed for the first time since dashing out into the rain of Innsbruck, dressed as a maidservant. They went on, more gaily, to Bologna. Here Prince James's agent was waiting with courteous and affectionate messages for the betrothed, and the little girl was overjoyed, as with the trinkets—artificial flowers and the like—which the Cardinal of Bologna gave her.

And here, in Bologna, she was married by proxy. The ceremony was performed by an English priest, her husband was represented by his agent, Mr Murry. Even the unwilling Prince Sobiesky was duly impersonated by the Marquis of Monte-Boularois, and we can only guess at what his reaction was when he heard of this. The ring James had sent was duly placed on Clementina's finger.

A week later, on 15 May, 1719, she entered Rome. The tale of her romantic escape had preceded her, and the streets were full of shouting, cheering people.

Three months later, on 2 September, there was a public marriage, at Montefiascone.

Everyone concerned was honoured in various ways: the four

seventeenth-century English [ma]riner, Robert Knox, spent twenty [yea]rs as a prisoner of the King of [Cey]lon. After his escape he wrote [a v]ivid account of the experience [and] became a prosperous and res[pect]ed author. At that point, this [por]trait was made of him. His book, *[An] Historical Relation of Ceylon,* [was] published in 1681. It divides [into] four parts, only the last of which [dea]ls with his own adventures: the [oth]er three deal in the greatest [acc]uracy and detail with the island [itse]lf, the King, and the people.

Knox noted a great many customs, some of which he approved and others, like this ritual execution by elephant, which he deplored. He was a tolerant if unwilling visitor to the island of Ceylon and quite prepared to point out that many of the Ceylonese ways of doing things were at least as effective as those in Europe. He admired and respected the King of Ceylon, although his prisoner. This drawing is one of a great many Robert Knox made, illustrating the island of his captivity. But he was a man of many other abilities and grew prosperous, as a prisoner, by trade and agriculture and usury.

Jack Sheppard was the greatest escaper of his time—perhaps of any time. Here (*right*) we see him being helped in an escape by his two mistresses, Edgworth Bess and Poll Maggot (who, surprisingly enough, were very good friends). They paid their guinea each to see the "notorious criminal" and smuggled him in a small saw. With this, as we can see in this representation of the two ladies' next visit, he removed one of the prison bars. Then, while one of the girls flirted with the warder, he flung a girl's cloak about his shoulders and made his simpering exit. He was not above chucking the delighted guard under the chin as he passed.

Destiny, in the end, caught up with Jack Sheppard. In these three little engravings by George Cruikshank he is being taken out of the Newgate Prison from which he so often and so brilliantly escaped there are scenes of disorder on the way: and at a calmer point in the proceedings he is allowed, by an old custom, to stop and drink a quart of ale. But the procession moves inexorably on, to Tyburn and the gallows. There have been demonstrations along the way and an attempt to free the prisoner while, at the tavern where Jack has his ale, there are cheers for him and he drinks the health of the crowd. Yet this profession of sympathy with the condemned man does not prevent the usual enormous crowd of tens of thousands of men, women and children assembling at the end of the road at Tyburn. Here they will share the great excitement of seeing a fellow Englishman breathe his last at the end of a rope.

Irishmen became baronets; and Wogan was even appointed by the Pope to be a Roman Senator. A medal was struck to commemorate the flight from Innsbruck to Rome.

Poor old Prince Sobiesky fared less well. Suspected of complicity in the escape, he was disgraced by his Emperor—though, as we have seen, he had done his best to make it extremely difficult.

The one who, it seems, deserves better reward than she got was Jeanneton, who had risked imprisonment and worse by impersonating the Princess—even though, when she crept into Clementina's bed, she believed her to be only an heiress. Had she been discovered there, muttering about headaches while the Princess drove madly across the frontier, one shudders to think what her penalty might have been. But Jeanneton managed to escape and was subsequently made personal maidservant to the Duchess of Parma. A pleasant post, no doubt, but one feels she might at least have been raised to some rung of a peerage, or given a nobleman for husband.

But she went quietly back into her high heels, not bothered about a reward.

Our story ends in a minor key. After so much trouble and risk and exertion, one might have hoped the marriage would be a huge success. It was not. James was a stolid, lugubrious husband, who spent the rest of his life less in trying to please the little girl who had risked so much to join him as in bemoaning his ill fortune in not being King of England.

No doubt Clementina, too, was sorry about that: it would have been nice to be a queen. But, for her, the thrilling memory of pursuing a husband, however dull he proved to be, remained with her through life. She became the mother of Prince Charles Edward—"Bonnie Prince Charlie", and well he might be, with a mother so beautiful—and his own spirited and colourful attempts to seize the throne denied his father carried the spirit of adventure and romance into another generation.

Chapter 10

NEWGATE FAILS TO HOLD
JACK SHEPPARD

DARKNESS fell, and with it silence. It was as if a hundred shouting, screaming, obscene men and women had all been struck dumb, or dead.

And now he made his final bid for freedom, and an escape from the hangman's noose. He had been retaken only a day earlier and he was lodged, loaded with irons which in turn were bolted to the floor, in the strongest wing of the prison, a wing now christened, from its shape and its security, the "Castle". In three days' time he would be taken from this cell, loaded into a tumbril, and taken on that long last journey through the packed and gaping streets of London to the gallows at Tyburn.

It was now or never. Slowly at first, then faster, he began to twist and pull at the irons which secured him to the floor. At first all he did was chafe wrists and ankles so that the skin broke and the links were stained with blood, but eventually, after two hours' patient manoeuvre, he broke the padlock, a huge, cumbersome thing weighing nearly seven pounds, and was free of the floor, albeit with a hundred pounds weight of chain still wound possessively about his slender body.

Using the broken link at one end of this he began to chip away at the plaster above his head in the wall of the cell. Bit by bit it came away, and after forty minutes he had removed not only a square foot of it but a dozen bricks to boot. Through the hole thus made a thin man, a very thin, lithe, long man— Jack Sheppard—could squeeze a way through into the chimney which ran up from the floor below, and through the floor above, to the roof.

To his dismay, he encountered a stout iron bar in the filthy cavern of the chimney as he entered. Sweating, gasping with the exertion, he tried again and again to budge it, and failed. And even a man like Sheppard would be unable to squeeze a way past, for it blocked all exit upwards to anything larger than a rat.

Most men would have given up.

Jack Sheppard, still manacled at wrist and ankle, began to use the same broken link of chain to cut into the mortar, inside the chimney, which held one end of the bar in place.

At first he made no impression at all, save for clouds of soot and stones which descended and choked him, and a sudden hateful scourge of black spiders, one of them the size of a sparrow, which dropped from the darkness above and wrapped him in one vast, sticky, choking web.

Half an hour later he had removed sufficient mortar from one end of the horizontal bar to wriggle it out, and to pass his slim body through the gap and up the narrow chimney.

Now, using the bar as crowbar, he tapped his way up the inside of the chimney, feeling, as a surgeon feels, for a hollow space in the solid framework of the ancient stone building. He found it and now—having been more than an hour in a black and choking cavern, unable to see, almost unable to breathe— he began again with his new "crowbar" to ease out a few more bricks.

This was easier. Only a few minutes and he had made his exit, was out of the hateful cavern, black but undaunted, and in the room immediately above his own cell. He must hurry, for the warder would soon be peering into that cell and would give the alarm. He shuddered for a moment as if a cold wind had burst in down the chimney: there would be a gasp of surprise, then a shout, then the ringing of a bell, then the hysterical shouts and cheers of the other prisoners and the barked orders of the gaolers and soldiers.

Then he took possession of himself. He was in the so-called Red Room; he could see the whole of the vast empty chamber, a chamber which had once been blood red, was now blue and peeling, like an ancient cheese. A rat the size of a terrier ran over his foot.

He made an involuntary move and almost screamed with pain.

He had put his entire weight on the foot, and a nail, perhaps three inches long, had pierced it and was projecting, rusty and blooded, through the upper of his shoe. With a gasp of agony he lifted the foot, at the same time pressing down with his hand on the projecting nail, and succeeded in freeing himself. The nail was in a rotted plank, almost as if it had been left there to wound a man trying to pass through the locked Red Room, and he tore it out from the wood and put it, hot and slimy, in his pocket. Limping as the blood gushed from his foot over the floor, he made his way to the door.

With practice made perfect by years of crime, he removed the cover plate from the lock, slid the bolt back with his fingers.

He was now in a long, echoing corridor. At the end of it he could just make out, in the semi-darkness, three large doors. He approached them, still limping, and studied them carefully. They were, to all intents and purposes, identical, but a little thought and a little guesswork made him decide on the right-hand one of the three. This, unless he were much mistaken, would be the one to the prison chapel—the chapel where, only the day before, he had heard his own, condemned man's, sermon. The door was vastly thick, far too thick to be damaged with his crowbar or with the broken chain, and it was easier—though it took more than another precious hour—to make a hole through the stonework in which it was set and pass a hand through, to undo the bolt on the other side.

There was a clatter of footsteps below, and he stiffened. He could hear his heartbeats, like the thunder of some giant clock, some satanic timepiece by which the Devil himself would gauge the roasting time of Hell's inmates. They drowned the noise of the footsteps below on a stone floor.

The footsteps vanished, he was left alone with his pounding heart; then that too seemed to vanish. There was no shouting, no sound of panic, and he decided that the noise had been nothing to do with his own escape. Closing the chapel door behind him, he studied the room, and the pew, only a yard or so away, where he had sat the day before to hear his soul commended to a distant and unhelpful God.

He walked down the little narrow aisle, came to the chapel's other door at the far end of the room. The next move was simple to a man of his strength and agility, for this second door was in fact a gate of oak, with half a dozen iron bars projecting vertically from it. With little effort, he bent two of these apart with the faithful crowbar, then slid through.

The next door, at the far end of this corridor, was the heaviest he had ever encountered, and he drew in his breath with a gasp. It had a massive lock, visible, attainable, and he was nothing if not an expert locksmith—but this monster was an iron box some eighteen inches square and six deep.

He set to work with his fingers, his crowbar and his piece of broken chain, but nothing would make the monster yield. Then, driven suddenly by a combination of despair and panic, he struck again and again at the doorpost with his iron bar, and it moved just sufficiently for him to squeeze past.

Yet another door, even thicker; but the same treatment sufficed to let him past, and he was outside on a flat slate roof. A crescent moon was shining, creeping up in the east, past a massive chimney, and he realized that this block of masonry was the very chimney up which he had struggled. Ruefully he looked down at his blackened clothes, the torn knees of his breeches, but there was no time for self-pity, and he vaulted up to a still higher roof and was at last on the very top of the hateful prison which had enclosed him.

For a moment, with the cool night air soughing past his ears, it seemed he was free, could lie back in comfort on this pleasant flat surface, watch moon and stars go by. He lay several minutes in this fashion, before realizing the error of his ways. He got to his feet, walked to the edge of the roof and looked down.

The drop was enormous: he'd had no idea how high he was. He looked round frantically for a pipe or a buttress, as his head swam and his heart pounded.

There was a lead pipe which ran vertically down the side of the building, and he gingerly clasped it with one hand and began to lower himself over the edge with the other. Then with a faint scratching sound which became a creak, a sudden, frightening crack, the pipe came away from the wall, and he was only just able to save himself from falling with it. There was a pause that seemed minutes as he clung with both hands to the ledge, his feet in space. Then, with a thundering crash, the pipe collapsed into a courtyard.

He was able to pull himself back on to the roof, just as a door opened below and two men rushed out. He lay flat on his face, not daring to look over the edge and observe them, listening to the muffled sound of their comments on this strange occurrence. But even as he lay in a semi-panic, his agile mind had moved on to the next step, a step other men might have been slow to take, but which Jack Sheppard knew was the only one open to him. He would have to retrace footsteps over the entire journey, get back to his cell.

And from his cell he must gather up the filthy blanket which had sufficed him as a bed, bring it up here to the roof, and use it as a rope down which to descend to freedom.

The journey from cell to roof had taken no less than four hours, he had checked them off by the chiming of a church clock half a mile away to the north, but the return should, with luck, take considerably less, as doors had been forced and holes made in the masonry. There was, however, the considerable risk that his absence had already been noted, that he would descend into the arms of the warders.

But one could not stay forever on the roof.

He made his way back, the whole way, down to the lower roof, in through a doorway, then on and on in the dark, through a succession of half-open, damaged doors, into the chapel, the Red Room, the choking chimney, and his own small cell. He sat for a moment on the floor and the yellow eyes of a rat stared at him from a yard away.

There was a sound of footsteps outside the cell, and a face

seemed to press itself against the bars. "Good night," said Jack, though indeed it was nearly morning. There was no reply, only the sound of feet retreating down the stone passage.

No time to ponder this circumstance. Wrapping the verminous blanket round his body he struggled back through the hole he had made in the chimney, scratched his way up again to the Red Room. He found himself humming softly, for the rest of the journey was a simple one which he could have done, he decided, with both eyes closed and one arm in a sling. The fact that arms and legs were still in chains, and might be for some time, till he came to a blacksmith, was of no importance at all. Half young Sheppard's life seemed to have been lived in chains, and by and large it had been a good one.

Back on the roof, he slit the filthy blanket down the middle, tied the two halves together. Then he looked down.

Still it was far too short. Cursing, he undid it, slit it again, knotted the four threadbare pieces together into a long rope. Then he fastened one end to a projecting brick, and let the rope drop down to its full extent.

In the light of the moon he could see it was still some ten feet short of the ground, but it would have to do. The thing that mattered was to get down it quickly, before it tore and flung him into the courtyard on top of the tangled mess of lead he had already dislodged. It would be unable to kill him—nothing could kill lucky Jack—but he might break an arm or a leg and be unable to negotiate the last hurdle over the low prison wall.

A moment later, his hands burning and chafed, he was in the courtyard. His blanket, when he jerked hard at it, tore near the top and came down into his hands, and with it he was able to negotiate the last hurdle of the perimeter wall.

A fantastic escape, by any standards, but a futile one. A few months later, young Jack Sheppard was captured again, and this time there was no chance. On 16 November of 1724, a few days short of his twenty-first birthday, the greatest escaper of his own time, and perhaps any other, was led off in a tumbril, westward down Holborn, followed by his two weeping mistresses, Poll Maggott and Edgeworth Bess. Destination Tyburn.

At the Crown Tavern, the procession stopped, by hallowed custom, to give the condemned man a quart of ale. There was good-natured banter, in which Jack shared, and then an ugly rumbling of rebellion in one corner of the crowd which showed ominous signs of spreading.

The tall thin, youthful figure held up an arm, the rumbling ceased. For a moment there was silence as the crowd wondered what he might do or say, but Jack held his peace, and the crowd did likewise.

Drinks over, the procession went on, getting longer every minute, with mothers rushing to keep up, a child or more in their arms, determined not to miss the fine spectacle of a man gasping his last against a grey and misty sky.

At Tyburn tree the procession halted. The mob was quiet as a prayer was said, and after the "Amen", Sheppard's voice could be clearly heard saying: "My poor mother. I shall join her in Heaven."

There were mingled boos and cheers at this sentiment, and the noose was slipped over his head.

And now it was as if the whole of London—for surely all of it was here?—had been struck dumb, and still. Not a sound was heard for fully a minute: not a creature stirred.

Then, with a terrifying suddenness, there was a hoarse cry of "Cart!"

The cart lurched forward, there was a gasp, a cheer, then a terrible groan from the crowd, and the slight body of Jack Sheppard, kicking against the grey sky, was suspended from Tyburn tree.

And so perished, before the eyes of as large an audience as had ever gathered together in one spot to see a man breathe his last, a brave and in many ways gallant young man—not yet twenty-one—who had escaped more times from more "impregnable" prisons than any other man in history. Had he lived in more enlightened times he would not have been hanged, for none of the robberies he committed—none of them with violence —would have earned him more than a few months' imprisonment.

Like father, like son. That had been the philosophy that dogged him. His housebreaker father, Tom Sheppard, had been executed for that crime on November, 1703, the very day that his son Jack was born to Tom's weeping, twenty-year-old wife. Or was she already, by a matter of minutes, a widow?

No one seemed to know. But within weeks, pretty little Widow Sheppard had found herself a protector, the stolid Mr Wood, who had known and disliked her husband, while being violently attracted to his pretty, dark-eyed wife. Mr Wood, who was appropriately enough a carpenter, made Mrs Sheppard an allowance and visited her regularly in the one-room dwelling she was now able to afford. And both Mr Wood and Mrs Sheppard were on more than one occasion nearly knifed by a wildly and, understandably, jealous Mrs Wood.

Somehow, all four managed to survive this, and when young Jack had grown to a tall, thin, immensely strong lad of fifteen, he was apprenticed to Wood, to learn the trade of joiner. But a life of petty crime appealed far more: it was pleasant and easy, with his lithe, muscular frame, to wriggle in through windows and down chimneys, and make away with valuables which could be sold across the river and give badly needed food and little luxuries to his mother. His first recorded theft is of a pair of silver spoons which had caught his fancy. He found their removal so easy that he was soon helping himself to two or three trinkets a week, selling them—often in haste, for some derisory sum—and buying presents for his mother. Soon there was no time left for carpentry, and he left his apprenticeship to go and settle in a district of Southwark by himself, a district known as "The Mint". A Royal Mint had once been established there, by Henry VIII, and here, by one of the peculiarities of English law, no magistrate had jurisdiction. The place abounded in criminals, many of them colourful, and had included at one time or another both the notorious highwayman Dick Turpin and Captain MacHeath of "Threepenny Opera" fame.

But Sheppard, though he had left his mother to dwell in this no-man's land by the river, still loved her and paid regular, foolhardy, visits to her, bearing money and food; or, in his wilder moments, some trinket he had actually stolen and preferred to give her, rather than trade it in for something less incriminating.

Magistrate or no magistrate in "The Mint", Jack Sheppard had been imprisoned eight or nine times by his late teens, with successively longer, more unpleasant, sentences—and he had managed to escape each time. On the first occasion, after being caught robbing a church in Willesden, he was put into the nearest lock-up, known locally as "The Cage". This was a massive building of stone, windows and chimneys heavily barred and doors a foot thick and double-bolted. He found a piece of rusty metal in his cell and with it cut—infinitely patient—a small hole in the plaster ceiling, just sufficient to allow his thin body through. A few deft shoves and he had removed enough tiles from the underneath of the roof to continue his progress to the open air and freedom.

He was soon recaptured and put into the New Prison at Clerkenwell, where he was hung with fetters and locked into the strongest part of the prison. This time he was fortunate in having the services of an attractive young woman he had recently met and who was soon to become his mistress. (Sheppard never had sufficient time or freedom to get married, but his intentions, he stoutly maintained, were "honourable, most honourable, I swear it", and his grateful and devoted mother, as well as half a dozen hero-worshipping ladies, would swear with him to the truth of it.) This lady, Edgeworth Bess by name, was arrested with him, and was able, through local friends, to get a file, a chisel and two gimlets smuggled in.

That very evening Jack broke out of his fetters—a feat which, owing to amazing muscle control, he was able to perform without the aid of any tools, merely by contracting wrists and ankles—and started work on the window bars with his file. The file broke after five hours' work, with the bar still unbreached. Indismayed by this unexpected and alarming stroke of bad luck, Sheppard abandoned the fruitless work on iron bars, with scarcely a sigh of regret, and started work on an oak beam with his gimlets. This beam blocked another window: by infinite patience he drilled a hundred holes along its length until it disintegrated.

He clambered through the gap and then, sweating with this new exertion, dragged the amply-proportioned Bess out after him and dropped with her to the prison yard. Finding their way blocked by a twenty-foot perimeter wall, Jack instantly screwed the two gimlets into a stout oak gate post, one above the other, and, using them as rungs of a ladder, moving lower to upper and so on, dragging the gasping, cursing Bess behind him, got them over the gate and to freedom.

But all this, of course, was child's play to Newgate, from which, as we have seen, Jack Sheppard was to make his last escape. Yet, even Newgate held few terrors for him: his last escape was his third successful one from that most impregnable of gaols. It brooded over London where the present Old Bailey now stands, and it was reserved for capital cases—for men and women sentenced to death. This, in 1723, was the fate decreed for Jack Sheppard. He was flung into a condemned cell and exhibited to gaping visitors at a guinea a time. It is a measure of his notoriety that people were prepared to pay what, in those distant days, was a considerable sum, just to stare at him. It was while posing as a pair of these well-heeled customers that Bess and another female friend of Jack's (who surprisingly, like all his lady friends, got on famously with the rest), by name Poll Maggott, bribed the gaoler to let them speak to the condemned man. They had already smuggled him a tiny watch-spring saw and he had, over several days, nearly severed a door bar to his cell. Now with one young woman flirting with the warder down the stone corridor, the other—Bess—lending her strength, he removed the bar completely. Bess took off her cloak and gave it to him, and while Poll took up the whole of the amorous warder's attention she made her way out of the prison, unseen.

A moment later Poll, remarking that it was late, broke off her flirtation and escorted "Bess" out of the cell. As they passed the warder, Jack was unable to resist chucking him under the chin, and the delighted man bowed low as they went past and out to freedom.

But Jack, beloved of women and loving his mother, was incredibly stupid at large. Each time he paid an absolutely predictable visit to his delighted mother, and each time—during his short periods of freedom—he went out with either Bess or Poll, frequently both, and made an exhibition of himself in some public place. Always it was London. Never did he leave the town he so loved long enough to let a little of the hue and cry die down. His recaptures, his subsequent escapes, became so numerous that men were unable to say how many had been effected, and we are even less certain today. One thing is certain: he had been caught and condemned, by the age of twenty, more times than most hardened old lags of three times his age. Once he was recaptured blind drunk with his mother, in the "Black Jack" pub in Southwark, but escaped just as he was being led away, by a fantastic leap through a high window. From then on the pub was rechristened "The Jump". On another occasion, he was picked up, having somehow gate-crashed a Guildhall banquet in stolen finery and yet remarking cheerfully, to all who would listen, that he was indeed just humble Jack Sheppard: the clothes, an hour before, had belonged to another.

A week later he was free, having made yet another escape, and more convinced than ever—with reason—that no prison in the world would be able to hold him more than a day.

That was true: but fate in the end caught up. He was put in prison and taken out again, within twenty-four hours, for the long, wild ride to Tyburn.

Chapter 11

BONNIE PRINCE CHARLIE OUTWITS
THE ENGLISH ARMY

As the reader may have noticed, escapes in this volume are sometimes linked together—and not just for caprice. One of the most cherished legends of Scotland remains that of "Bonnie Prince Charlie"—but it is more than probable that the charm, the vivacity and resilience, to say nothing of the beauty, descended to him from his Polish mother: not from his dour Stuart father. She figures in our pages as the little Princess Clementina. The "Old Pretender" lacked fire and imagination: with a bit more of both qualities—and, of course, a bit more luck —he might have regained his family's throne.

His son, in the fullness of time, would have succeeded him peacefully as King Charles III—and Scotland would have been denied a real tale of adventure. Perhaps it is well the " '15" petered out in failure.

James II, as every schoolboy knows, was driven from his kingdom by dissatisfied subjects in 1688, and replaced by his stolid daughter Mary and her still more stolid Dutch husband

William. They had no children and were succeeded by Mary's younger sister Anne—who had quantities, none of whom survived her.

The most logical choice for a successor might well have been her half-brother James, son of the deposed James II by a second marriage. But he, apart from being an uninspiring sort of fellow, was a devout Roman Catholic, and this the people of England and most of Scotland distrusted. James was refused his birthright and the German George, great grandson of James I, was invited in his stead.

And George, as a king, was inadequate: so inadequate that we must thank him for our Prime Ministers—for he spoke no English and somebody had to do the work. We can also thank him for the fact that some of us say "eye-ther" and not "ee-ther", some of us "n'eye-ther", not "nee-ther". And that is the extent of it.

The dullness of George, coupled with the half-hearted military adventures in which England was now embroiled on the Continent, gave James, "The Old Pretender", his chance. In 1715, he landed in Scotland from France.

He failed and crept back to France, thence to Rome where he set up his "Court". There, some four years later, he married little Clementina after her whirlwind escape from captivity in the east. A year later, Prince Charles was born.

And Charles, beautiful baby, grew up to be a young man with astonishing good looks, coupled with great physical strength and skill: he was the best horseman, the best swordsman, the best shot in whichever circle he chose to move. He was also a young man with imagination; and a conviction, which had been implanted in him from birth, that some day he would be king.

He also had a mind of his own. When he decided to risk his own landing on the west coast of Scotland, in 1745, he never even bothered to tell his father, for fear that that dour, discouraged individual would try to stop him. He landed at Moidart, as bleak and rocky a coast as any in the world, on 23 July, and from all over the Highlands chiefs rushed to pledge him their allegiance —though there was markedly less enthusiasm among the Lowlanders (and, of course, the English). At first it seemed as if this second rising might well succeed. The Prince's charm, his obvious courage and what today we would call his "personality", won over all who saw him and many who had not—for the legend of "Bonnie Prince Charlie" was as infectious as the plague.

But this, too, failed. There are glorious chapters in the short tale, like the fall of Edinburgh, the victory of Prestonpans, moments when it seemed England lay waiting like an excited bride, watching rivals for her hand being killed off, one by one, by a knight in shining armour. But it was his own Highlanders who let Prince Charlie down. One of the less edifying spectacles in Scottish history is that of Prince Charlie's Highlanders, gorged with loot and refusing to move farther south until they got it all home. From this moment the rising was over. The remnant of a Scottish army, after fighting many a gallant rearguard action was finally routed at Culloden on 16 April, 1746.

The " '45" had been entirely a personal campaign. The strange fascination of the young Prince had rallied men behind him in their tens of thousands, in a cause which most had believed dead and hopeless. Now the thoughts of his dwindling supporters were for the safety of the young man who had made all this possible and been so cruelly let down, with victory in sight and the panic-stricken burghers of London evacuating their homes. All that was over: the burghers were shamefacedly going back, and the English army which, as in '15, had been engaged in disputation on the Continent, was returning. It had been a comparatively easy matter for the Old Pretender to slip off at dead of night and head for France: he had left himself plenty of time. It would be a more difficult problem for his son. For Charles had fought at Culloden while he had a remnant of an army to fight with: his horse was shot out from under him while he was shouting at stragglers, trying to shame them into coming back to the attack. He had been brought another horse, but by now the battle was utterly lost, the clans routed. He was alone.

He must have felt as alone as any man in the world on that April afternoon. The whole of England was against him and now a large part of Scotland, which had wavered, seen how the campaign was faring, and taken its decision. There was nothing for it but to get to France, as his father had.

The difficulties were a thousand times greater.

The route of the flight is a Scottish geography lesson and not all of it need concern us here. The Prince soon learnt that George ("the Second" now, only son of George I and, if anything, even less attractive) had placed a reward of £30,000 on his head: he gaily responded by asking his few supporters to spread the word that he, Charles, offered £30 for that of George II. But there was little time for practical joking: a boat had to be found in a countryside now swarming with Government troops, and, with it, boatmen. On the stormy night of 26 April, after ten nights in the open air, Prince Charlie in an eight-oared boat made the perilous journey to the island of Benbecula in the Outer Hebrides, avoiding Skye on the way, for the larger isle had now filled with George's troops. A few nights later he was forced to cross to the Island of Scalpa, and for weeks he was dodging from island to island as Government vessels landed search parties after him. Several times the Prince's boat, all hands to the oars, was actually pursued in a frantic rowing race along the jagged coast-line—races which were always, but narrowly, won, with the Prince's little boat vanishing round a bend or disappearing between massive rocks.

Day by day the hunt grew more intense. It was obvious that George II was running no risk of further rising. Prince Charles would be captured and executed in the most public and degrading way, a deterrent to the romantic fools who clung to the hope of a new Stuart monarchy. The reward offered was so great that the young man stood no chance of getting away—and in any case, never had there been such a swarm of Government soldiers and sympathizers on Scotland's territory.

It was then that the daring plan was hit upon of getting him from the Outer Hebrides, where the Government forces knew him to be in hiding, to the unlikely sanctuary of Skye, where these forces abounded. For this very reason, if the Prince could get there and be received into a friendly house, no one would suspect his presence: but the whole coast of Skye was patrolled and guarded; no man could land there unseen.

No man could—and thereby hangs our tale.

One of the Prince's sympathizers, though he was in the awkward position of being commander of a company of Government troops, was Hugh Macdonald. He had a young stepdaughter living with her brother on the island of South Uist, in the Outer

Hebrides. Hugh Macdonald's own home was in Skye, and there his wife and servants resided. Skye, as we have seen, was a difficult place to enter, but with a pass from her father young Flora Macdonald would be able to go there, pay a visit to her mother.

And, as lady's maid, she would take no less a personage than Prince Charles Edward, Pretender to the throne of England and Scotland.

This episode is usually dramatized in Scots history as the tale of a loyal young girl eagerly putting her own life in jeopardy for that of her Lawful King. John Buchan, master story-teller, has perpetuated this attractive myth; but we are more likely to get the truth from the eminent Scots historian Professor Mackie, who says she did it "only reluctantly". One cannot blame her. Poor girl, the escape had became a desperate business, and the penalty for helping Charles would be death. (In fact, while he was endeavouring to make his escape, and, for a period after it, his suspected supporters were being led away in droves: over a hundred and twenty were executed, a thousand more banished or transported, and another seven hundred taken away, whose fate has never been revealed.)

But Flora agreed.

A rendezvous was arranged on Benbecula. Government forces were here too: there was no place within striking distance where they were not. Midges and mosquitoes were in still greater force, and the Prince, who spent several nights in the heather awaiting his protectress, was attacked so unmercifully by them that he cried out with the pain. Yet his spirits never flagged and when the assault ceased momentarily, with a gust of wind or a sudden shower, he was able to joke about it.

At last, on the evening of 27 June, Flora arrived with her brother and Lady Clanranald, who was to be in charge of the Prince's disguise.

No sooner were they all met than it was reported that Government troops were advancing, closing in on the little party from less than a mile away. The meal which everyone had begun was left behind untouched, and the party made haste across the waters of a loch to hide until five in the morning. Then, reckless with hunger, they returned and ate it.

A little later, with the sun scarce up in the sky, Prince Charles had become Betty Burke, expert with the spinning wheel. He was to carry a letter from Hugh Macdonald, in addition to the safe-conduct—a letter which extolled Betty's skill as spinner and suggested she be put to spinning a quantity of lint which was in the Macdonald home.

This, should the little party be apprehended, would help them bluff a way through. The Prince, delighted with his disguise, hoped fervently that no one would ask him to spin.

There was the little matter of Betty's unfeminine gait; and before the little party of Flora, Betty and the Prince's loyal Neil Maceachain set off by themselves, Lady Clanranald implored the Prince to do something about it. He assured her he would try.

It was the evening of 28 June when the three of them set sail in a small boat with a few oarsmen. At dawn of the 29th they were off the coast of Skye, and straightway they spied a sentry. As they began to row silently away, he caught sight of them and roared, "Halt!"

It would have been madness to do so, for their travel through the night would have brought suspicion on their heads, safe-conduct or no. They began to row frantically along the coast, hoping the sentry would become tangled and lost in the under-growth which came to the water's edge. He fired, ran, shouted again and fired twice, narrowly missing each time. The noise had brought other soldiers, fifteen of them, to the shore, all of them shouting, firing, running along it to waylay the boat when it came to land.

But the undergrowth was thick, and gradually the boat out-distanced the soldiers. It evaded them and managed to land at a deserted spot on the north of the island. From here Flora and Neil went off to a house where they hoped for sanctuary, leaving Betty Burke, Pretender to the throne, in the boat with the boat-men. These had instructions to explain to anyone curious that Betty was "a lazy jade" who refused to go with her mistress.

It was as well that Flora reconnoitred their intended stopping place, for one of the two guests staying there was the officer in charge of a party searching for Charles. She managed to explain her predicament to the other guest, whom she knew and trusted, Macdonald of Kingsburgh, and he immediately excused himself and prepared to smuggle the Prince from the boat to his own house. In the meantime, the unfortunate Flora was forced to dine with Lieutenant McLeod and answer all manner of questions about her trip from Benbecula and about reports of Prince Charles.

After dinner she managed to get away: she had not seen her mother for a long time, the good lady would be upset and worried if she did not reach home soon. Reluctantly, Lieutenant McLeod let the pretty, strangely overwrought, girl go, and she set off on horseback and soon caught up with Kingsburgh, Neil and Betty Burke. It was still light, and a gaggle of villagers were following them on foot, much interested in the tall girl with the manly walk, her brazen way of lifting skirts when she forded a stream. They were also indignant at the way this serving-wench seemed to chat so familiarly with Kingsburgh, even after her own mistress caught them up.

They arrived at Kingsburgh House at midnight and the lady of the house was woken by the excited shriek of one of her daughters, "Och, mither, my father's brought in *such* an odd, muckle, ill-shaken-up wife as ever I saw!" A startled Mrs Macdonald could only agree, when she clapped eyes on Betty Burke, but at her husband's suggestion she went off to get supper. He followed her to the kitchen and explained their unusual guest. There was, understandably, an air of excitement verging on panic, but this did little to damp the Prince's good humour or his appetite. We are told that he went on to demolish two bottles of beer, a bumper of brandy and a huge plate of eggs with bread and butter, after which he took out his pipe. His host, seeing it was broken, gave him another, and they sat for a while and smoked, breaking off their conversation every few seconds to listen for sounds of pursuit.

The plan now was for Charles to leave Skye again, which was turning out as dangerous as the Outer Hebrides, and move towards the mainland—for a start, to the island of Raasay. Already there were people talking, all over Skye, about the strange tall girl with the "wide, lang steps"; it was more than likely that the oarsmen who had brought them, and who were in the secret, would be bribed or tortured to reveal it. Charles left the next morning, still in women's clothes—and in the nick of time. Government troops under General Ferguson burst in the moment he left and the unfortunate Kingsburgh was arrested. He only just escaped with his life, being sentenced to twelve months in prison for "negligence", rather than outright treason, for it could not be proved that he had known he was harbouring a royal guest.

Meanwhile, in a wood, Charles changed back into male Highland dress and headed for Portree, whence he and Neil Maceachain would sail for Raasay. Flora's last service to him would be to go on ahead to Portree and make sure of his reception.

They met for the last time in the inn at Portree—Charles, Neil, Flora and three or four others—and the Prince made his farewells. Before this he had brought suspicion down on his head with the landlord, who was not a Stuart sympathizer, by absent-mindedly waving away the change after he had bought a quarter of a pound of tobacco. One of his party had to insist that he pocket it as a poor man should, and reluctantly he did so, leaving the landlord to retire to his room and puzzle over the behaviour of this shabby, good-humoured fellow who threw away his money like pebbles on a beach.

Charles's last words with Flora were spoken in some emotion. "For all that has happened, Madam, I hope we shall meet in St James's yet."

They never met again. And perhaps we can spare a thought for Flora, who had agreed, and undertaken, as dangerous a mission as it is possible to imagine. She had wandered about the Hebrides for three days in the company of a wanted man, a man with £30,000 on his head and death for his helpers, and had in fact been involved up to her neck in the plot for nine long days, at any moment of which she could have been arrested. Whether or not she had undertaken it "reluctantly" at first, she was considerably moved when they parted, and took a lock of his hair as keepsake.

She lived a long and honoured life, marrying the son of the Kingsburgh who had given them shelter; so that in later years that very shelter became her home. She emigrated to North Carolina with her husband but returned when the War of Independence broke out, to die in her native Skye in 1790.

When she and the Prince parted, that midnight at Portree, he had insisted on sending his faithful Neil to accompany her home, so he lost his most faithful follower. He made his way, with one or two others, to Raasay, but a little later, with Government troops there as well, he got back to Skye. Weeks followed of a nerve-chilling hide-and-seek about the endless inlets and coves of Skye. He became a servant again, but a man-servant now, with the name of Lewie Caw. He took off his periwig, placed a dirty kerchief on his head and went about, with the shuffling peasant gait he found easier to adopt than the mincing walk of a maidservant, cheerfully humping another's baggage about the island.

But this could not go on for ever, if only because no French ship would be able to drop anchor unseen off Skye, and news had come that the French were doing everything in their power to rescue the Prince. He must get to the mainland, guarded though it was. This, with one or two others, he achieved on 5 July, just as dawn was sliding grey and purple over the hills. They were about to disembark when a party of militia appeared and they hastily put out to sea again and began another of the breath-taking boat races along the coast. They made no progress at first: the bigger boat which came out in pursuit caught up with them, minute by minute. Then, as they rounded a bend, Charles leapt ashore, plunged into the trees.

Ultimately he made his way to the house of the faithful laird of Borrodale, only to find it burnt to the ground by Government troops, and the old man himself living in a hut nearby. Most of the Prince's party had been captured and the old laird quickly tucked him away between two large rocks where he had built a shelter for just such a purpose.

But this too became risky, and on 17 July Charles set off again. Time was running out, the chase was getting more frantic every day and the Prince, if he were to survive, would have to get to a port—and find a French ship—very soon. It was as if the whole of the English Army, back from its Continental wars and supported by half of Scotland, was spread thick up the whole of the west coast and scattered throughout every island in the sea. A walk of a quarter of a mile in any direction sufficed to reach a Government detachment. Every day there was some hair-raising escape: one day the Prince's money was found to be missing after they had given four shillings to the boy who brought them milk. They could obviously not afford to lose the entire Privy Purse, though it was down to a few pounds, and they went back. Here the boy's father, recognizing the Prince and wild with rage and shame that his son should have tried such a thing on such a personage, seized a rope and threatened to hang him. At this point the money was speedily returned. But this retracing of footsteps had saved the Prince's life. Had he gone on as he was going, he would have been seized by a body of troops coming in the opposite direction.

They were making now for Poolewe where French ships had been sighted, and the pursuit was slackening. The tireless energy of the Prince and his few supporters had worn down the opposition so that "Butcher" Cumberland had handed over the task to the Earl of Albemarle; a little later the noble earl wrote of the hunted Prince: "I cannot help suspecting he is gone off, either in some of the small French vessels that have been hovering along the coast, or in a boat. . . ."

But there were still weeks of flight ahead for Charles, doubling and redoubling on his tracks, wearing down the pursuers with never as much as a half-day's rest. Throughout it, ill and tormented with insects, sleeping night after night in the soaking heather, he yet kept up his own and his friends' spirits. When they felt they were out of earshot of their pursuers, they threw their bonnets in the air and shot at them, at which sport Charles "far exceeded" the others.

On 20 September, back in the barren waste of Moidart, where he had landed over a year previously, he was taken off in the French frigate *Prince de Conti*, transferring at sea to the larger *L'Heureux*. Both ships had been off the coast, anxiously waiting, for a fortnight.

So ended a personal campaign which proved, perhaps, very little—except that one young man could keep the bulk of the British Army in a state varying between alert and panic for a year.

Back in Paris, Charles was fêted as the hero of the hour. though rather later, under the terms of the Treaty of Aix-la-

Chapelle, he was expelled. He spent the remainder of his days on the Continent. His marriage many years later to Louisa von Stolberg was childless and unhappy, and both before and after this marriage his life in exile was dissolute and unworthy.

But with one crowded, breathless year, he has left us a legend and a memory to efface it.

Chapter 12

NAPOLEON SAILS
FROM ELBA

SOME escapes have been easy to make; others have been extremely difficult. Few escapes have made a bigger impress on history than that of Napoleon.

One little man left an island at the dead of night. A hundred days later, as a direct result of this, half Europe was plunged in battle.

The island, of course, is Elba—a tiny mountainous blob on the map, a pimple rising up from the coastal shelf of Italy, through the surface of the Tyrrhenian Sea, to squat alongside the west coast of that country, and at six miles distance. Tunny and sardine are caught; grapes and olives are grown; iron, lead, sulphur and alabaster are found: but there is little wealth.

If it were possible to reduce the area contained by its ragged coastline to measurable dimensions, one would not be far wrong in describing the island as twelve miles high and seven wide.

An insignificant place, judged by the standards of empire.

And yet, for rather less than a year, at the start of the nine-

120

teenth century, the island of Elba was an empire, ruled over by a man who, while renouncing the throne of France, still regarded himself as her Emperor—a man held in mixed awe, love and hatred by half the world.

"Able was I ere I saw Elba", as the schoolboy palindrome goes. The short sentence, reading the same from either end, is attributed, tongue in cheek (and who else would be likely to come out with such a thing?), to Napoleon Bonaparte. But Napoleon, even had he been able to muster sufficient English to produce this *mot*, would hardly have done so.

For Napoleon, from that humiliating morning in May of 1814 when he arrived at the capital of his little Empire, believed himself every bit as able as before. He believed, with an absolute certainty, that he would regain the larger Empire he had lost—and regain it soon.

The words in which he had been forced to abdicate still stuck in his gullet: they were hateful, meaningless words, and he had no intention of abiding by them: "The allied powers, having proclaimed Napoleon to be the sole impediment to the re-establishment of peace in Europe; he, faithful to his oath, declares that he abdicates, for himself and his heirs, the throne of France and Italy. He is ready to offer any personal sacrifice, to his very life, for the welfare of France——"

Never was affidavit made with less conviction; never was man more determined to regain the throne he had been forced to abdicate "for the welfare of France". Never was man planning more earnestly, even as he signed the document, to go back on it, than Napoleon Bonaparte, the little Corsican who had become the greatest general of his time.

He had also become one of history's most over-rated men. The Napoleon Myth had already taken root, would flower and grow to the end, even as the man himself withered and died.

But in May, 1814, there was no thought of death. There was too much else going through the Corsican's mind as the British frigate and its icy, courteous crew delivered him to Elba. On the way to his port of embarkation he had paid a last visit to his old regiment, had kissed the colours. The men and officers had wept, without shame.

But after that touching ceremony, as he continued his journey across France to the port of Fréjus, he was treated quite differently by the peasants through whose villages he passed. These poor people, sickened by years of wartime austerity and personal tragedy, disillusioned by defeat, had mocked and insulted him, had spat on him as he passed. For most of the way he had been forced to adopt a disguise.

And now—rather as if the English, in a fit of pique, had downgraded their First Sea Lord to Admiral Commanding the Round Pond in Kensington—the greatest general of his time was banished to a tiny island, with his own tiny private army. Small wonder that Napoleon settled into his new home with bitterness and hatred, and began immediately making plans to escape from it.

He was forty-five years old. Men—particularly generals—are then often at their prime, and the forty-five years had been stuffed with drama and speeded by ambition, almost from the day he had been born, in Corsica. His father had managed to get him into the military school at Paris, and a year later he had been gazetted to a regiment of artillery and begun his extraordinary military career. The discontent which had seethed for years among the peasants of France now rose to an angry head. The monarchy was overthrown and Napoleon, for reasons which may have been idealistic or the reverse, ardently and promptly supported the new revolutionaries. They, for their part, promoted him in 1793 from an unknown and junior officer of artillery to lieutenant-colonel, and dispatched him to the Mediterranean port of Toulon, which was royalist in sympathy and in occupation and was holding out, with the help of a British fleet, against the revolutionaries.

It was here that the fledgeling colonel laid foundation for his military reputation. He devised and put into effect new and untried methods of attack, and soon reduced the town and captured or killed its defenders. Immediately the grateful revolution promoted him to general.

And now in Bonaparte's eyes the future was clear. He had attained the highest rank in his country's army: he would achieve the same in its government. Louis XIV had been able to say, *"L'Etat, c'est moi"* : Napoleon would say the same, and with greater justification.

122

He was sent, as a general, to Italy, and from the start of this campaign a new era began in the strategy of the new Republic. From now on, wars would be fought for plunder and aggrandizement: no longer would Frenchmen bleed and die simply for what they held to be the principles of their revolution. Wars in future would pay for themselves.

And for Napoleon. Inspired by prospects of incredible loot, and by an absolutely ruthless commander, his men swept on. Their nation's recently arrived rulers, back in Paris, were delighted with the splendid gifts and huge sums of money Napoleon sent them from the front. Steadily he found greater favour. The general became commander-in-chief.

And in 1799 his moment came—the moment he had worked for. He had embarked on a romantic and apparently pointless campaign in Egypt. And while the commander-in-chief was out of Europe, military affairs, as he had no doubt anticipated, went from good to bad to worse, as the nations joined forces against a hated French régime. France was now fighting on several fronts, and doing badly on all of them—including the Egyptian one, but news from that side of the Mediterranean took a long time in coming, and Napoleon had no intention of letting it precede him.

He left his army in Egypt under command of General Kléber and rushed back to France, where the revolutionary government, beginning to lose a war, was losing popularity. The moment Napoleon landed on French soil, the people rallied to him: here was the man, the greatest in France, who would lead them back to victory. He advanced in triumph on Paris and with little difficulty took over the government, making himself "First Consul", with two other Consuls to share the task of governing. These he ignored.

He decided to present himself, the new ruler of France, as man of peace. He offered peace terms to France's enemies, and these were accepted. In 1802, as reward for having virtually dictated peace to the world, he was made First Consul for life.

He was already, in all but name, the King of France. With this fact established, he looked round for opportunities for war.

Soon France was fighting again, a little reluctantly at first, but by now his hold over the country was absolute. In 1804 he declared himself Emperor, had himself crowned at Notre Dame. He had reached—did he but know it—the zenith of his powers. He embarked on a war with Spain, which did badly. He then elected, in 1812, to invade Russia and, suffering one of the most crushing defeats in history, withdrew from the gates of Moscow, losing five-sixths of his army in the long retreat to France. In the following year his forces were utterly defeated during three days in October by an alliance of Russians and Austrians and most of the German states. He refused to admit the defeat, and, while these allies continued to sweep into France from the north, the Duke of Wellington attacked from the south, having cleared the French out of Spain.

The invaders demanded not only complete surrender, but the abdication of Napoleon. While his armies collapsed about him, Napoleon did so.

It was decided—foolishly—to banish him to Elba, and on 4 May, 1814, he arrived there to take up the ridiculous appointment of its "King". He had with him the regalia of Empire, and a small army, with a collection of ageing and decrepit ships.

He would have to bide his time before regaining the mainland —though there was no doubt in his mind of that final objective. He began to devote his great energies to improving the island's fortifications and to organizing the protocol and other matters of his new domain. At the same time he dispatched informants to the mainland, to keep him in touch with every development that took place.

One of the first items of news that reached him was that the French Government, led by Talleyrand, was plotting with the allies to have him assassinated. A man like Napoleon was too great a danger, so close to the shores of France.

When he was told this, Napoleon smiled. He was indeed a danger, and he knew it. How great a danger, time would soon reveal.

The allies had re-established the Bourbon monarchy after his forced abdication, putting Louis XVI's brother on the throne as Louis XVIII. (The son had ruled, in name only, for a short time after his father was guillotined. Then this "Louis XVII" vanished.) The new monarchy now attempted to eliminate Napoleon's support by retiring his loyal troops on half pay.

Napoleon's anti-clericalism—or rather, that of the Revolution, for Napoleon had no time to worry about such matters—was hastily reversed and non-Catholic army officers were cashiered. Church estates were restored, and the gentry who had been quaking in fear of their lives were reinstated on the land.

But Napoleon—even in exile—inspired respect, and Louis XVIII did not. The new king was fat, ridiculous and unpopular, and as Napoleon watched this rising tide of discontent from his tiny kingdom, he realized the time was getting close when he would oust this crowned buffoon and re-establish himself as ruler of France.

One evening in early 1815 he announced to his mother, who shared his exile: "I go to Paris."

The following night, he sailed. His little army of a thousand men embarked in a navy of seven frigates, set course for the coast of France.

He landed a few days later near Cannes and straightway marched north towards Paris.

At Grenobles, a thousand of the King's soldiers faced him, blocking his path.

Napoleon rode out in front of his force, the familiar cocked hat on his head, arm tucked between two buttons of his tunic, and confronted the royal troops.

In the utter silence that followed his appearance, he said simply, "I am the Emperor."

A further silence—then a cheer, which rose to a roar. The officer commanding the King's troops rode forward, saluted, there was a greater burst of cheering, and the army of Napoleon had swollen to two thousand men.

By Lyons, the number had risen to seven thousand.

Suddenly, over all Europe, there was panic. The first intimation had reached Vienna on 7 March, where the statesmen of Europe were gathered to settle the future of a world without Napoleon. A message was read to the appalled delegates: "The English Commissioner Campbell is inquiring in Genoa whether anyone has seen Napoleon. He has disappeared from the island of Elba."

Europe was aghast. How had the man escaped? Everyone blamed everyone else.

But, of course, there had been nothing to stop him. The man had been given his comic army and navy and told to stay there with it. The fact that he had sworn to "abdicate for himself and his heirs, the throne of France——" was ludicrous, knowing the character of the man, ludicrously irrelevant.

While the statesmen of Europe pondered and panicked, the King of France, poor Louis, fled. Napoleon continued his advance toward Paris, with the numbers and enthusiasm of his army growing hourly. He reached Paris, and the crowds carried him, in triumph, shoulder high.

The Congress of Vienna declared thoughtfully that "Napoleon has placed himself outside the pale of civil and social relations". This seemed damning and well-phrased and they sat back, confident that they had struck a blow in the defence of Europe against Napoleonic aggression. While they did so, more troops from all over France were rallying to Napoleon's banner.

Eventually the English Duke of Wellington was ordered to take command of an allied force and deal with the situation. This force would, in a final shove, put paid to Napoleon and his threat. But the Duke seemed oddly apathetic, took his time over getting to Brussels where the force would assemble, and when he got there seemed more interested in enjoying the attractions of that gay capital than in deploying an army. While Wellington dined and danced and made ladies swoon, Napoleon assembled his own. From the thousand men brought in from Elba, it had swollen to a quarter of a million.

At the head of this huge and loyal army, Napoleon now marched into Charleroi, on 15 June. That night the Duke attended a huge ball thrown in Brussels by the Duchess of Richmond. Had he then, three days later, lost the Battle of Waterloo—as he so nearly did—he would to this day be held in contempt and disgrace as a fool and a womanizer. Such are the fortunes of war.

But his 110,000 British, Dutch, Belgians, Hanoverians and Braunschweigers, aided mightily by Blücher and his 117,000 Prussians, defeated Napoleon and his army at the little village of Waterloo. By the evening of 18 June the cream of the French Army was in headlong retreat, leaving behind all guns and ammunition. The final thrust had been made by Wellington and his Guards, and by nine in the evening when Blücher arrived on that sector it was agreed that he and his Prussians would take over the pursuit. Wellington retired to a comfortable inn for dinner.

The One Hundred Days of Napoleon's escape and triumph had come to an end. Elba, Cannes, Paris, Waterloo—it was all over. He abdicated again, then tried frantically to escape to the United States, but failed, and at last was forced to surrender himself, at Rochefort, to Captain Maitland of the British ship *Bellerophon*.

The allies, bleeding and angry from their exertions at Waterloo, resolved that there must never again be a question of escape for Napoleon Bonaparte. But how could it be prevented, this time?

After much discussion it was decided to banish the little King of Elba to another, farther, island. He would be taken to the South Atlantic, to the barren rock of St Helena, given comfortable quarters and a personal staff, and left there.

Probably right up to the end of his life, six years later, Napoleon plotted and schemed to leave St Helena. But this distant spot in a southern ocean was a very different affair to the Isle of Elba, and he never succeeded.

It was easy, very easy, to escape from Elba. But could any other man have done so and then gone on, in a hundred days, to raise an army of a quarter of a million and defy the world? Has any other escape by a single man—statesman, soldier, train-robber—had so devastating an effect?

Chapter 13

WINSTON CHURCHILL PLAYS HIDE-
AND-SEEK WITH THE BOERS

T HE South African War was one of the less praiseworthy
exploits of the British Army. Quite apart from the question-
able morals involved, much of the affair was handled with an
amateurishness which makes the Charge of the Light Brigade
seem a masterpiece of strategy.

A French-and-Indians mentality and Crimean equipment went
hand in hand with a wide-eyed interest in the blossoming wonders
of technology.

One such wonder was the Estcourt Armoured Train.

It consisted, reading from left to right, of two wagons, an
elderly engine, and another three wagons. The last of these (or
the first, depending on which way the driver operated his steam
valve) sported a seven-pounder gun, muzzle-loaded.

It also carried, on the occasion we are about to relate, a
number of soldiers commanded by Captain Haldane of the
Gordon Highlanders; and no less an individual than the young
correspondent of the London *Morning Post*, Mr Winston

Churchill. The train—one of the most improbable "armoured patrols" in history—was to probe along the railway beyond the town of Estcourt, nibbling into enemy territory, into the land of the Boers.

Hardly surprising that when it had penetrated fourteen miles it was ambushed.

The driver reversed, but, as the Boers had sabotaged the track behind, this achieved little. Soon half the wagons were derailed, with bullets thudding into them, ricocheting off into the veldt.

It was now that Winston Churchill, ex-officer of some experience though only twenty-four, decided to take charge. He persuaded the frightened engine driver not to desert his post but, in response to his directions, to butt and shove the derailed, upturned wagons out of the way.

Eventually this was done, and the engine, with the *Morning Post* correspondent on the foot-plate, started back home without wagons, while the surviving troops marched in its scanty shelter.

But somehow engine and driver got out of control, put on more and more speed, leaving the infantry unprotected and far behind. Churchill, having at last made the driver slow down and stop, jumped off to go back and see how Captain Haldane and his troops were faring.

He was immediately shot at by Boers. Bullets screamed past his ear, but he jogged steadily along the track, doing his best to ignore them.

Suddenly, out of nowhere, a horseman galloped up, stopped his horse in its own length and shouted a command.

Many thoughts chased each other through the young Churchill's mind. But as he wrote later of this episode: "'When one is alone and unarmed,' said the great Napoleon, in words which flowed into my mind in the poignant minutes that followed, 'a surrender may be pardoned.'"

He raised his arms in surrender.

He was sent—a prisoner-of-war of an unusual sort, for he was a civilian—to a detention camp in Pretoria. The trip, on foot and by train, took three days, and at the end of it officers were separated from men, and Churchill, ranking as the former, was put with sixty British officer prisoners-of-war into the so-called "State Model Schools".

This school—for it was only one large building—stood in a quadrangle and was surrounded on two sides by an iron grille and on the other two by a wall ten feet high. "These boundaries," Churchill wrote later, "offered little obstacle to anyone who possessed the activity of youth, but the fact that they were guarded on the inside by sentries, fifty yards apart, armed with rifle and revolver, made them a well-nigh insuperable barrier."

But a plan was made, and, with Lieutenant Brockie and Captain Haldane (who had shared the alarms and futilities of the Armoured Train), Churchill prepared to put it into effect. It involved a careful analysis of the times sentries on the beat passed a certain point. From this point they were unable to see the top of a few yards of wall. It was arranged that the three of them would one at a time pull themselves to the top, lie flat against it till the sentries were again out of vision, then drop to the other side.

On the evening of 12 December, 1899, Churchill, as the first of the three to make the attempt, strode over to a little circular lavatory hard up against the wall and, as arranged, hid himself inside. He watched the sentries carefully through a small aperture, then took his chance. Using a suitable ledge inside the open lavatory, he "seized the top of the wall with my hands and drew myself up. Twice I let myself down again in sickly hesitation, and then, with a third resolve, scrambled up and over. My waistcoat got entangled with the ornamental metal work on the top. I had to pause for an appreciable amount to extricate myself. In this posture I had one parting glimpse of the sentries still talking with their backs turned, fifteen yards away. One of them was lighting his cigarette, and I remember the glow on the inside of his hands as a distinct impression which my mind recorded. Then I lowered myself lightly down into the adjoining garden and crouched among the shrubs. I was free!"

Free?

He waited several minutes for the arrival of his two comrades, then learnt that the sentries had been alerted and there was no hope of their getting over the wall. In fact, they now urged him, in loud whispers from the other side of it, to come back while there was still time: he would stand no chance of getting out of Pretoria.

He refused to come back—and, in any case, there was no means of scaling the wall from this side. He prepared to make his way eastward to Portuguese territory and its seaport, Lourenço Marques, on Delagoa Bay. "I walked on leisurely through the night, humming a tune and choosing the middle of the road. The streets were full of burghers, but they paid no attention to me. Gradually I reached the suburbs, and on a little bridge I sat down to reflect and consider. I was in the heart of the enemy's country. I knew no one to whom I could apply for succour. Nearly 300 miles stretched between me and Delagoa Bay. My escape must be known at dawn. Pursuit would be immediate. Yet all exits were barred. The town was picketed, the country was patrolled, the trains were searched, the line was guarded. I had seventy-five pounds in my pocket and four slabs of chocolate, but the compass and the map which might have guided me, the opium tablets and meat lozenges which should have sustained me, were in my friends' pockets in the State Model Schools."

As a piece of planning, this seems on a par with the Armoured Train: we are lucky that Churchill's abilities as an organizer increased as he grew older.

He decided to find the railway leading to Delagoa Bay. In order to do this, he headed south and within half a mile struck a line. There was a chance that it was not the eastward one but another going north to Pietersburg. Yet it was pointless to stay still, and he began to walk along it, preparing to leap aboard the first train that passed. He was fairly certain this was the right line, and if it proved to be nothing of the kind, he could always hop off again: at least he would be out of Pretoria.

But after two hours no train had appeared. He came to the lights of a railway station and here he cautiously circled round behind it and rejoined the line two hundred yards farther on.

He crouched in a ditch, waiting.

An hour passed. Then, to his immense relief, a train could be heard. A moment later its great yellow headlights lit up the rails.

It stopped at the station. The young fugitive wriggled closer to the edge of the line and waited.

After five minutes, the train started up. "The rattle became a roar. The dark mass hung for a second above me. The engine driver silhouetted against his furnace glow, the black profile of the engine, the clouds of steam, rushed past. Then I hurled myself on the trucks, clutched at something, missed, clutched again, missed again, grasped some sort of hand-hold, was swung off my feet—my toes bumping along the line—and with a struggle seated myself on the couplings of the fifth truck from the front of the train. It was a goods train and the trucks were full of great sacks, soft sacks covered with coal dust. . . ."

He burrowed in among them and went to sleep, still uncertain whether he was heading for Delagoa Bay and safety, or northward into enemy territory. He was almost too tired to care.

He awoke a few hours later. It was still dark, and he knew he must leave the train before dawn to find a pool to drink from, and a hiding place, before the sun got up. A moment later, shaken but unhurt, he had flung himself from the fast-moving train and landed in a ditch.

He found some water, drank and drank again, far more than he wanted, in order to give himself enough for the whole day.

That day duly dawned. He sat hungry and depressed, watching the trains go by and deciding to board another when night fell. But darkness came and no train.

At last, a little before one in the morning—14 December—he decided to walk rapidly along the line and cover as much as possible of the journey on foot: perhaps another train would never come. But he made little progress. "Every bridge was guarded by armed men: every few miles were huts. At intervals there were stations with tin-roofed villages clustering about them. All the veldt was bathed in the bright rays of the full moon, and to avoid these dangerous places I had to make wide circuits and even to creep along the ground. Leaving the railway, I fell into bogs and swamps, brushed through high grass dripping with dew and waded across the streams over which the bridges carried the railway. I was soon drenched to the waist."

He got to a station. There, laid up on sidings, were three goods trains.

He was about to board one of these when a sound of voices

alarmed him: quickly he slipped into the long grass of the veldt and was soon out of sight and earshot of the station. By now he had made out fires in the darkness to his left. Wondering whether they might be a Kaffir camp, a "kraal", and believing that these black men hated the Boers, he headed bravely in that direction. A moment later, panic overwhelmed him. Suppose it were not a Kaffir kraal, but a Boer settlement? He decided to press on, with caution.

It was three in the morning when he realized he was heading for the mouth of a coal mine. A few houses were grouped round it, and now he saw that the fires towards which he had been heading were furnaces for the steam-engines which operated the mine equipment.

With some desperation, coupled with a knowledge that a number of Englishmen had been retained in the country to operate mine equipment for the less mechanical Boers, he walked up to a door and struck it hard with his fist.

"*Wer is da?*' cried a man's voice.

"I felt a shock of disappointment and consternation to my fingers.

"'I want help: I have had an accident,' I replied.

"Some mutterings followed. Then I heard steps descending the stairs, the bolt of the door was drawn, the lock was turned. It was opened abruptly and in the darkness of the passage a tall man, hastily attired, with a pale face and dark moustache, stood before me.

"'What do you want?' he said, this time in English.

"I had now to think of something to say. I wanted above all to get into parley with this man, to get matters in such a state that instead of raising an alarm and summoning others, he would discuss things quietly.

"'I am a burgher,' I began. 'I have had an accident. I was going to join my commando at Komati Poort. I have fallen off the train. We were skylarking. I think I have dislocated my shoulder.'

"It is astonishing how one thinks of these things. This story leapt out as if I had learnt it by heart."

The stranger, after some hesitation, invites him in. Then, as they stand warily at opposite ends of a table, lit by the oily light of a kerosene lamp, Winston Churchill decides to tell the truth. He is war correspondent of the *Morning Post*, and he has escaped from Pretoria.

His host is relieved and delighted. His name is John Howard, he manages the Transvaal Collieries, and this, as chance would have it, is the only house for miles around where an Englishman might be offered sanctuary. Yes, the soldiers have already come, making inquiries about him, but the fugitive will get all the help it is possible for Howard to give. Already some three thousand pictures of him have been printed and telegrams have been sent to all railway stations. A reward has been offered for him, dead or alive.

Howard sends him down the mine, for he needs time to think. If he is caught helping a prisoner to escape he stands to face a firing squad himself. One problem has already arisen. The generous Mr Howard has allowed the young man to polish off most of a leg of mutton, and this, because Howard is a light eater, will be noticed by his Dutch serving girl.

Churchill is shown the cage, introduced to Mr Dewsnap, who operates the rig, and enters it with Howard. They drop down through the earth. There, at the bottom of the mine, he finds two men with lanterns and a big bundle which turns out to be a mattress and blankets for his own use.

He is led through the darkness until they reach some sort of a chamber where the air is cool and pleasant, at which point the kindly Mr Howard presents him with two candles, a bottle of whisky and a box of cigars before taking his leave.

"I do not know how many hours I slept, but the following afternoon must have been far advanced when I found myself thoroughly awake. I put out my hand for the candle, but could feel it nowhere. I did not know what pitfalls these mining galleries might contain, so I thought it better to lie quiet on my mattress and await developments. Several hours passed before the faint gleam of a lantern showed that someone was coming. It proved to be Mr Howard himself, armed with a chicken and other good things. He also brought several books. He asked me why I had not lighted my candle. I said I couldn't find it.

"'Didn't you put it under the mattress?' he asked.

"'No.'

"'Then the rats must have got it.'"

Churchill was more careful after this, but the three days he spent down the mine were memorable for the constant sound of little feet and the occasional sensation of a rat scurrying over his body. "Luckily for me," he wrote later, "I have no horror of rats as such——"

After three days during which a search for the *Morning Post* correspondent took place a few hundred feet above his head— for police had been sent to the mine—the hue and cry died down. Mr Howard said he might come out and spend the rest of his confinement on the surface, in a back office.

Meanwhile, Howard arranged with a friendly wool-grower to hide Churchill in a load of wool going by rail to Lourenço Marques. At two o'clock on the morning of the 19th he was led by his host to a siding where three large railway trucks were standing. Without a word being spoken, he was inserted in the first, where there was a space between bales big enough to lie down in.

Some time later, the train was coupled up, started off.

And now, though danger is still only too real and near, discomfort for our fugitive is largely over. His kind host has provided him with two roast chickens, some meat, some bread, a melon and bottles of cold tea. He consumes some of this, then wriggles his way along the truck to where he can see out through a chink in the side, to keep a check on his progress. He has carefully memorized all the towns on the way, so that he will know exactly where he is and how far from safety.

Late on the afternoon of the 20th, the train reaches Komati Poort, the last Boer town before the frontier. Here it stands every chance of being inspected by customs officials as well as police. He covers himself with sacking, lies flat on his face, and people actually stick their heads in and do not see him. He stays this way, sweating and miserable, for hours. At last the train starts up again.

He has begun to wonder whether the last station really has been Komati Poort. If so, he is now safely over the frontier and into neutral, Portuguese, terrirtory, heading for the port of Lourenço Marques. If not——

"But all these doubts were dispelled when the train arrived

135

at the next station. I peered through my chink and saw the uniform caps of the Portuguese officials on the platform and the name 'Resana Garcia' painted on a board. I restrained all expression of my joy until we moved on again. Then, as we rumbled and banged along, I pushed my head out of the tarpaulin and sang and shouted and crowed at the top of my voice. Indeed, I was so carried away by thankfulness and delight that I fired my revolver two or three times in the air as a *feu de joie*. None of these follies led to any evil results."

Late that afternoon the train reaches the coast at Lourenço Marques: and Churchill leaves the hiding place where he has spent three uncomfortable and anxious days. He slips unnoticed off the train and mingles with the loafers in the station yard, "which my slovenly and unkempt appearance well fitted me to do", and thence, via the main streets of Lourenço Marques, makes his way to the British Consulate which he has recognized by its Union Jack on the roof.

"The secretary of the British Consul evidently did not expect my arrival.

" 'Be off,' he said. 'The Consul cannot see you today. Come to his office at nine tomorrow, if you want anything.'

"At this I became so angry and repeated so loudly that I insisted on seeing the Consul personally at once that that gentleman himself looked out of the window and finally came down to the door and asked me my name: From that moment, every resource of hospitality and welcome was at my disposal. A hot bath, clean clothing, an excellent dinner, means of telegraphing —all I could want.

"I devoured the file of newspapers which was placed before me. Great events had taken place since I had climbed the wall of the State Model Schools. The Black Week of the Boer War had descended on the British Army. General Gatacre at Stormberg, Lord Methuen at Magersfontein, and Sir Redvers Buller at Colenso, had all suffered staggering defeats, and casualties on a scale unknown since the Crimean War. All this made me eager to rejoin the army, and the Consul himself was no less anxious to get me out of Lourenço Marques, which was full of Boers and Boer sympathizers. Happily the weekly steamer was leaving for Durban that very evening; in fact, it might almost be said it ran in connexion with my train. On this steamer I decided to embark.

"The news of my arrival had spread like wildfire through the town, and while we were at dinner the Consul was at first disturbed to see a group of strange figures in the garden. These, however, turned out to be Englishmen fully armed who had hurried up to the Consulate determined to resist any attempt at my recapture. Under the escort of these patriotic gentlemen I marched safely through the streets to the quay, and at about ten o'clock was on salt water in the steamship *Induna*.

"I reached Durban to find myself a popular hero. I was received as if I had won a great victory. The harbour was decorated with flags. Bands and crowds thronged the quays. The Admiral, the General, the Mayor pressed on board to grasp my hand. I was nearly torn to pieces by enthusiastic kindness. Whirled along on the shoulders of the crowd, I was carried to the steps of the town hall, where nothing would content them but a speech, which after a becoming reluctance I was induced to deliver. Sheaves of telegrams from all parts of the world poured in upon me, and I started that night for the Army in a blaze of triumph.

"Here, too, I was received with the greatest goodwill. I took up my quarters in the very platelayer's hut within one hundred yards of which I had little more than a month before been taken prisoner, and there, with the rude plenty of the Natal campaign, celebrated by a dinner to many friends my good fortune, and Christmas Eve."

And so a great escape concludes. A little later, having basked in the glory of being a hero, having rejoined the army for a few more months campaigning, in which the tide turns in his country's favour and Pretoria falls, he is invited to return home and stand, once again, for the Oldham constituency, where he has previously been rejected by the electorate. Things now have changed completely. "I entered the town in state in a procession of ten landaus, and drove through the streets crowded with enthusiastic operatives and mill-girls. I described my escape to a tremendous meeting in the Theatre Royal. As our forces had now occupied the Witbank Colliery district, and those who had aided me were safe under British protection, I was free for the first time to tell the whole story. When I mentioned the name of Mr Dewsnap, the Oldham engineer who had wound me down the mine, the audience shouted: 'his wife's in the gallery'. There was general jubilation."

Here is an escape, remarkable in itself, which started the greatest man of his generation on a career which would some day save his country—and the world.

Chapter 14

THE CRAZY ROAD OF
LIEUTENANTS JONES AND HILL

ANYONE—like me—who has been fascinated by the work of spiritualists, mediums and mind-readers, who has in fact believed these powers exist and are fairly widely distributed, will be hard put to it maintaining such a belief after he has read the tale of this escape.

That is, if he believes in the escape. For it is one of the most "impossible" ones since biblical times. Moses himself, organizing plague after plague on the luckless Pharaoh, in his attempts to get out of Egypt, might have bowed in the direction of the Bosphorus on hearing of the mental tortures brought down by two young British officers on their Turkish captors. Mohammed reaching Medina after the kindly intervention of a dove and a spider, might also have marvelled at the spectacular results achieved by mere human intellect. Aided, of course, by human greed and human fear.

But there is every sort of corroboration; for the number of prisoners-of-war who escaped from the Turks in the First World

War was comparatively small, and, the details of each other's methods were soon common knowledge.

Lieutenant Jones from Wales, and Lieutenant Hill from Australia, found themselves, half-way through that war, in the hell of one of Turkey's worst camps. The place was Yozgad, run by an unscrupulous staff who sold P.O.W. rations on the black market, robbed incoming parcels of comforts and wore without embarrassment English home-knitted gloves, socks and caps in their everyday dealings with English prisoners. Most of the prisoners-of-war had been force-marched long distances to reach the place, many of them were ill, some desperately, and the general feeling was one of utter resignation: this was hell, but who would be fit enough, fool enough to try an escape over three hundred and fifty miles of mountains to the coast? The few attempts had brought misery on the heads of those remaining: escapers, in short, were not popular.

One of the would-be escapers had been the tough and wiry Cedric Hill. He made an unsuccessful bid and brought down such trouble on himself and others that he had now given his "parole" to the Senior British Officer that he would make no further attempt.

It was at this point that Jones got his postcard. It was only a postcard, from an aunt—and there should have been letters galore, from wife and mother and father, which were bogged down in the Turkish Post Office. But this postcard, with its kindly, helpful suggestion, was to alter the lives of a number of people.

For it suggested that the bored lads in prison camp might like to make themselves a "ouijah" board. The name came from the French and German for "yes" and they were devices very popular among fortune tellers. Even ordinary people fiddled with them, trying to get "messages" from Beyond, from "The Other Side". The construction was easy: one took a round, flat shiny surface, like the top of a polished table, or a tin tray, and carefully glued paper letters round the rim, exactly like the hours on some horizontal clock face. Except that one used, instead of numbers, all twenty-six letters of the alphabet. Then, one placed an upturned tumbler in the centre of this circle. Two or more people, blindfolded and sitting well back from the table, would rest a finger on the upturned glass.

Sometimes nothing happened. But sometimes the glass would move, as if guided by some supernatural force which no one at the table was able to control or stop. Then, as it touched letter after letter, someone not blindfolded would start noting them down, one by one.

Usually the sliding glass, apparently without human help, would register a meaningless series of letters. People could, if they wished, try to make something of this cypher. Sometimes, though, the board produced whole words, even sentences. Then excitement mounted, and people would bark questions. If they were lucky, the board replied.

Jones was a highly unusual man. He had spent years in the Indian Civil Service, that intellectual élite of Empire, and he understood most things: in particular, human nature. He found a method of getting replies from his board. It was a simple matter to memorize the position of all the letters round the edge (they were not in order) so that even blindfolded he could "read" each one as the glass, with his finger resting gently on it, came by.

As for the glass's movement—he found, as others have done, that a very slight physical persuasion, after one has mastered the knack, will make it move in any desired direction. All the other, anxious, arms can feel is a powerful force they seem unable to resist.

The inhabitants of Jones's barrack-room made many attempts to get sense from the board, but it had continued to produce meaningless rows of letters. Then, one evening as they sat there, the blindfolded Jones touching the glass and a bored officer saying, "Come on, for the last time, Board, what's your name?" it replied.

"S-A-L-L-Y."

Everyone jumped up. Two men put fingers on the glass, others blindfolded them. The glass, now well into its stride, shot rapidly from letter to letter and no one was able either to stop or control it.

"Sally" grew cheeky, then affectionate, and they loved her. Then they found that the board could become at will all sorts of personalities. They named it, to cover them all, "The Spook".

Jones at this time had no intention of doing more than have a harmless game with his toy until he was found out—after which he would cheerfully accept the abuse and the pummelling. He was a little startled by the fact that no one even guessed what he was doing. Some of the more sceptical "verified" the genuineness of the messages by extravagant schemes of covering up letters, using the board upside down and so on, but Jones had the act well organized: the Spook was soon accepted without question as a supernatural being. And only Jones (who "learnt it from the head-hunters of Burma") had the power to evoke him.

The harmless game went on, week after week. Then they learnt that the camp interpreter, a pale young Levantine nicknamed "The Pimple", who regularly stole from their parcels and always wore a British-knitted balaclava helmet, had asked that Jones come and see him.

" 'Good afternoon, Jones' he said familiarly as I came in. He had never greeted me before—he kept his salutations for *very* senior officers.

" 'What do you want?' I asked.

"He led me a little to one side, away from the crowd.

" 'You are a student of spiritism?' he said, eyeing me sharply. 'The sentries have told me.'

" 'Well?' I ventured.

" 'Have you studied the subject?'

" 'So-so,' said I.

" 'How much do you know about it? I too am interested.' "

And soon, very soon, Jones found that he had not only the odious Pimple, whose real name was Moise, but the Commandant himself, absolutely at his mercy.

But to do this, he had to let a few friends into the secret. He did so, they were suitably amazed and annoyed by the way he had fooled them so long, then they all sat down together to devise a way of fooling the Pimple. The little man had presented a list of questions he would like answered by the Spook, and although he had made every effort to disguise their intent, it was immediately obvious to the band of conspirators that he was trying to find out details of young women interned in another part of the camp.

The rude answers Spook provided, which were a huge leg-pull, impressed the Pimple enormously. Up to this day he "had not believed in spiritism": from now on he would be a firm believer. (And perhaps, to this day, he is—out in Egypt where the Spook later told him to go. That was one of the more preposterous "revelations": Go to Egypt, it said, and you will become a leader of the stature of Buddha, or Jesus of Nazareth. You are the one, the Chosen One. Mon Dieu, the Pimple said, and wrote it all down.)

But this was later. In the meantime, an important question, the most important question of all, had to be answered. The Pimple explained, gasping with anticipation, that there was a large sum of money buried in the camp grounds. Everyone, from the Commandant down, knew it. The money had been put there by a rich Armenian family just before they were led away to massacre. The Pimple enjoined Jones and his two assistants to secrecy. He would give them ten per cent each, if only they would make the Spook tell him where the treasure was.

But in the meantime—so greatly had this miracle seized the minds of the camp—the Turkish Commandant posted an Order, forbidding prisoners to communicate home in their letters, any "news obtained by Officers in a Spiritistic State". Some humorist had told Moise, the Pimple, that the Spook regularly attended meetings of the Turkish High Command and the idea straightaway took root.

Tension mounted on all sides. The Pimple, at a long séance, was told exactly where to look for the First Clue to his treasure. Not for the treasure itself, just for a First Clue: that was the way Spook liked to do things. All sorts of hilarious conditions were imposed, including a companion for the Pimple during the hunt, who must, like him, have "naked steel against the skin" (and the Spook helpfully suggested a bare bayonet up the trouser leg); a bottle of ink; some string; a basket of wood shavings; and a few more oddments as well.

All this was rapidly arranged by Moise.

They had discovered, weeks before, an old and rusted pistol half buried in the grounds. This they now carefully reburied at a special spot and the Spook announced that the treasure would be "By Arms Guarded". Finding the arms: that would be the First Clue.

"Day dawned for the search. The Pimple had brought the

camp cook as his required companion. The cook was walking awkwardly on account of the bayonet up his trouser leg, and he spoke rapidly in Turkish to the Pimple, who turned to us and translated.

" 'The cook wants to know what we are to do if the Spook leads us to a harem.'

"Mundey and I had the utmost difficulty in keeping our faces straight. We had not thought of such an enterprise.

" 'We can stop outside, I suppose.' "

By now they had the Pimple so much at their mercy that they were able to indulge in something more convenient and rapid than simple Spooking. Spook ordered Jones to go into a trance: in this state he would get his orders direct, without the board. Jones did so and immediately saw an invisible being who gave him inaudible instructions. There was a pregnant wait while the Pimple complained that he could see and hear nothing. Then suddenly,

" 'South!' I shouted, and started off at a great pace down the lane. 'South! South!'

"Mundey kept step with me. The Pimple and the Cook trotted (uncomfortably because of the bayonets) close behind us. With eyes fixed on the 'spirit', I rushed past the astonished sentry, who obeyed a signal from Moise and made no effort to stop me. As I went, I called to the spirit to have mercy on us poor mortals and not to go so fast."

They got, of course, to the spot where they had buried the revolver—and in the most roundabout way possible. Here they indulged in hilarious mumbo-jumbo, getting Moise to burn the shavings, pour on his bottle of ink and listen while Jones mumbled incantations (in Welsh) before they allowed the almost hysterical little man to find a revolver underneath his fire of shavings.

This manifestation put the Pimple into a permanent frenzy of excitement which mounted every day. He knew that, having found the "arms", he would be given information leading to the actual treasure. The Spook had promised that he would, in good time, and in the meantime Spook congratulated Moise on having discovered the First Clue. There were one or two little improprieties, of course, in the way he had done it—did

144

he not remember being told not to use his shovel that way?—and this had rather annoyed the spirit guardians of the treasure.

Jones suddenly hit upon a method of escape. It was a diabolical method.

It depended on the Commandant, Kiazim Bey, becoming interested in the treasure hunt, and now Jones grew daily more anxious for him to attend a séance. The man must know all about it, he had probably seen the chase for the First Clue, but he was staying in the background.

But as Jones had hoped, the Commandant was interested. The summons came, and Jones, in the man's office, studied him.

"He played nervously with a pencil while he spoke to me through the Interpreter, but never took his eyes from my face throughout the interview. He began with western abruptness and plunged *in media res.*

" 'Before we go into any details,' he said, 'I want your word of honour not to communicate to anyone what I am now going to tell you'."

He got it—but, before he was able to come out with what he had planned to say, Jones staggered him: "You are going to ask me to find for you a treasure, buried by a murdered Armenian of Yozgad. You want me to do this by the aid of spirits. And you are prepared to offer me a reward."

The Commandant gasped. When he had recovered, he agreed this was the case. Jones left his presence with high heart and a plan taking shape in his head. Already he had decided on a companion for his escape: it would be Cedric Hill. Quite apart from the man's courage and eagerness to get out of Yozgad, he had many skills—like an ability to make cameras and all sorts of complicated equipment out of virtually nothing.

Hill agreed. There was only the little matter of the parole he had given not to escape—but Jones had plans for this. They would, using Hill's home-made camera, get some incriminating photos of the Commandant digging for treasure with a gaggle of his own prisoners-of-war—an absolutely forbidden state of affairs on at least two counts. The camp could then blackmail him if there were any question of punishment.

The actual plan of escape was involved and ingenious, and

Jones allowed delays to play their part. Weeks went by in which the Spook refused to tell where the treasure lay, weeks in which the Pimple and the Commandant nearly went mad, but during which Hill became accepted as a second man with the "gift". The Spook decreed that only these two mediums would be able to find the treasure. It was quite beyond his, the Spook's, ability: there was too much interference in the Beyond.

For the mediums to develop the necessary degree of concentration, enough to pierce the mystery, they would have to be alone together for a few weeks—away from the hurly-burly of the camp, having no interference with their vital thought-processes. They would not enjoy it of course, the Spook said, but having now given their word to find the treasure, they would have to do it. It would entail, the Spook suggested, their being put together into confinement *à deux*. And outside the crowded camp, away from the noise, the distraction.

Jones's complex reasoning was that if he and Hill were out of the camp proper when they made their escape—however they made it—there could be no question of implicating the other prisoners-of-war. And of course, outside camp, even heavily guarded, they stood a better chance of making a getaway.

But as the Senior British Officer must be warned of any escape—he had forbidden them all—it must be made clear that Jones and Hill were being punished by the Turks, had not simply wangled themselves a transfer to a new quarters.

This, incredible as it seems, was done by having the Spook produce an incriminating letter, proving the two mediums had communicated "spiritistic information" home—against, as we have seen, express orders to the contrary. Absolutely nonplussed, the Commandant took the Spook's advice and put the two of them into "solitary confinement".

From Jones's and Hill's point of view, this imprisonment, which could easily be shown, if necessary, to be unjust, could have a disastrous effect on the Commandant's standing with his own High Command. Constantinople had no desire for the Turkish nation to be branded as a lot of savages, particularly when half the world was saying this already. It could be a second form of blackmail against Kiazim Bey. It could even result in the two prisoners-of-war being repatriated: this had already happened with another officer who was proved to be unjustly treated by his Turkish captors.

Yet even these were supplementary plans. The real one was to get Kiazim Bey, on the Spook's instruction, to send them both to Constantinople, whence they could steal away and find a ship to freedom. This should be possible, for the Commandant was prepared to do anything the ingenious Spook told him. If it could be represented that the final clue to the treasure had somehow or other got to Constantinople, there would be little difficulty. It was a bore that the Spook, in a moment of hilarity, had decreed that Commandant, Pimple and Cook must always be present at the unearthing of each clue, or of the treasure itself: they would simply have to be escorted to the coast by their Commandant.

But in the meantime, in confinement outside the gates, they were soon living better than ever before. Their Commandant smuggled in food and drink while hoping daily that their confinement was beginning to have the desired effect on their powers.

A suitable time elapsed—and the Spook arranged for all five of them, Jones, Hill and the Turks, to engage in a search for the Second Clue. This was a buried tin with a gold coin inside, and some meaningless writing on a piece of paper. It was duly found, to the Commandant's delight, and at this point his photograph was taken secretly and three times. The pictures, when Hill developed them, were excellent.

After a further suitable lapse of time the Spook announced that the next and final clue would be found in Constantinople.

This was a tall order, even for one as completely hypnotized as Kiazim Bey. For that reason, Jones and Hill had been quietly mugging up the symptoms of insanity. With their reputation for dabbling—indeed, practising—in the occult, they had but to produce symptoms stranger still to be acknowledged as lunatics by both Turk and Englishman. And as mental cases, they would *have* to be sent to Constantinople.

The Commandant knew nothing of this second plan: he was working on the first. Thanks to the impending transfer of staff and prisoners from another camp to his own, it had begun to seem simple. He had but to arrange his own journey to the coast on medical grounds and take with him as Interpreter and

Orderly the pair whom the Spook so tiresomely insisted on, the Pimple and the Cook. There would be no trouble taking the two prisoners: there were plenty of reasons why they should be going, under heavy escort, to Constantinople.

And the places of Commandant, Interpreter and Cook would be taken by their opposite numbers on the incoming staff.

Any private doubts Kiazim Bey might have had about this fantastic arrangement were swamped by information from the Spook who now told them they would find, in Constantinople, a clue to treasure far greater than they had dreamed of. As for the Pimple, it was at this point that the Spook told him of a "call" in Constantinople which would take him to Egypt and thence to leadership of the world. Some equally farcical encouragement was offered the cook, and the three fools were ready to set off, with their British companions.

They would have felt differently if they knew that Jones and Hill, delighted with their plan, had decided to improve it. They would not only hire a boat on the coast: they would kidnap the Commandant, take him with them.

But all this was foiled by a piece of bad luck. An already complex story is made quite un-understandable, in our little allotted space, if we go into details. Suffice it to say that the Commandant panicked. He knew Jones and Hill would not try to escape—but it came into his head that the hostile folk "On The Other Side", the ones the Spook so often—and, as it turned out, so foolishly—referred to, might kidnap them.

And with these two gone, there could be no further hope of finding treasure.

The Spook took charge. If by careless talk of unseen forces wishing evil to the treasure-hunters he had sabotaged the original plan, he would get the alternative, "madness", plan into action, and fast. The Commandant was suddenly persuaded that the treasure could still be obtained and he himself run no risk of embarrassment, if the two Englishmen be certified insane by the camp doctors. They could then be rushed off—for this was one of the things the High Command most dreaded, sudden insanity among prisoners-of-war—without any questions, to Constantinople. They would travel under very heavy escort which would prevent the "Other Side" seizing them, and Kiazim Bey, in case anything went wrong, would be spared the embarrassment of travelling with them. The Spook agreed that it was no longer necessary for him to be present.

As the Spook pointed out, it was this or nothing: Hill and Jones had to get to Constantinople to find the clue. Only there could Spook give final orders.

By now, having convinced almost all their fellow P.O.W.'s that they were clairvoyant and a dozen other things besides, it was easy, as their behaviour grew strange, to get sincere corroboration that they had "always been odd" and were now out of their minds.

They set off with a large guard and the Pimple. They soon realized they would have difficulty in convincing specialists of their insanity. They would have to build up their dossier of madness by a series of adventures on the way, adventures for the guards to report on arrival. One of these was actually to hang themselves during an overnight halt. This, they had been told, would stand them in good stead—if they survived.

By a masterpiece of ingenuity they got Spook to inform the Pimple of their plan to hang themselves. (Jones had become— without knowing it of course—the Voice of the Spook, when he twiddled his coat button. And when he stopped twiddling and became Jones again, he had no idea of what he had been saying. The Pimple was hard put to it, replying politely to both "Jones" and "Sir", keeping a wary eye on the button.)

They hanged themselves, almost too well, and were cut down in literally the nick of time by the well-warned Pimple and the sentries. By this time Moise had begun to believe they really *were* mad: he hoped fervently this would not affect the outcome of the treasure hunt. He hoped they would survive: days after this foolhardy move they were unable to sleep or eat solid food, for the pain round neck and throat.

They reached Constantinople, where the investigation of their sanity was even more exhaustive than they had feared: they found themselves under observation twenty-four hours a day, surrounded by linguists who could tell as soon as they tried to converse in English, French or any other language. They were soon separated, and the unfortunate Hill nearly died of ill-treatment.

They—just—carried off the deception. Perhaps the hanging did it, after all.

Jones saw Moise once more, when he came to the ward in an effort to consult the Spook about his treasure. The Spook said there would be some delay.

(After the war, Moise pestered them both with letters, until Jones sent him a copy of his book *The Road to En-Dor*—"the oldest road and the craziest road of all," in Kipling's verse—from which our excerpts have been taken. After this, the letters stopped.)

Segregated in hospital, the two met again on the way home, in Alexandria. By this time, not daring to relax their deception, they had fooled literally thousands of people, including a kind lady from the Dutch Embassy in Constantinople who went away in tears. An Englishman, also an escaper, who saw Jones in hospital, described him in all sincerity as "a ghoulish figure. He wore a black overall, a yard of which he had picked into threads. His hair was long, he wore a beard, and his white, sunken cheeks gave him a ghastly appearance". Francis Yeats-Brown, whose own escape is in these pages, noted that he saw "the two madmen" on his way home.

They reached Alexandria separately, a fortnight before the survivors from their own camp passed through. The war was over.

By any practical yardstick, their effort was pointless. But it has left us a unique tale of escape.

Chapter 15

FRANCIS YEATS-BROWN AND
THE "WHITE LADY"

I MAKE little apology for the fact that both First World War escapes in this book are from the Turks. For in the years 1916-18 a Turkish prison camp was as horrible a place of confinement as any in the world—and very hard to escape from. The guards were less competent than those which guarded prisoners-of-war in Germany (they were often old men) but the hazards outside—the terrain, the climate, the bandits ready to murder anyone for the shirt he wore—made get-away virtually impossible.

For this reason and for the fact that starvation and brutal treatment had often destroyed the will and physical strength to try, the numbers escaping were few. One finds, on reading the literature of the period, that most escapers, in their long journey to the Turkish coast and to British territory, came in contact with the others. Francis Yeats-Brown, whose escape we consider here, came across "the two madmen Jones and Hill", subjects of another chapter, and firmly believed they were.

Yeats-Brown was educated, like Churchill, at Harrow and Sandhurst, and like Churchill, who was twelve years his senior, went to India as a newly commissioned officer. There, like Churchill again, he spent a lot of time reading. Yeats-Brown's great interest was in that strange, athletic, branch of the occult, Yoga.

War came when he was twenty-eight and on leave in England and he quickly reported to Aldershot and joined the Royal Irish Lancers: his own unit, the Bengal Lancers, was in India. With the rank of Captain he saw service in France, hoping all the time that the Bengal Lancers would be posted to the western front so that he could join them there.

They were not. He decided to transfer to the Royal Flying Corps. He was given his Observer's wings, sent to Basra on the Persian Gulf.

It was November, 1915, when he was sent on a highly dangerous mission with his pilot. They were to land behind the Turkish lines at Ctesiphon, where the British were launching a big attack, and cut the telegraph wires.

They made a perfect landing on what seemed deserted ground and taxied across it. It was just as Brown bent down in his cockpit to grab some of the gun-cotton he would use for this task that the machine came to a grinding, shuddering halt. They jumped out—only to find they had hit one of the poles they were sent to destroy. With poetic justice, it had destroyed the leading edge of their wing.

There could be no question of taking off again—but there was no point worrying about it. Calmly, they fixed explosives to another pole, detonated them, watched it crash into the sand. Then, with more explosive, they splintered the insulators, ripped away the wires.

By now they were being fired on at close range, and even if their machine had been airworthy, one doubts whether they would have got away to safety.

They were captured by Arabs, almost beheaded on the spot, then taken over by Turkish cavalry and dragged off to Baghdad. Here the populace spat in their faces and a not-unfriendly Governor questioned them about British dispositions and took their obvious lies in good part. A little later they were sent on to Mosul and from there to Afiun-Kara-Hissar, the "Black Opium City", with its dreaded prison camp on the outskirts.

Here, conditions were appalling. He watched men die like flies, deep in maggots. In fact, of the fourteen thousand prisoners-of-war in Turkey, only three thousand ever survived to get back to England, a record as shocking as any in modern times. He took up Yoga again to get his mind off the fleas and lice which infested him, and the Yoga gave him much spiritual comfort. Probably, with its rigid discipline of body as well as mind, it did much to keep him in reasonable health while all around were dying. He had been very ill on the long march to camp, but now he slowly mended and made plans to escape. He refused to give his word, as the Turks demanded, not to do this: so his confinement was made more difficult, escape less likely.

By Christmas, 1917, with snow deep on the ground, and a bitter cold over the whole Anatolian plain, he had managed to strike up some sort of friendship with the Cypriot interpreter in the camp, who was an opium addict and for whom Brown, incredibly enough, had managed to arrange supplies. And a little later, helped by this man, he was able to get a medical certificate to go to the big Haidar Pasha Hospital outside Constantinople for an operation on his nose.

A two-day train journey and he was there. He was searched and a letter found on him to the Dutch Minister in Turkey, who was acting as British representative. It was from all the prisoners-of-war in camp, complaining bitterly about their treatment and particularly about the perverted cruelty of the Commandant. (The week before, the man had raped a young prisoner while he was being held down by two guards.) Although he was within his rights to convey this to the Dutch, he knew it would do little to ingratiate him with the hospital authorities, and he was lucky enough, after they had taken it and torn the envelope, to distract them, remove the letter, and substitute a blank sheet.

A little later, as he had hoped, his close friend Robin Paul arrived in the hospital for treatment to a "bad ear".

Brown's medical examination was cursory indeed. The specialist took one look, said "Deflected septum—breathe through your mouth". Then moved on.

This was a disappointment: he would be on his way back to camp within a day unless he could produce some other affliction. It came in a blinding flash. He announced suddenly that he had decided to become a Mohammedan, but was aware that this would necessitate a small operation.

By virtue of the fact—which he knew—that the Chief Doctor was just perfecting a new technique for this very operation, he was seized upon as guinea-pig. In a gleaming theatre, before an appreciative audience of students and professors, Captain Yeats-Brown was painlessly circumcized.

Now officially convalescent, as he had planned, he was transferred with Robin Paul to the former Armenian Patriarchate in the suburb of Psamattia. From here they were allowed a certain amount of freedom. They had heard of a certain "White Lady", a girl of Polish descent who had been adopted by an English family in the Middle East. She was therefore an enemy alien, but a loved and respected one, allowed freedom within Constantinople because of the work she did for the sick and needy of all nationalities. Knowing where she lived and the fact that she attended the nearby English church, they got permission to go under escort to the church themselves.

After the service they recognized the girl and managed to have a few furtive words with her. Yes, she said, if they could only meet her again, she would give details of a hiding place in the town and means of getting from it to freedom.

This was wonderful news. But first they had to meet her again at the rendezvous. In order to do so on the date she laid down (there had been no time to discuss suitable ones) they had to arrange a visit to the dentist. They had managed this before and their faces were slowly filling up with the gold which a delighted dentist stuffed into their teeth, in return for lavish payment. (He sent inspired progress reports on their treatment to their Commandant at Psamattia, explaining that they would need a great deal more—for the "teeth of these Englishmen" were in a shocking state.)

On this all-important dental sortie they gave their two Turkish escorts lunch in a restaurant. It was a good lunch and the men were delighted to wander into the Seraglio Gardens afterward. They paid no attention when Brown strolled off to a far bench and sat down by himself: moody fellow; he would be thinking about that Yoga, and the rest of it.

Moments later, a European lady came into the Gardens, glanced round her and came to the bench. She sat as far away as possible from Brown and began to read her book.

Still reading it, she said softly, "I have found you a place to hide——"

"Thank you—thank you——"

"But how will you get out of Psamattia?"

He told her.

She got up, closed the book and walked away. As she did, a little screw of paper dropped from her hand and he bent to pick it up.

When he had a chance to study it, he read the name of a Greek restaurant.

At the next visit to the dentist they led their delighted escort into the restaurant where the White Lady (whose name was Eveline Whittaker) had directed them. By furious signs, embarrassed excuses, Brown managed to slip out of the dining-room and meet the proprietor, Themistoclé, in the kitchen.

Terms were arranged and they shook hands. For fifty pounds, Themistoclé would lodge them both in his own house.

And where was the house?

Ah—Themistoclé would show it him. Now.

Now was too soon. Wait.

Brown got back to the table, announced to the well-wined guards that he needed cigarettes. They allowed him to go out with the proprietor to be shown a suitable shop. It was no distance, Themistoclé explained to them all: only a little way down the road.

But by the time Brown got back to the table the guards had begun to fidget: his trip down the road had taken a long time indeed. He had trotted, with Themistoclé, all the way to the Greek's house, memorized the route and sprinted back, buying cigarettes on the way.

The proprietor followed, more decorously. When Brown, Robin Paul and their escorts had left the restaurant he found a note under the plate. The two Englishmen would make an escape at full noon on 27 July.

They had chosen a date: all they needed was a method.

By the appointed evening, they had one. They collected a rope and enlisted the aid of an accomplice. At a quarter to ten, with the moon not yet up, they crouched below the window-sill in their room, and at this pre-arranged time their accomplice engaged the sentry outside in conversation.

Silently, and only a few feet above the sentry, they climbed from the window, found foothold on a narrow ledge which ran beneath it, began to inch a way along the blank wall of the building. They halted and barely restrained a fit of coughing; cigarette smoke from a man immediately below in the street had blinded them.

Farther on they managed to drag themselves to the roof and crawl along behind the low parapet, among the debris. Leaves, anonymous filth, the stinking body of a cat.

There was a shout in the street, and they froze. Then the alarm died as suddenly as it had arisen.

Inch by inch they moved on. It was an hour and a half before they were out of sight of the sentries along the front of the building and as they slowly raised their heads and prepared to drop their rope to the ground, they found themselves staring, across the narrow darkened street, into the eyes of a man.

This was the end. He was ten feet away, looking out of his window, obviously stunned by their sudden appearance. Any moment now and he would give the alarm.

But the man did nothing. He continued to stare and they realized his mind was miles away, eyes out of focus: if they remained absolutely still, he might not notice.

But the slightest distraction would alert him: a shrieking cat, the cry of a bird—or the approaching moonlight. It was sliding along the roof, a great pool of it, inch by inch, and now there was no question of their ducking behind the parapet. They stayed there, necks stiff, arms in agony, not daring even to change the expressions on their faces.

Just when moonlight was licking the parapet an inch from Brown's hand, the man shrugged his shoulders, went back into his room, out of sight.

No time to lose. Feverishly, they tied the rope to a hook in the parapet, threw it over into the street below. A vault over the parapet, a painful, skin-tearing slide down the rope, a noisy mishap as one of them dislodged the sign-board of a shop and it crashed like a million tea-trays into the street—and they were free.

They walked away as nonchalantly as possible, lighting cigarettes with a trembling hand. A moment later they struck up a German song.

They reached the Greek's door, knocked on it. Nothing happened. They knocked again, flattened themselves in the shadows.

The door opened an inch and they saw one eye, low down, level with their waists.

"You're the prisoners?" said the child. "You should have been here hours ago." It opened the door.

Inside, there was friendly welcome from Themistoclé and his entire family. Brown handed over the promised fifty pounds and they were led upstairs, where their badly damaged hands were treated with ointment, and a short "service of thanksgiving" was held at a portable altar inside a cupboard. Then they were allowed to sleep.

At dawn they were aroused, shown the emergency hideaway. It was a trapdoor in the *basement*—a refinement few western homes can boast—revealing a forest of pillars, extending all ways as far as the eye could see. There was an immense stone cistern immediately below them.

"What is it?" Robin asked.

It was the ancient underground water system, installed twelve hundred years before by the Emperor Justinian, and now Brown lowered himself carefully into this underworld. All around were skeletons of men and animals: he climbed up again.

That day they managed to write a letter to Eveline, telling of their escape. Towards evening, they noticed that Themistoclé had begun to look furtive; and Robin, deciding suddenly that the man was debating whether to hand the two of them over to the Turks and claim further reward for his activities, urged Brown to come away with him, now.

Brown refused: he would keep his faith with the "White Lady".

Robin Paul made his escape the next morning, dressed as a

rather improbable Arab, carrying a bowl of curds and a cucumber.

For Brown, more romantic methods of escape were being planned. At another rendezvous with Eveline, he was given the uniform of a German governess. Dressed in this fashion, she explained, he must report to a certain Russian Prince who was being repatriated and could take this "lady" with him.

He put on the clothes, reported to Prince Avalov, and was sent away; repatriation orders had not yet come through. But before he went, the Prince would be grateful for a small loan.

A little later he learnt from Eveline that the Prince's orders, once postponed, were suddenly brought forward and he had been sent to Russia that very day—taking with him Brown's immediate hope of escape, and his loan.

But he was not disheartened. He was still, more or less, at freedom and now he changed his extraordinary female disguise for that of a Hungarian mechanic, in spectacles, with shabby bowler hat and dyed red moustache. This might get him near a garage and the chance of a stolen car. He was also able to get hold of a forged Turkish passport.

He had found many kind companions among the little Christian community of Constantinople. They were anxious to further his escape—anything that would bring down this infidel government—and they cheerfully cashed cheques for him, cheques which he wrote on pieces of paper lying about. (These were all subsequently met, in London.) His intention, now that his free "repatriation" had fallen through, was to amass sufficient money to buy a passage to Russia. Everyone, in fact, rallied round with a childish enthusiasm, an enthusiasm which in the end was Brown's undoing, for somebody spoke too loudly. He had almost obtained a motor-launch, was actually discussing terms with the owner, when the police burst in.

No chance now of escape. He was led off to military prison— for now he was not only an escaped prisoner-of-war, he was in possession of a forged passport and had in all probability forged it himself.

Weeks followed in a crowded underground dungeon, a pitch-dark room infested with squealing, ravenous rats. He managed to buy his way into solitary confinement which was more hygienic, and from which he could see daylight through a small window over the courtyard. From here he had the doubtful privilege of seeing one prisoner beaten to death.

One day he was amazed and delighted to hear Robin's voice in the passage. Obviously he had not made good his escape, which was a pity, but now with the two of them reunited they could prepare a better plan, in concert. Although in solitary confinement, he got in touch by scribbling notes in the prison latrine, and they began to plan.

But first Captain Yeats-Brown had to be court-martialled as a forger. Almost any penalty might have been exacted for this crime, but in the nick of time the forger he was suspected of being was captured in another part of Constantinople and he was released from solitary confinement.

The war, had they but known it, was nearly over: this accounted for the growing leniency of the Turks, as they looked with foreboding towards an armistice. Soon Paul and Brown were being allowed so much freedom that it was an easy matter for them simply to walk out of the prison grounds. They got to Eveline, who had kept in touch throughout their adventures, and she confirmed that the war was nearly over. Far from running risk of being re-imprisoned, they could find sanctuary with a British unit.

Scarce believing their luck, they did so. Their first job for their own side was to get hold of a fast car for the use of the British fleet when it entered Constantinople.

A puzzling order, but they set out as good officers to obey it. (In fact, the car was required to take a naval advance party round ammunition dumps reported by Intelligence, and make sure these were not destroyed.)

By now they had so many contacts throughout Constantinople that it was a simple matter to get not only a car, but the type they wanted—and to get it in time for them to go joy-riding before handing it over for its official purpose. The gleaming Mercedes was delivered, the price paid, and they set off in it to do a little shopping.

They had parked it outside a shop. When they returned to the shining juggernaut, a Turkish policeman was standing there.

"This," he said, "is the property of the German General Liman von Sanders."

They got in, started the engine. "That is not your affair."

"It *is* my affair. It is a German car—see, here is the German eagle—and I believe you have stolen it from General von Sanders——"

They drove off with a roar and a cloud of smoke. No further effort was made by the authorities to retrieve it.

The story has a happy ending. They were repatriated, recovered their health, and kept in touch with the "White Lady", who had done so much to help them.

A few months later Robin married her.

Prince Charles Edward was greatly helped in his escape after the abortive
'45 rising, by the gallant Flora Macdonald. She was not at first entirely
keen on the idea, for the penalty, if she were caught, would be extreme.
The Prince, for his part, had doubts—and all this is accurately depicted
in this painting of their first encounter. Winston Churchill (*below*) went
out to cover the South African War as a newspaper correspondent, and
while accompanying an "armoured patrol" was captured. The Boers
rushed him to Pretoria and to prison camp. He was soon to escape. In
this picture, taken right after his capture, he stands with other
prisoners-of-war, angry, defiant, planning the next move.

When Italy's fortunes wer
waning in the Second World Wa
the King relieved Mussolini of hi
office as dictator and put hi
under arrest. After a series c
lightning moves—in order to fo
any possible attempts at rescue—
he was confined in a hotel hig
up in the mountains. It was fro
this hideout that a German tean
of airborne troops released hin
The troop-carrying gliders whic
crash-landed on the mountai
were followed by a light aircraf
into which the astonished Duc
was loaded (*above*) to be flow
via German-held fields, to Hitle
The rescue was carried out by th
young German captain, Skorzen
seen (*left*) in Spain today.

Chapter 16

THE MARCH OF
MAO TSE-TUNG

PROBABLY there has been no mass escape like it—not since the time of the Israelites. And whereas the trip from Egypt to the Promised Land is clothed in pleasing, Old Testament ambiguity and garnished with miracles, the Long March of Mao Tse-tung and his Communists from the south-east of China to the north-west, has been documented as fully—and as repetitively—as any undertaking in history. No miracles here, just 100,000 men (if we consider only Mao and his main column) desperate for physical survival and the survival of an ideal.

That Mao should have got his column to its destination, even though 80,000 of his 100,000 died *en route*, got it there across six thousand miles, is a huge achievement. That Mao should still be the leader, six thousand miles and a year later, is perhaps still greater.

Our story begins in 1919. That was the year of the "Fourth of May Incident". The last dynasty of China, the Manchu dynasty, had fallen, seven years earlier, and Dr Sun Yat-sen formed the

National People's Party, or "Kuomintang". But it was in May, 1919, that the people of China learnt the Versailles Peace Conference had no interest in China; that the extra-territorial rights held by foreigners would be retained—and that encroachment by Japan would be accepted, even recognized.

The country rose in anger. On the fourth of May, thousands of students in Peking marched on the legation quarter to protest. They were not allowed in the legation quarter: it was extra-territorial.

They turned to Russia. If the western powers would not help them in achieving self-respect, the Russians must.

The Russians did: and, naturally, respect, not only for China, but for Russia and Communism, spread. One of those most impressed by Communism was the young school-teacher, Mao Tse-tung.

The stage for present-day China was set in May, 1919.

Sun Yat-sen died and his place was taken by one of the war lords, Chiang Kai-shek, who now styled himself "Generalissimo". And although Chiang had visited Russia and was in favour with the Soviet union, it was soon apparent that he had no intention of toeing the Soviet line. His Kuomintang Party was adamant in favour of retaining the age-old Chinese relationship of big landlord, little peasant. This, of course, was the reverse of Marxist-Leninist thinking: it was the reverse of Mao's thinking, and that of the rapidly growing hard-core of dedicated Communists.

In 1927, Mao, now a Party official, submitted a report on his own province. It was a "Report on an Investigation into the Peasant Movement in Hunan", and it advocated no less than bloody revolution to overthrow the landlords and divide their land among peasants. It was eagerly studied by the Communist movement.

Nothing could have been more calculated to estrange them from Chiang's Kuomintang: Chiang set out frankly and ruthlessly to destroy Communism in China. By the middle of 1927 the Movement had gone underground and, when really big attacks began to be launched against its sympathizers, the whole Communist community retired to the mountain ranges between Hunan and Kiangsi. From here, ambushing pursuers, they were able to maintain an existence and at the same time capture large quantities of arms, and even recruits from those sent to destroy them. With these arms and recruits, Mao set up his "First Red Army".

Chiang's determination mounted. In his eyes, Communism was now a more serious menace to the well-being of China than the Japanese threat from east and north. He launched a series of major campaigns against the First Red Army. Each attack involved more troops than its predecessor: each was flung back in disorder, with the loss of huge quantities of arms.

On the fifth campaign, Chiang staked his all. He brought in military experts from Germany, assembled a million men, hurled them at the Reds.

A million men went into the mountains of Kiangsi. The rest of China waited.

The wait was long and it seemed as if Chiang had again been repulsed, for there was no sign of Communist collapse. Then the outcome became clear. Mao's forces had not been defeated—they would never be defeated—but against such overwhelming superiority in numbers and equipment they had been forced to break into small groups.

Chiang was triumphant: small groups could be wiped out, one by one: Communism as a military force was finished.

Nothing was further from the truth, and Mao knew it. But for his force to become effective, it would have to coalesce, and this it was unable to do, surrounded by Chiang's armies. It would have to escape, get to a distant part of the country where, even if the Kuomintang followed, it could not be surrounded.

The only place was the extreme north-west. Here, in the provinces of Kansu and Shensi, with backs literally against the Great Wall of China, built to prevent barbarian invasion from the north, they could resist any attack. They would be able to regroup, speed up the recruiting which even in the blackest hour had never slowed, contain Chiang. After all this, they would drive the Japanese out of the country.

To Mao Tse-tung, though not to Chiang Kai-shek, this, and not civil war, was the main objective.

And so the Great March began.

There could be no question of trekking north-west to the Great

Wall, for that would mean fighting a way through the whole of the Kuomintang armies. They would head west, get to the Burma border, wheel sharply north.

It would be six thousand miles. On foot.

Would it not be wiser to go underground and hope to build a force at a more propitious time? Many leaders would have taken this decision.

It is an indication of Chinese political and military thinking that this second way never occurred to Mao. He was quite prepared to lose eighty per cent of his force: he knew they could be replaced.

There were in fact a number of Communist groups involved, but Mao's "First Army" was the largest: to all intents and purposes its journey can be regarded as the definitive "Long March".

There was careful preparation. The Communists in Hunan and Kiangsi had been split into little groups, the whole area ringed by a *cordon sanitaire* of Kuomintang. These groups, not all of them soldiers, for whole communities, men, women and children, would be travelling, had to be secretly alerted; mules, ponies, carts, guns, ammunition, had to be secretly assembled, including as much equipment as could be taken away from factories. The new land, the promised land in the north-west, must grow into a thriving, twentieth-century nation.

While all this fantastic preparation was being made, secrecy was maintained.

At the end of October, 1934, the Long March began.

The Communists broke their way out of encirclement and headed west. They were followed by thousand upon thousand of peasant households, factory workers carrying equipment, the families of soldiers and Party officials, heading bravely into the unknown.

From the moment they broke through the Kuomintang cordon they were ceaselessly attacked by Chiang's forces and by warlords who either sympathized with him or had their own reasons for trying to destroy the seemingly endless column. It has been calculated by George Paloczi-Horwarth, in his penetrating study of Mao, that: "The distance they travelled was similar to that from Mexico to Alaska, with the difference that the natural barriers on their way were more formidable. They crossed eighteen mountain ranges, twenty-four rivers, several deserts, swamplands and six territories inhabited by wild and hostile aborigines. They fought more than two hundred battles and hardly a day passed without a skirmish or two. The troops covered about six thousand miles on foot. They passed through twelve provinces, inhabited by two hundred million people. They occupied more than sixty cities and several hundred towns. While parts of the Red Army pursued the local troops, in the cities and towns political instructors taught the people how to form Soviets and start to govern their own districts. The travelling theatres of the Red Army gave performances. Posters proclaimed the liberation of the slaves, the abolition of taxes, the 'expropriation' of the landlords, the destruction of land-deeds, the distribution of the lands of the absentee landlords. Before they left a district, guerilla zones and peasant partisan units were organized. Some of the rifles confiscated from the war-lord arsenals were distributed among the peasantry."

An astonishing picture, this endless travelling circus, fighting its way mile by mile, yet insisting on a show at every stop.

At first, few of those taking part, even among the leaders, realized how far Mao was taking them. Most believed they were getting out from Kuomintang encirclement and going a little way to the north, where they would join up with other Communist groups. Had they known what was in store, it is possible that many would have refused.

But the advance continued. Each time starvation seemed certain to wipe out the entire force, they came to a city which they captured or persuaded to feed them: then, for a few days, the whole force rested and gorged. By January, 1935, they had captured the large city of Tsunyi, in northern Kweichow. Here, apart from rest and food, they got four thousand recruits.

Here, too, one of Mao's greatest political battles was fought. Unlike the soldiers of his column, who had only to concentrate on defeating an obvious enemy, Mao and his Party colleagues had to watch each other day and night, lest one stab another in the back. Everything in Communist history has to have a label, from the "Fourth of May" to the "Autumn Crop Uprising. The "Tsunyi Conference" is one of these. It was in this city, while his troops spent twelve days resting, that Mao overcame his opponents, overrode Party leadership and forced it to acknowledge him Party leader as well as military leader. He gained the support of men like Chou En-lai and Liu Shao-chi.

After Tsunyi the First Army fought and won a battle against twice its number of Chiang's forces and war-lord allies. One of the most amazing things about the Long March is that while the soldiers were beating off an almost endless series of attacks, industry began to hum. At every halt, temporary factories were set up: uniforms, footwear, even weapons, were made in them.

Money in huge quantities was confiscated from banks on the way. If we ignore this little irregularity, we can state that the finances of the travelling nation were sound, and expertly conducted. Everything provided by peasants and merchants *en route* was paid for.

They came next to the land of the fierce aboriginal Lolos, had to pass through it in order to reach the next objective, Szechuan. Before Mao, no Chinese had ever succeeded in taming these wild men—but Communist ideology, pointing out that Communists were just as much enemies of earlier Chinese governments as were the Lolos themselves, won them not only safe conduct but Lolo recruits.

Guided by Lolo scouts, they reached the most formidable barrier of the entire journey, the Tatu River. The river was crossed by the skeleton of an old, swaying bridge, missing the all-important footboards beneath. It could be crossed by swinging, monkey-fashion, underneath it and this a number of volunteers set out to do, while being subjected to merciless fire from Kuomintang positions on the far side. Most of the volunteers were killed, plummeting into the foaming waters, but a handful got across and were able to destroy the Kuomintang positions. The bridge was repaired and the force got over it in a procession which took several days.

The Tatu River was followed by a climb to 16,000 feet over Great Snowy Mountain, a climb in thin cotton uniforms, which killed off many from cold and the unaccustomed lack of oxygen —for most on the March were plains-dwellers and all of them southerners. By the time the climb was over, Mao's force of 100,000, which had been joined by 25,000 recruits, was down to

45,000: high casualties indeed. At this point it was joined by the "Fourth Front Army" under Chang Kuo-t'ao, a deadly rival of Mao, and the nightly political wrangles and intrigues grew more bitter. Eventually Mao overcame this opposition, too, and although Communist history now tells us everyone joined up immediately with "right-thinking Mao", facts suggest he led only a small minority. It was only after more months of intrigue that he achieved the leadership.

If you glance at an atlas you will see one of the largest areas of "swampland" in the world, marked at longitude 95 East: the last lap of this fantastic journey was made across it. Many men and animals were lost, sucked from sight into the mud and sand. The survivors picked a way across this for weeks in continuous driving rain.

But it was this very barrier which made the escape possible. Mao's army was down to only 20,000, and in no shape to do much fighting: the Kuomintang, faced with the swamp, gave up the chase.

Twelve months from the date of starting—on 29 October, 1935—Mao's force reached its destination. The community set itself up in the north of Shensi province, hard up against the Great Wall of China.

Had it been worth it? Was it worth losing so many thousands of men, women and children, in order to set up a Soviet state in the north of China?

For Mao Tse-tung, yes.

History has still to tell us whether, in the final analysis, it was good for the Chinese people.

167

Chapter 17

THE SMALL WOMAN LEADS
THE CHILDREN TO SAFETY

THERE are three women in this book of twenty-odd escapes—
a fair percentage, perhaps, reflecting the comparative needs
and opportunities of men and of women to escape from fate.
There is little similarity between them: Princess Clementina
escaped from her prison in search of love; Mary Stuart left hers
in an ill-starred bid to gain a kingdom.

But our third feminine escape is different. For whereas the
historical ladies had only themselves to look after, and were much
helped by others, little Gladys Aylward led a mass escape of no
less than a hundred children.

It is a strange and heartening tale, this one of the girl from
North London who insisted on going out to China as a
missionary. Leaving it at that—a girl who saved up her tiny
wages as domestic servant, week after week, to pay for a passage
to Tientsin and finally made it—the story captures the
imagination.

But Gladys Aylward's finest hour was yet to come—the day

when she set off with her band of Chinese orphans to cross the hills and escape from the invading Japanese.

To start at the beginning: she was born in Edmonton, in North London, and as a young girl went into domestic service. The fact is almost totally irrelevant, but it has always caught journalistic fancy that a "parlour-maid" should find herself in such a situation. But in those distant 'tween-war years there were thousands of girls who went cheerfully into domestic service, and Gladys Aylward was not the only one who felt an urge to change from serving a few people in a tiny world to serving the world itself.

But now, with the English domestic virtually a thing of the past, a horse's toe or a human tail, the fact has a certain piquancy.

She was twenty-six, a tiny brown-eyed thing with dark hair in a no-nonsense bun at the back of her head, when she heard the call. Perhaps it was in church, or at a Missionary lecture, or looking up at a man on a soap-box in Hyde Park, when the seed was sown. Wherever it was, the seed took root and flowered. Gladys Aylward, domestic in a comfortable, kindly, house in Belgrave Square, decided to become a missionary.

And in China.

She went along to the China Inland Mission.

It was good of her to come, very good indeed. What exactly was it, though, that made her think of China?

She wasn't certain herself—but China it would have to be.

Puzzled, they agreed to accept her as probationer, teach her the job she would have to do—if she were passed satisfactory when the time came up. Gratefully, Gladys Aylward gave up her position in Belgrave Square.

But things went less well than she had hoped. Three months training and her theology was, to say the least, "very poor indeed". In the view of the Principal, it would be a long, long time before Gladys Alyward was fit to go to China and spread the word of God. By that time she would be older, and if her abilities as theologian were any guide, she would find it impossible to pick up the Chinese language.

She swallowed the rebuff. Still determined to be a missionary, she became a "Rescue Sister" in Wales, trying with diminutive size and irrepressible determination to "rescue" young girls from the Swansea docks; catching them outside pubs, befriending them when their money was gone, getting them somehow back to Mum and Dad. Occasionally she got them into church.

But though she did this with all her might, a part of her was elsewhere. She had to get to China.

Getting to China took money: she went back into domestic service to earn it. A month later she startled a travel agency in London by going in, sliding three pound notes across the counter. She would like a ticket to China, please, and here was the first payment: if they would book it now, she would bring in a little more every week. She had heard the railway to China was cheaper than the boat.

The clerk agreed, but a puzzled look crept into his eye. It cost less—of course it did, only half as much—but not only would it take many weeks at this rate of saving to pay for the ticket: it would be little use when she got it. There was a full-scale war going on at the other end, between Russia and China.

To Gladys Aylward, if not to the man behind the counter, these two facts cancelled each other out: by the time forty-seven pounds and ten shillings had been saved, the silly war would be over. It stood to reason.

Shaking his head in wonder, the booking clerk made out, very slowly, a receipt for three pounds.

This, to Gladys, was a tremendous step; she was on her way. It only remained to fix up a job, some sort of missionary work, at the other end. And from what she'd heard, they were crying out for that sort of thing, she wouldn't have much trouble.

She was right. Long before the money was saved she had a post. Mission friends put her in touch with old Mrs Jeannie Lawson in Tientsin and the reply came that if Gladys could get herself to that city, someone would meet her. She would be taken up-country, join Mrs. Lawson in her work, and if all went well prepare to take over that work at some future date. Mrs. Lawson had no intention of leaving China, but she was not as strong as she had been. One of these days—she made no bones about it—she would drop in harness; that was the way she intended to go. But there must be someone to take over.

Eventually Gladys had saved the magic total and she accepted with trembling hands a fistful of railway vouchers. They entitled her to travel the whole way across Europe and Asia to Tientsin; and she duly presented herself at Liverpool Street Station. It was September, 1930.

We have no space for the manifold horrors of that journey. Having been re-routed to Vladivostok to avoid fighting near Dairen she at last found herself on a Japanese ship. The friendly captain understood her problem; he would arrange for her to get to Japan, then travel south to another port and sail back to the mainland, to Tientsin.

A fortnight later, having been shown every kindness and courtesy by the Japanese, she was steaming into Tientsin harbour.

She was made welcome by missionaries (really, Asia seemed more civilized than many parts of Europe she had been through, like Russia for instance) and a little later she was on a train to Peking.

After Peking, much of the journey was by mule, but this did nothing to damp her enthusiasm. She rode proudly into the walled town of Yangcheng.

The first weeks with Jeannie Lawson were a trial. The old lady was a hot-tempered, irritable seventy-three, and the local Chinese, far from wanting the two women's help, regarded them with loathing and fear as "Foreign Devils". Although Gladys immediately adopted the Chinese dress of smock and trousers which she was to wear for the next twenty years, she was, for many weeks, spat at and insulted when she went out.

Prospects for spreading the word of God were poor: even tough old Jeannie admitted it. But every so often one made a convert and that was worth all the mud and spittle and frustration. And Gladys, despite the grim prognosis of the China Inland Mission, was learning the language, beginning to get into the minds and hearts of the people of Yangcheng.

Shortly after she arrived, the two of them had an idea. They would open an Inn. In fact the house in which they lived with old Yang, the convert-cook, had originally been one. By persuading a few of the muleteers who passed each day to come in for a meal, they might be able to chat with them in their Shansi dialect, tell them a little about God.

At first there was markedly little enthusiasm about visiting

171

the Inn—but by standing in the street, much like girls outside a house of easy virtue, the two ladies were able to lure in a few wanderers. And—just as they had hoped—the men liked the good food, the clean surroundings, even the stories from the bible. The clientele enlarged.

But Jeannie Lawson died, in harness as she had always sworn she would, and it was lonely work after she had gone. The local mandarin asked Gladys to pay him a visit.

Did she know the Government had now decreed it illegal to bind the feet of girls?

She did. She thoroughly approved. It had been a cruel, crippling custom.

It was good she approved the Government's edict. And now he wished her to undertake some work for him, in that connexion.

She would do her best.

He would like her to be his Foot Inspector.

Somewhat discomfited, she agreed to undertake this strange work. It would give her a chance to meet people in far-flung districts and try to convert them, at the same time making sure their feet were unbound. She left the work of the Inn to Yang and set out.

On one of her first journeys she came upon a woman with a naked child, so dirty one could not even discern its sex. The woman offered to sell her the child for two dollars, and Gladys, profoundly shocked, rushed to the Mandarin and reported the fact.

There was nothing to be done. Go back to your work, ignore such things.

She went back, bargained with the woman and bought the little girl for nine pennies—the first of five children Gladys adopted, and forever "Ninepence".

In 1936 she took out Chinese citizenship. It made little difference to her life, she was trusted by the people and allowed to go about her work, but it gave her a feeling of belonging. She went on cheerfully with her work and became known, from her success in quelling a prison riot, as *Ai-weh-deh*, The Virtuous One. She paid no attention to rumours that the Japanese, those pleasant people who had befriended her, brought her to this land,

172

were invading from the north, had entered her own state of Shansi.

But in the spring of 1938 the little snub-nosed bombers swooped in over the hills. While everybody ran out to admire them, they made a terrible attack on Yangcheng. Casualties were very heavy, and Gladys organized rescue operations among the terrified people, set up a dressing-station, a refugee camp, brought some sort of order and calm out of chaos and terror.

The Japs came a little later, khaki-clad men on foot, and the citizens, or most of them, dispersed to outlying districts. The enemy left after a few days and the townspeople came back.

To their horror, and Gladys's, for she had gone and come back with them, every soul foolish enough to stay behind in Yangcheng had been butchered, most by the bayonet. Women and children lay in heaps against the city wall: dogs were feeding on human flesh.

Now she had to take charge of a huge burial operation, gathering bodies and laying them in a communal grave outside the West Gate. She was puzzled and distressed: how could the Japanese, the people she had known and liked, behave this way?

The tide of Nippon ebbed and flowed. Jap soldiers came back to Yangcheng and this time she stayed, was able to control them by her presence. There was only one disgraceful occasion when a body of them burst down the door of a women's quarters and swarmed in, bent on rape. In an attempt to save the women— an attempt in which she was successful, and the men slunk away —she was struck by a soldier's rifle butt and suffered injuries from which she never completely recovered.

The Japs left again—and a little later an orderly brought a message from the Chinese commander. Chinese forces would be evacuating the whole area in a day or two, the Japs would move in, probably in large numbers, and it would be foolish for anyone to stay.

Gladys Aylward refused to move. She felt she had the measure of the Japanese, could deal with them in her own way. She had a large band of orphan children, in addition to her own five: she would stay here and look after them.

"But, Ai-weh-deh, there is more than that——"

"Oh? What is it?"

173

"Yes, Ai-weh-deh. Much more."

He unrolled a poster from inside his shirt and she took it.

On it was a list of names for whom reward was offered by the Japanese Army. Her eye ran down the sheet.

There it was. "For the Small Woman, known as Ai-weh-deh, a reward of One Hundred Dollars."

She felt the blood drain from her face. So this was it—the end. She would have to go. She had no illusions about her safety: a sum like a hundred dollars was enough to subvert quite a few people she trusted. A hundred dollars was a fortune.

Yes, she would go. It was brought home to her in sickening panic by the sudden appearance of a Japanese patrol. With the words of the notice ringing in her head, she broke into a run and they, not knowing at that range who she was, opened fire for the fun of it. Bullets screamed past her. With a white-hot, searing, pain across the shoulders, she felt one hit her.

This, then, was dying. It might have been worse. Then she saw she had only been grazed, the Jap soldiers were only using her body for target practice. Gasping with horror, she managed to wriggle out of her padded coat and crawl like a caterpillar into a ditch. The bullets thudded into the empty coat for a few more seconds, then the soldiers went away.

And it was as she lay in the ditch that she realized she could never go away and leave the children. The Japanese would simply use them—Ai-weh-deh's children—as hostages. They would have no compunction about butchering all of them, if she did not surrender.

But where did one go—with a hundred children?

There was only one place. Madame Chiang Kai-shek had started a children's fund in Chungking, and the nearest place where children could be cared for by it was Sian. It was hundreds of miles away, across the Yellow River.

They set off, a few days later, hardly knowing which way they should travel, but with the children, at least, regarding it as the greatest possible excitement. There were twenty girls between thirteen and fifteen, half a dozen boys between eleven and thirteen, and seventy-odd others between four and eight. She paid a last visit to the Mandarin of Yangcheng, who bade her a sad farewell and gave her two coolies carrying baskets of millet on shoulder poles. The party assembled at Gladys's Inn, now ruined by bombing, and set off boldly through the West Gate.

They walked all day and stayed the night in a Buddhist temple where the priests made them welcome and the children were overjoyed at being so close to forbidden idols and beautiful ornaments. The next night was bitter, in the open, with an icy wind. Already some of the smaller children were exhausted— and the trip had scarcely begun. By following the road, they might have been able to reach the Yellow River in five days, but with Japanese planes about and the possibility of meeting Japanese patrols this was out of the question. They would have to cut straight through the mountains. This, even if all went well, must take about a fortnight.

Soon they had run out of food and were weakening fast. Gladys and the older children were carrying as many of the little ones as they could, resting a bit, struggling on, falling down.

They had got on the move again after one of these halts when a child at the front held up a hand. The message went back along the column and everyone scattered into the wood on either side of the path: "Soldiers!"

They hid in the wood and then, to their delighted relief, saw the soldiers were Chinese. The children came out and generous soldiers emptied their own pockets and haversacks of food.

An hour later, both sides were on their separate ways. The children were soon out of food again, but she managed to keep up their strength and determination till the twelfth day when, as Gladys had predicted, they saw the mile-wide barrier of the Yellow River. Now in the deserted village of Yuan Ku—deserted save for one man who did not care that the Japanese were coming; he was an old, old man, what did it matter?—they managed to scrape together sufficient food for a meal. For the first time in twelve days they were able to wash, and the little ones, recovering their strength and spirits as only children can, splashed delightedly in the water.

But, search as she would, Gladys could find no sign of a boat. With sad heart and worried mind she got the children to sleep, then lay awake all night, pondering the next move. The Japs were not far behind, all evidence pointed to the fact that they were hardly a day behind. They were marching far faster than one middle-aged woman and a hundred children could hope to go.

It was dawn when a body of Nationalist troops came up the river bank. They heard the sound of children singing, could hardly believe their eyes when they confronted a hundred of them.

"Where are you going?" the officer asked Gladys.

"I am taking my children to Sian."

"*Sian!*"

"Yes, Sian. That is the only place they will be safe from the Japanese. For you see, the Japanese want *me*—and they are pursuing me out of Shansi, right into Honan. If we can cross the river and get to Honan. If not, they will capture us here."

The officer whistled, barked an order, and boats were brought out from among the reeds. A few minutes later the "Small Woman" and her charges were heading across the muddy Yellow River to the province of Honan. From here, from the town of Mien Chi, they would be able to head by rail for Sian—if the railway were still running.

But immediately on disembarkation they were arrested by a policeman. They had no right to cross the Yellow River: did they not know that the river was closed to all traffic, because of the war?

A comic-opera situation—but to exhausted Gladys and her weary, puzzled children, no laughing matter at all. She managed to demand they be tried officially, by the local Mandarin, and this was arranged.

The next day the Mandarin of Mien Chi, after a suitable display of gravity, agreed with her that she had had no alternative but to cross the river. There was no case to answer. But could she, perhaps, keep those children outside the window a bit quieter, so the court's proceedings became audible?

He arranged for them all to board the train—and this, for the children, was the most exciting adventure of all, for few of them had ever seen one. Gladys admitted they had no money and would be unable to buy tickets, but he only laughed: with the enemy so close, no one bothered about money.

There were four happy, soot-filled, days on the back of the train, as far as Tiensan. There, the bridge had been blown up and they would have to get off and march over more hills, to Tung Kwan.

It was now, as they clambered off the train and contemplated another cruel march, that their spirit nearly gave out on them. The children began to cry—first one, then two, then a hundred—and she sat down on a rock and nearly wept with them.

Then she took hold of herself. "Come on," she shouted, "let's sing." And they sang. One by one they got up, still singing, and followed her up the dusty road toward the mountains.

No one knew or cared the date, but it was April, 1940. Europe had been at war for half a year, and soon a British army would be embarking, at Dunkirk, on an escape not unlike their own across the Yellow River. But there was no time to think of what might be happening elsewhere: grim, slogging determination, and a faith in God's help, were needed, if they were to get to Tung Kwan, over these cruel mountains.

Miraculously, they did, and at dead of night got on another train, within shot of the Japanese, and reached Hwa Chow. They spent a few days here, gathering strength, then found another train to Sian. It took days—and Gladys Aylward, by this time desperately ill, had no idea how many elapsed. It was a hot and stinking April and she just managed to get her children settled in a refugee camp before she collapsed.

The small foreign woman—some said she was dying, others that she was dead—was taken on an ox-cart by some peasants to the Scandinavian-American Mission at Hsing P'ing. Here, though utterly baffled as to who and what she was, the doctors brought her back from the jaws of death.

She lived in China for another ten years. Then, with Communists over-running the country, her orphans dispersed and her own five children married and away, she returned to a strange and unfamiliar England. Immediately, she went back to her work of "saving souls"—at home.

She left behind children, growing into adult-hood, and much else besides.

But in Shansi and Honan, Ai-weh-deh is remembered as that quite indomitable person—the Small Woman who led a hundred frightened children to safety.

Chapter 18

THE LONG WALK
OF SLAVOMIR RAWICZ

THIS has been called, with justification, the most amazing journey ever recorded. A young Polish officer, captured by the Soviet Secret Police and taken to a Siberian labour camp near the Arctic Circle, makes his escape and walks, inside a year, four thousand miles to freedom in India—the India that another of our escapers in this book is making such strenuous efforts to leave.

The story is excitingly told in the man's book of his adventure and it has been called "The best adventure story I have read for years", "A new classic of escape" and "An unbelievable epic". Most of us would agree, and for that reason I include it here.

But one must add the slightly numbing rider: his story has been doubted by those who know the terrain over which Rawicz claimed to travel. There was no doubt that the man and his party had been through hell, that they were living skeletons—and only just alive at that—on being admitted to hospital in Calcutta.

Without doubt Rawicz hid his food under the hospital pillow. But having neither met Rawicz nor travelled his route I can offer no personal comment.

And whatever happened to "Smith"? The U.S. Consulate in Calcutta seemed to have no record of such a man.

Yet because the story has at least a very real basis in fact, and has been accepted as truth by millions of people for a dozen and more years, I cannot leave it out.

I want to believe it *is* true.

It was during the Second World War. When, men taken by the Russians in their little campaigns of "liberation" against the Finns and the Poles and the rest of them, were tortured if there seemed a chance of getting information. Sometimes, Communist-style, they were "tried" and "punished".

One of these unfortunates was a lieutenant of Polish cavalry, Slavomir Rawicz. He was twenty-four when he was captured in November, 1939, and the Russians chose to believe him a spy on the grounds that his mother was Russian and that her home was near the Polish border with Russia. In an attempt to make him sign a confession to this effect, he was brutally tortured, outrageously "tried", and sent for twenty-five years to a Siberian labour camp.

The torture and trial lasted twelve months and it was late 1940 when Rawicz found himself on board a train of sealed cattle-trucks heading east. He and the thousands of prisoners with him wore light canvas prison clothes: the temperature was arctic.

At railhead, the Siberian town of Irkutsk, the survivors were issued with more suitable clothing, chained to lorries and force-marched behind them.

Rawicz tells us the prisoners staggered along behind lorries for forty days, being given no shelter at night, while the snow grew ever deeper. When the lorries could go no further, Ostyak tribesmen were employed to take the camp supplies on by reindeer-sledge, the prisoners still marching behind.

They reached their destination—"Camp 303" in Siberia, north-east of Irkutsk and 350 miles south of the Arctic Circle. They were immediately put to work building their own huts.

Once with a roof over their heads, the five thousand prisoners found life not entirely unpleasant. Rawicz volunteered to work with sixty others in the big workshop which made skis for the Russian Army. The place was reasonably heated and the work was interesting.

And, warmed at last, the urge to escape began to grow.

To succeed, he would have to find out everything about the camp, the people who ran it, the possible exits, a route of escape. He volunteered again, this time to repair the Commandant's radio. He knew little about radio, but luck was with him and he was able, secretly, to diagnose a loose battery lead. Like a fashionable, expensive physician, he refused to divulge the fact until the third visit, and when at last it burst into life with a concert from Moscow he won the admiration of both Commandant and wife.

The set worked well after this third visit, but a little later he was asked to return: it seemed to be less powerful.

This was true; the batteries were running down. He explained this and suggested the Commandant order a spare set. The man agreed, then left to attend a meeting and Rawicz found himself alone with the lady.

She was a woman of about forty, handsome, tall, with her hair wound, halo-style, Russian-fashion, about her head. She was, in addition, a kind person, who seemed to have every sympathy with the prisoners in her husband's camp. She made him a cup of tea.

Rawicz was only half listening as she spoke, when it suddenly dawned on him: she was urging an escape. He sat up with a jerk.

They talked for a long time, and she spoke of the things she thought "a man" would need. Friends, for a start: no one could do it alone. He would also need food, and to this end he would have to dry and store a part of his daily bread ration. He would have to "acquire" some of the animal skins, deer, fox and sable, which officers shot and which hung on wires in the open, waiting to be made into clothes. Perhaps a man intending to escape —she never gave him a name—might steal them—one a day, as he passed by.

In which direction, Rawicz asked, would this hypothetical escaper travel?

She thought. East, to Kamchatka—no. West, back into Russia —obviously not. South, to India or Afghanistan, that would be the only route.

That night he assembled his team of escapers. He had been studying his fellow prisoners for weeks, and he knew those he wanted. They were the thirty-seven-year-old Pole, Makowski, precise, clear-thinking; the twenty-seven-year-old Latvian, Kolemenos, blond six-footer and immensely strong; another Pole, Sergeant Paluchowicz, aged forty-one; Zaro, the cheerful, mischievous, thirty-year-old Yugoslav; Marchinkovas, the thoughtful, twenty-eight-year-old architect from Lithuania; and an American, "Mister Smith", aged fifty, wise and fit-looking, who had been engaged on the construction of the Moscow Underground until his arrest in 1936.

Having developed a respect for Commandant Ushakov, as well as his wife, Rawicz planned not to escape until the Colonel went to attend his Senior Officers' Course in Yakutsk. In the meantime he and his associates spent their spare time together in the barrack hut, making moccasins out of stolen skins (big Kolemenos took one every time he was sent to collect birch logs for the ski-shop), and making warm sable waistcoats and gaiters. Rawicz made a long knife in the ski-shop from a broken saw; the Commandant's wife, when next he saw her, silently presented him with an axe-head.

On the evening of their escape, they arranged to keep awake until midnight by attending the Wednesday evening political indoctrination class, which was voluntary. At the end of it they wished the instructor a cordial goodnight and made a way back to their hut.

Most of the other inhabitants were snoring when they got there, and they lay in the darkness listening to the noise and to their own pounding hearts.

Then Rawicz felt a tap on his shoulder. It was Smith, speaking in his perfect Russian. "Now."

It was just after midnight—and a day or two before Easter of 1941—when the seven set out. There was a heavy snowstorm at the time, which helped cover their tracks, but they had brought a sheepskin which they dragged behind to achieve the same effect. It was a fairly simple matter to get through the wire—simple in comparison with what lay ahead—but it took twenty nerve-rasping minutes. Then they began a slow routine of jogging, walking, jogging again, for half a day. With the arctic sun crawling up, they scraped out a snow shelter at the foot of a large tree. Rawicz remembered the cheerful remark of the Ostyak reindeer-driver on the way to Camp 303. "Don't worry about the snow—wrap it round you like a featherbed." They did.

They made a start on the rations. It was too near camp to risk a fire, but they ate bread, and it was here that they made a discovery about Paluchowicz. His false teeth had been stolen by the NKVD: he was unable to eat anything hard. By moistening his bread in melted snow, he was able to get it down.

Hardly the most suitable of companions—but it was too late now.

They lay till the pale daylight of that first day had vanished, then started their jog-walk-jog routine again. Keeping direction south would have been a problem, for the sun was often invisible, but they guided themselves by noting the moss on the north side of each tree.

Ten days after leaving camp they were a cheery crowd, laughing and joking and now daring to travel by day. They reached the River Lena, and here Smith, as the eldest and by common consent the leader, counselled a wait until dawn, when they would trot over the half-mile of frozen water. In the meantime, they would light a first fire and make gruel.

At dawn they crossed, but in the middle of the river Rawicz showed his six companions a Polish trick for getting fish. Laboriously, he broke the immensely thick ice, and suddenly four herring-sized fish shot out on a gusher of icy water, flung up by the sudden release of pressure. They collected them, drank a little of the water, moved on.

They were reaching higher ground now, with the next objective, Lake Baikal at an altitude of 1,500 feet, many hundreds of miles to the south. There were fewer trees and the snow was thinner on the ground. They caught and killed a hare, and a little later a stag with antlers tangled in a tree-root. They were well and in good heart.

Spring put in an appearance: it was May. Then, after having smelt it for two days—a strange, damp smell like mildew—they

182

found themselves looking down from their mountain-pass on the three-hundred-mile length of Lake Baikal. Along the rim were fishing villages, a main road with telegraph-poles, a distant factory.

They feasted eyes on this glimpse of civilization and decided they were approaching the north-east corner of the lake. They would have to travel due west to escape detection and continue their southward journey parallel to the shore, but miles from it.

Suddenly Zaro held up a hand and they froze.

They looked to where he was pointing and saw a movement. It might have been an animal: it might have been a human. They saw it again for a fraction of a second, decided it was a man. He had seen them, was trying to get out of their way.

But if he had seen them, they would have to kill him. Grimly, they stalked him.

And it was when they got to the bushes the figure had entered that they saw, to their utter astonishment, a young girl. She was cowering and weeping, dressed in tattered clothes, part man's, part woman's, with a small gold crucifix gleaming at her neck.

Satisfied that they meant her no harm, she poured out her long story through the tears. She was Polish and her parents had been butchered by the Russians on their farm in the Polish Ukraine. That had been two years before, in 1939. She had been deported to a collective farm in Siberia, a *kolhoz,* and she had been working here ever since.

Until two days ago. Then the foreman of the *kolhoz* sent for her, tried to rape her. She fled.

Now, two days later, having been given lifts by kindly truck drivers, she was nearing Irkutsk. There she would be safe. She looked imploringly at them: she *would* be safe, in Irkutsk, wouldn't she?

"Mister Smith" fixed her with a piercing, not-unfriendly, stare. "We are not going near Irkutsk."

But now she insisted on coming with them, wherever they went, and the older, more cautious Smith gave in to the urging of the rest.

They were eight.

For a bit, the journey was pleasanter. Seventeen-year-old Kristina treated them all like jolly older brothers except for the grey-haired Smith who was a respected father. With her torn-up petticoat she bandaged the sores on their feet, though her own feet, as they soon discovered, were in worse state. They made her a pair of little moccasins: she was childishly delighted with them.

In late May they crossed the River Bargusin. By now they were short of food: there had been fewer wild animals, and those they saw they were unable to catch. Then, miraculously, they came to a village and, not daring to reveal themselves, stole a pig at night, took it to a cave and cooked it.

They crossed the Trans-Siberian Railway, flattening themselves to the ground as a passenger train roared by. A little later they had left Siberia, were into Mongolia, and carrying as their last gift from the Soviet Union a sack of potatoes harvested from a convenient field.

They had covered twelve hundred miles in sixty days.

On they went, still cheerful, managing to find just enough food to live on, water to drink, passing to the west of Mongolia's capital, Ulan Bator. They helped a river-boatman whose sampan was in difficulties and he gratefully threw melons at them, which they dug out of the mud and carried off.

Then—the Gobi Desert. Four days they found no water, no food. At death's door they came to an oasis, with water in plenty, and drank and washed themselves. They moved on, prepared to risk thirst again in the hope of finding something to eat.

And now the first, perhaps the greatest, tragedy. Kristina had been weakening daily, she stumbled often, had to be carried part of the way by big Kolemenos, though she implored him to leave her and go on. She died and they left a small wooden cross over the grave.

Two days farther, Makowski collapsed, dragged himself to his feet and went on. A little later he, too, was dead.

They were growing desperate now; they had carried a little water in their only container, but they were literally starving. They overcame their reluctance to sample the only living thing in the desert, the great black snakes that slithered across their path and vanished into holes in the baking sand. They made a forked stick and Rawicz trapped one by the neck while the rest of them frenziedly beat it to death, cut off its head and skinned it.

The meat was pleasant and this, Rawicz writes, saved their lives. A day later, the sand gave way to scrub, low hills, a stream. Six of them had survived the Gobi Desert.

Nothing they hit after this seems to have equalled the torture of those weeks across the waterless wilderness, but from here on their health had suffered so badly that everything they encountered took its toll. They struggled on through the Chinese province of Kansu, into Tibet.

Here they found a Circassian who was delighted to converse with them in Russian and pointed out that they would soon reach a fork in the road. One way would lead to India over the ice of the Himalayas; the other, easier, road led to Lhasa, capital of Tibet. He urged them to choose the latter. They ignored the advice.

The path grew even steeper, the air more rarefied. Their strength grew less. They woke, lungs aching after a bitterly cold night's rest in the open, to find that young Marchinkovas, the Lithuanian, had died in his sleep. There was no earth in which to bury him; they laid the body in a rock-cleft, covered it with stones.

Kolemenos carved a third cross.

The five pressed on across Tibet and in January of 1942 crossed the frozen Tsangpo River which flows into India as the Brahmaputra.

In March, with India only just over the next mountain, they lost Paluchowicz. There was a strangled cry and he disappeared from view. They stumbled to the spot and found themselves looking through a crack in the rocks into swirling mist below, a drop of untold thousands of feet. It was as if the earth had suddenly opened and Paluchowicz had fallen to the very centre.

Kolemenos made his fourth cross, stuck it in the ice.

They never knew when they crossed the frontier into India. It was spring again, though the weather, high up in the Himalayas, was as icy as Siberia. In their last weeks they had hardly slept, knowing that if they did, in that rarefied atmosphere, they might never wake. They had seen, in the distance, a pair of creatures eight-foot high, walking on their hind legs. Rawicz at the time had never heard of "Abominable Snowmen" but he later came to the conclusion that he had seen a pair of them, just as his party crossed the frontier.

185

The surviving four, Rawicz, Kolemenos, Zaro and "Mister Smith"—who never revealed his first name and might well have disguised the second—got to India and were picked up by a patrol of Indian soldiers. Smith was an old, old man, gaunt and pale with a white beard down to his waist; the rest were little better.

After listening to their fantastic story of a four-thousand-mile march from Siberia, the young British lieutenant took them gingerly to a delousing station. They stood naked to watch their tattered clothes, their shorn hair, burn quickly in a fire of cloth and petrol.

The Medical Officer examined them and prophesied gloomily that although they now felt hilariously, unbelievably well, they would soon be very ill.

He was right: they were very ill indeed. Rawicz was in delirium for a whole month in a Calcutta hospital, grabbing his rations and stuffing them under the pillow, fighting with doctors, orderlies, nurses. At one stage he was lucid enough to be interrogated, and as we note earlier his story failed to please all the authorities.

Perhaps, after such a march, preceded by eighteen months of prison, one can only wonder humbly that Rawicz was able to produce any sort of coherent tale: one can wonder that he was alive to say anything.

After long convalescence the party split up, Rawicz to go to the Middle East and join the Polish forces, the others to be united with their own countrymen, wherever they might be found. It would be interesting to know what has since happened to "Mister Smith". To the best of my knowledge, nobody does.

But, judged as fact, or even part-fantasy, Slavomir Rawicz's tale is as remarkable as any ever told.

186

Chapter 19

"SAFER THAN A
KNOWN WAY"

THE Japanese in Burma and in the Pacific were regarded, with justification, as sub-human opponents. Not since the days of Genghis Khan had their sort of savagery been practised: it was as if a thousand years of civilization had passed them by. Every form of brutality, from the ripping open of pregnant women to the bayoneting of children, the burning alive of whole families, was gleefully indulged in. It is doubtful whether even the Khan himself would have stooped to the level of mid-twentieth-century Japan.

Controversy has raged since 1945 about the wisdom, the morality, of dropping the bomb on Hiroshima.

Only *since* 1945. Memories are short.

For at the time there was little doubt—particularly in the minds of those aware of what was going on in Asia. A blanket of barbarism had descended, civilization was swept aside, replaced by a savagery which put Huns, Vandals, Mongols and the rest to shame.

187

Without the Japanese Army, it is likely the nuclear deterrent would still be just that: an immensely, cruelly, powerful weapon, tested, developed, refined—and never used.

There would have been no question of dropping it on Germany, even if the allies faced imminent defeat. The Germans were dedicated adversaries, yet capable of a rational human reaction. But the Japanese, winning or losing, would drag down civilization with them. Unless they could be put out of the war—and now —thousands, perhaps millions, more innocent people would be destroyed. Japan was already in sight of defeat—but if war against such an opponent could be shortened by a single week, it would be worth it.

I no longer subscribe to that view. In 1945 I did.

The bomb destroyed Hiroshima and Nagasaki, and hundreds of thousands of people. Those of us who have known the Japanese people in peacetime and in war can only shake heads in horror. For as little Gladys Aylward felt, in a China being overwhelmed by Japanese soldiers, it was impossible to reconcile the behaviour of the Japanese Army with the people of Japan.

We cannot afford to be superior. The Second World War taught us that mankind—and we are all a part of it, no man is an island —has progressed a very short way. It took the Japanese to show us, the bomb to underline it.

So when young Ian MacHorton, member of a British column in Burma, moving on foot through the Japanese lines, was wounded and left behind by his friends, we cannot begin to picture the agony of mind that assailed him. He knew the rules —every man was a volunteer who had agreed to abide by them —but no man had really believed it could happen to him.

He was patched up, made as comfortable as possible. His brother-officers tried to be light-hearted: he would be taken care of by the Burmese, he would miss the rest of the war, it was a piece of cake.

The last person to linger a moment with him was his Gurkha orderly, Kulbahadur. "Goodbye, sahib. We will meet again—I know we will."

Kulbahadur left and it was only then that MacHorton felt the terror, the helplessness, of his situation.

This first expedition under General Wingate had gone into

Burma at the start of 1943. The main body had crossed the River Chindwin and a diversionary force, which included MacHorton's 3/2nd Gurkha Rifles, crossed a few miles farther south. MacHorton, in fact, had joined the force only a day or two before it set out, as a reinforcement: he was untrained in the sort of fighting the column would meet.

They entered Burma, did their job, suffered heavy casualties and prepared to fight their way out again. But by now, April, 1943, the whole expedition was in trouble. All seven columns were east of the Irrawaddy and caught in the triangle formed by that river, and the Shweli River, and a motor-road. The Japs had brought up heavy reinforcement, and by covering the road as well as both rivers they were able to cut off movement in any direction. The Wingate force was unable to head either west for India or east for China.

I have a little experience of the terrain in which this took place, for in that year I was flown from India to join the Kachin tribesmen of that part of Burma and help build up a permanent force. Unlike Wingate's force, it would stay there and harass the Japs for as long as might be necessary.

Its role of course would be far less hazardous than that of Wingate's columns, for the Kachins lived in the area, could tell an approaching Jap miles away, and were already a source of alarm and distress to the Japanese Army, who avoided contact whenever possible. Working with them, one felt extremely safe. But these "Kachin Levies" operated in the same territory as the Wingate force, with its dense, packed, bamboo jungle, its rushing northern rivers, and the Levies were able to find and bring to safety a number of Wingate's stragglers, long after the survivors of the main parties had fought a way back to India. Fortunately for all of us, including Ian MacHorton, the Kachins were not only brave little fighters: they liked the British.

But when Kulbahadur had left him, only a few miles from the big Jap garrison at Mong Mit, the future seemed utterly hopeless. He knew the rules, had accepted them: but there was great black bitterness in his mind as the column went off without him.

He lay there, blood pounding through his torn and useless leg, wondering helplessly, hopelessly, what would happen. The Japs would find him, of that there could be no doubt. Should he take them on, from the prone position, with his tommy-gun, should he remain hidden until the last minute? Should he call to them and surrender?

Exhausted by the dilemma, he slept.

He woke to find the Japs had indeed reached him. A party of them was only a few yards away. He fumbled for the tommy-gun: he would wipe out most of them with one long burst.

Then he realized that the survivors—and there would be survivors in this thick jungle—would make their way around behind him. And that would be that.

The party got within feet of him before leaving, but the agony was prolonged, with patrols on foot, convoys of motor lorries, all passing by, some stopping to shout, some to point, so that a dozen times his heart was in his mouth.

Then they were gone: the jungle was quiet.

If only he could get to his feet! Then he would be able to walk, however slowly. A mile each day and there was a chance of getting to China. For a crippled man the river crossings back into India were unthinkable. Eastward there was a chance.

The first thing was to lighten his load. Carefully, he emptied out the contents of his pack, retaining half a mess tin, a pair of socks, morphia phials and anti-malarial pills, with a small square of silk from one of the parachutes which had been rationing the column since it left India all those weeks ago. There was a bit of cord attached to the silk.

Painfully with his kukri, and still lying down, he reached and hacked down a bamboo, made himself a crutch. One of the items he had discarded was a balaclava helmet and this he now retrieved to make a pad for the top of the stick, securing it with parachute cord.

But it seemed hopeless; when he struggled to his feet the agony was appalling and he dropped to the ground with a cry of pain.

He put a hand in his pocket to get a match and relight his pipe. As he did, it came in contact with a screwed-up piece of paper.

He took it out and read:

"I said to the man who stood at the gate of the year: 'give me a light that I may tread safely into the unknown.' And he replied: 'Go out into the darkness and put your hand into the hand of God. That shall be to you better than a light and safer than a known way!'"

It was something his mother had sent him, the quotation the King had read in that moving broadcast on the first Christmas of the war. He read it, read it again and carefully put it back in his pocket.

It took many more agonizing attempts, but at last he got to his feet. Once up, though almost fainting with the pain, he inched his way down the slope to a path and set off towards the east.

After three miles and as many hours he came to a track junction. Now he could see that the column which had left him behind was being pursued by Japs, for the unmistakable footprints were overprinted on the British ones. There was no time to consider the implications, and he hobbled a little way up one of the paths. Utterly exhausted, he lay down, went to sleep.

He awoke well before dawn and struggled to his feet with the crutch. He knew he would have to walk by night and sleep by day if he were to avoid detection. It would be hard work, an uphill climb all the way from now on, but the distant prospect of snow-capped mountains in the moonlight gave him hope.

At the same time he knew that if he went on climbing beyond the tree-line, towards the snows, there would be little chance of survival. He would have to find, or improvise, more clothes. He had left blanket and everything else behind, save for the tattered khaki shirt and trousers he was wearing. Already he had climbed a thousand feet: his lungs ached almost as much as his leg, and his body trembled in the unaccustomed chill.

He plodded on—sideways, for it hurt less that way—along a narrow path with a precipice on one side and a steep bank rising up on the other. As he came to each bend he forced himself on, determined to see what the next one hid.

Suddenly he was face to face with two armed men.

His hand leapt to his revolver holster, he whipped it out, started firing from the hip. Then complete exhaustion overcame him and he fell to the ground.

Much later, he regained consciousness.

"I turned my head cautiously. I became aware of a shaft of

golden sunlight slanting down to my right. I turned my head and saw that the sunlight came through a small grille high up on a stone wall. It was the sort of grille that one saw high up in the walls of story-book prisons.

"Good God! Was I in prison?

"Then I was aware of the gleam of a polished brass jug just beside my bed where my hand could easily reach it. I eased myself up in bed and raised it to my lips. I drank deeply. As I placed the brass jug back on the floor, which I could now see was uneven and hewn out of rocks, the gleaming bulbous metal rang like a bell.

" 'Shshsh'.

"I nearly jumped from the bed in fright at this new sound. I turned my head wildly to my left to see a yellow-clad figure arising from the floor on the other side of my bed. Forgetting all about my wounds, I sat up in bed and shielded my eyes from the brightness of the sunbeam.

"He was a tall and very thin man. From head to foot he was completely robed in yellow. I knew from this robe, which was made up of many strips of yellow cloth, that he was a Buddhist priest of one of the Upper Shan tribes. He had grey hair and was clean-shaven. His brown eyes were curiously penetrating and alive. I was aware that they glistened brightly as he fixed them on me. He looked me straight in the eye and, raising a long thin finger to his lips, repeated 'Shshsh'."

MacHorton felt for his revolver beneath the blanket which now covered him, but touched only bare flesh. He had been stripped. While he was considering this alarming development he heard commands, very close, in Japanese.

At this point the yellow-robed figure got up, went out through the studded teak door. MacHorton was alone in a cell, some thirty feet long by twelve wide, and six feet high—with Japs outside.

He lowered his legs to the ground, saw he had been rebandaged. The pain was bad, but less than it had been, and he managed to stand up and—wonder of wonders!—walk two paces, albeit agonizing ones, without his crutch.

A moment later his yellow-robed gaoler returned with two men, one bearing a basket of food. They stared at him. Then

The great German battleship *Tirpitz*, deep in its Norwegian fiord, behind booms and anti-submarine nets, was deemed absolutely safe by the Germans. Unarmed photo-recce planes could take pictures of her from a great altitude (*above*), but no bomber could reach her from an allied base. Yet midget submarines, exactly like this one (*right*), did the impossible, entered the fiord and crippled her with explosives. (*Below*) The British frigate *Amethyst* made a thrilling escape from Communist Chinese forces, down the Yangtse River. Here she enters Hong Kong harbour for refit after her ordeal.

Tibet has long been one of the world's most mysterious lands, high in the inaccessible Himalayas. But it was Tibet which the young German Heinrich Harrer chose as his sanctuary on escaping from a British camp in India. After many vicissitudes he reached the city of Lhasa and here in the Potala Palace (*above*) he was accepted and made tutor to the Dalai Lama.

The American Wendell Fertig, peacetime mining engineer in the Philippines and wartime soldier, refused to leave the island of Mindanao when Japanese forces invaded it. He raised a private army—promoting himself to "General", with home-made badges of rank in order to gain the necessary dignity—and kept 150,000 enemy at bay. Here he is (*left*) as the returning American army found him in 1945, and (*right*) as he is today.

one, dressed entirely in white, broke into a strange language. He went on for a few seconds and, seeing MacHorton understood not a word, dropped startlingly into Gurkhali.

But how did a Burmese villager speak the language of the Gurkhas?

The Shan headman—for this is what he was—explained that in 1915 he had volunteered for the Gurkha Rifles, been accepted to go to Gallipoli.

In a sudden wave of remembered panic, MacHorton thought of the two men advancing on him with weapons, of his own three revolver shots——

Ah yes, the headman explained. They had been Shan charcoal-burners walking through the forest, axe on shoulder. Fortunately he had lost balance as he fired and the three shots had gone wide. When the men had recovered from their fright, they picked him up and carried him to the village. And here he was hidden, in a cell deep below the village pagoda.

Last night Japs had come into the village, looking for British stragglers. They had spent the night and indulged in a little morning foot-drill before leaving. It was this which MacHorton had heard.

" 'And now bring the sahib his clothes!' he called in the voice of a man about to produce the *pièce de résistance*. The native who had brought in the basket of food stepped forward again, this time with my khaki drill slacks and shirt. They had been cleaned and pressed as neatly as though they had just been returned from the cleaners in a more civilized land, and the rents and gashes had been repaired. It was hard to realize that these now immaculate-looking clothes had been stained and filthy with blood and sweat, sliced by jagged mortar splinters and ripped by jungle thorns."

They laughed at his amazement and led him out to see their village. Already he was able to walk stiffly without aid, and he moved slowly with them up the steps from the cell, into the cool interior of the pagoda, out into the brightness of the morning.

He gasped at the beauty of the little village. "It nestled at the top of a long sloping valley, and straight up behind it rose two towering, thickly forested mountains, sloping steeply down to

each other to intersect immediately behind the village. Along
the full length of the valley on each side of it an almost vertical
strip had been cleared of trees and carved out beautifully into
terraces. On these terraces were grown the vital rice which was
the staple diet of the people. As my eyes travelled onwards from
the beauty of this valley, they took in next the grandeur of the
vast, glorious stretch of the Shan states. The glistening emerald
undulations of tens of thousands of acres of forests and jungle
dropped gently away to merge into the blue, shimmering, heat-
haze that lay along the lower foot-hills of the next range of blue-
green mountains. Beyond them rose fantastically the snow-
covered peaks of the Yunnan range, the sparkling spectrum of
dancing sunbeams softened by haze in the distance to a rainbow
glow in which the white peaks seemed to float in ghostly
majesty——"

MacHorton found a bond in common with the headman. His
own father had been to Gallipoli and been wounded and now, if
he had not already been, young Ian was an honoured guest. He
slept on the verandah of the headman's house, on a thick rug
woven by the village women, showing hunters in vivid colours.
The villagers brought him gifts and he was assured no Jap could
get within miles without an alarm being sounded. Then, of
course, he would be hidden in his cell.

He spent an idyllic fortnight in the village, planning and discussing his departure, and after the first ten days he was able to
walk almost normally. To his dismay, the headman assured him
escape to the north-east, into China, was quite impossible. Whichever path he chose, they all converged on to three or four heavily
guarded passes. No, the only way out would be to cross the
whole of Burma all over again and make a way westward into
India.

His hand was forced suddenly one afternoon. A young Kachin
burst in with a message that many British had been killed trying
to cross the Shweli: the Japs were moving on this very village
to use it as an HQ for mopping up the stragglers.

The headman implored him to stay: they could hide him
forever—why, the Japs could live in the village for a whole year
without his being discovered—but he refused. The temptation
was great, overwhelming, but as his health had recovered, so

had the conviction grown that he must get back to his own army, go on fighting.

He tried to pay with his few silver rupees but the headman waved them away. He was taken to the main gate of the village, given a guide for the first part of the journey, and sent off. If he changed his mind, he would always be an honoured, protected guest in the village. The headman saluted.

A few miles out of the village they saw the marks of British boots, but the guide assured him they were three weeks old. They marched a few miles westward and then, as arranged, the guide took his departure. If MacHorton continued in this direction he would find the Englishmen.

He was alone again; somehow, after the spell in the village, the near-recovery from his wound, it held no terrors for him.

But the terrain turned out worse than he had envisaged. He could find no water, the rations which the kindly villagers had put into his army pack were soon exhausted. Desperately he pursued a young hare, failed to catch it. He was staggering along in misery when the earth shook, and a herd of wild elephants thundered past, but he was too hungry to care.

He managed to kill a small lizard and eat it, and a little later he found water, a cool stream on the near side of an inviting teak forest. Here was a place where it would be pleasing to dally, but it was impossible—he had to press on as fast as possible.

Did he but know it, he was within half a mile of his column. Suddenly he was confronted by a village which materialized in its own little clearing in the jungle.

Could it be Tagaung? It was almost too much to hope, for Tagaung was on the very bank of the Irrawaddy which he would have to cross. Then again, were the Japs in Tagaung?

"By all that's holy! Look who's here!"

He dimly recognized the Irish voice, it seemed to be from some other world: then he almost wept with joy. It was the Column M.O., "Doc" Lusk. He staggered to his feet, ran to him.

He was back again with his column: and though there was every sort of hardship and danger ahead, and many of those who now greeted him so fervently on the east bank of the Irrawaddy would themselves soon be dead, we must leave him. The full story, from his book *Safer than a Known Way*, can hardly be condensed. There were times in the next few weeks when he almost wished death had overtaken him. But at last he reached Advanced British H.Q., west of the Chindwin, at Tamu. It was 16 May: a hundred days had elapsed since he passed in the opposite direction.

They sent him to his Regimental Depot, back to Dehra Dun (where at this moment Heinrich Harrer was planning his own escape into Tibet). He asked for the names of survivors of the Wingate columns, those who got back to India.

They handed him a list and he found it. But, as in the west highlands of Scotland, names from Nepal are limited: one may be shared by a dozen riflemen in the same battalion. Only the man's regimental number can clinch it.

What *was* Kulbahadur's number?

" 'Are you looking for me, sahib?' said a soft voice. I spun round. Kulbahadur stood just inside the tent, the rain streaming from his hat and groundsheet. His face beneath the shadow was one wide smile."

Chapter 20

"THE WOODEN
HORSE"

THIS escape of three men from a German prison camp during the Second World War is perhaps the classic escape story of that war. No collection would be complete without it. Apart from the ingenuity of the idea and the patience and determination of everyone involved, the backbreaking, desperately dangerous, preliminaries make one hold one's breath in awe. Men had to be very determined to get back home to fight another day, if they went this way about it. They could quite peacefully, not too uncomfortably, have spun out the rest of the war in Stalag-Luft III.

Peter and John got there in January, with thick snow on the ground. They had escaped from a previous POW camp and been recaptured and at first they were glad to be able to rest, not be hunted like animals over the countryside.

But as spring drew near, snow melted and there was warmth again in the air, their minds turned to tunnelling. This, of course, is the time-hallowed method of getting out of prison camp—but in their case every possible starting place had been used and discovered.

The camp consisted of single-storey wooden barrack-rooms raised three feet above the ground inside a barbed-wire perimeter. A few yards inside this impregnable wire was a single strand a foot above the ground: anyone crossing this was automatically shot at. Guards in their raised "goon boxes" kept twenty-four-hour watch; at night there were arc lights which flooded the whole perimeter and many yards outside in a brilliant white. There were searchlights as well, shifting, probing, through the night, and sentries who prowled with tommy-guns between the "goon boxes".

The main problem about tunnelling from Stalag-Luft III had been the unusual composition of the soil. Under a thin top layer of grey it was yellow sand which, when it dried, became snow white. Any interference with the earth, any disturbance of the top-soil, was immediately obvious, and from yards away. Yet there was constant talk in the barrack-rooms about tunnelling: some teams had got thirty or forty feet before their excavation was discovered, some had even escaped, only to be rounded up shortly afterwards when the tell-tale traces were discovered.

There had to be a way. Night after night they sat and argued about it.

And John had an idea. No man, no team of men, could possibly tunnel the whole way in one go, or even in dozens of goes, for a tunnel would have to be at least a hundred feet long to get an escaper out beyond the sweep of searchlights—and to start off under cover. There was no point making a damn great hole in the earth, out in the open: you had to start off underneath a barrack-room, or in the canteen, or some such place, clearing up the mess after you'd done a stint of digging, so that nothing should be discovered before the next bit began. It was all these possible start-points which had been tried and discovered.

But if a man were somehow able to start a hole in the open, fairly close to the wire, he would have that much less of a tunnel to dig and he would be starting in a completely fresh spot.

It was ludicrous, of course. The first scrape, and every guard in the camp would be on one's neck.

Perhaps one could have a little tent, or one of those shelters which telephone linesmen use to dig up wires and repair them.

Some hope.

The story, as nearly everyone knows, has been excitingly told in Eric Williams's book, *The Wooden Horse*. I can do no better than quote from that.

"'What about the wooden horse of Troy?'

"Peter laughed. 'The wooden horse of Troy?'

" 'Yes, but a vaulting horse, a box horse like we had at school. You know, one of those square things with a padded top and sides that go right down to the ground. We could carry it out every day and vault over it. One of us would be inside digging while the others vaulted. We'd have a good strong trap and sink it at least a foot below the surface. It's foolproof.'

" 'What about the sand?'

" 'We'll have to take it back with us in the horse. Use a kitbag or something. We'll have to keep the horse in one of the huts and get the chaps to carry it out with one of us inside. We'll take the sand back with us when we go in.'

" 'It'll have to be a bloody strong horse.'

" 'Oh, we'll manage it all right. There's bags of timber in the theatre. You'll be able to knock one up all right.' John could see it already. See it clearly and finished. As a complete thing. The wooden vaulting horse, the vertical shaft under it and the long straight tunnel. He could see them working day after day until they got the tunnel dug. And he saw them going out through the tunnel.

" 'Let's go and see the Escape Committee now,' he said.

" 'There's no hurry. Let's get the whole thing worked out first.'

" 'We'll go now,' John said. 'Someone else might think of it while we're still talking about it.' "

The Committee, somewhat incredulous, agreed. In a POW camp there must be co-ordination of escape attempts, or a maze of tunnels would be started, with an absolute certainty that most would be discovered. The Escape Committee's job was to see that only feasible plans were put into operation, and not too many at once. They were also responsible for seeing that escapers

199

were provided with whatever money and documents could be obtained.

The Wooden Horse had their blessing.

It was a splendid thing, four and a half feet high, covering an area of three feet by five on the ground. It had a solid wooden frame of great strength—it would need it—covered in plywood from Red Cross packing cases. The top was padded with blankets.

There were slots in the sides, through which stout pieces of wood, six feet long, three inches by two in section, could be inserted, so the horse could be carried.

The secret was soon out and there were plenty of volunteers to do the vaulting while others dug underneath. Obviously the horse would have to be seen to be used—and for its ostensible purpose—or the guards would wonder why it stayed out there in the compound. But there had to be a show of recruiting men to take part: posters were made and stuck round the camp, and "special prisoners were detailed to talk to the German guards, remarking on this typical English craze for exercise, and telling them, casually, about the vaulting-horse".

And a few days later a body of young men, dressed only in shorts, came out of the canteen door, marched over to a position near the inner, trip wire. Four other men carried the horse on its wooden poles, placed it in position.

The guards were fascinated by this strange English display. The vaulters were extremely good—with the exception of one man who frequently hit the top of the horse.

"Soon the guards in the boxes were leaning on their elbows waiting for him to make his run. It was not often they had the chance to laugh at the British prisoners. The boot was usually on the other foot. The more the spectators laughed, the more determined this man appeared to be to clear the obstacle. He took a final, desperate leap and in missing his footing he lurched into the horse and knocked it over. He knocked it over on its side so that the interior was in full view of the guards.

"The horse was empty. The vaulters righted the box and went on with their sport. Soon they carried the horse back into the canteen, where they left it until the following afternoon."

It was a week before the digging could safely begin and the calculation was that the total distance involved—to the wire, under it and out the other side to a safe spot—would be roughly a hundred and twenty feet. If they managed five feet a day they would do it in twenty-four days.

But there was no question of doing five feet a day. Every grain of sand would have to be taken from the tunnel, pound by pound, in cloth bags made from the bottoms of trouser-legs (suddenly everyone decided to have shorts) and disposed of inside the barrack-room. The complicated trapdoor would have to be replaced each time and covered with eighteen inches of earth, making sure none of the tell-tale yellow sand was visible.

A foot a day was more likely.

And so they began. "John crouched inside the horse. His feet were on the bottom framework, one on each side of the horse. In his arms he held the equipment. The horse creaked and lurched as the bearers staggered under the unaccustomed weight. They got the horse into position and began to vault.

"Inside the horse, John worked quickly. Scraping up the dark-grey surface sand, he put it into the cardboard box and started to dig a deep trench for one side of the shoring. He put the bright yellow excavated sand into the trouser-leg bags.

"As the trench grew deeper, he had difficulty in reaching the bottom. He made it wider and had to bank the extra sand against one end of the horse. It was hot inside the horse and he began to sweat.

"He finished the trench and put the plywood sheet in position. He replaced the surplus sand, ramming it down with the handle of the trowel, packing the shoring tight. The top of the shoring was six inches below the ground.

"Standing on the framework of the horse he carefully spread the sand over the plywood sheet, packing it down hard, finally sprinkling the grey sand over the whole area covered by the horse—obliterating his foot and finger marks.

"Calling softly to Peter, he gave the word that he had finished.

"The vaulters inserted the carrying poles and staggered back into the canteen with John and the bags of sand.

"Once inside the canteen they transferred the sand from the trouser-leg bags into long, sausage-like sacks made from the arms and legs of woollen underwear. These they carried away slung round their necks and down inside their trouser-legs.

"The sand was dispersed in various places around the compound, some of it finding its way by devious routes to the latrines, some of it buried under the huts, some of it carried out in specially made trouser pockets and dug into the tomato patches outside the huts."

And so the fantastic operation began. They realized straight away that everything depended on the speed with which they could get the sand away and that therefore the diameter of the tunnel must be as small as possible. This of course meant that the man excavating would not be able to turn round, or even sit up: he would get into the tunnel with arms in front of his head and stay like that, not even able to crawl with them doubled up. For the first few horizontal feet this was not too difficult, for he would be able to crouch in the vertical shaft as he scraped away sand with his trowel. Later, when he was entirely in the tunnel, he would have to scrape, then crawl backwards to the vertical shaft bringing the sand with him.

Bringing it back this way, ounce by ounce, it took a long time to fill twelve trouser-leg bags.

The heat, the lack of ventilation, were appalling and the excavator (who was either John or Peter: they took it in turns while the other supervised the vaulting) worked naked. Day after day it went on, and while the weary vaulters were given an extra ration to keep up their strength, there was none allotted for the excavators. One day Peter collapsed and was ordered by the British M.O. to spend a week in bed. During this week no digging was done, but the vaulters took their horse out every day.

There was a terrible afternoon when a part of the tunnel collapsed, with John in it. On seeing the hole one of the vaulters lay on it to prevent it being seen by the guards. As he did, he grimaced with pain from a "bad leg".

They could get no reply from John, and as there were no airholes in the tunnel there was every chance he was suffocating. They wanted to kick over the horse, start frantically digging to drag him out, but they restrained themselves: if the tunnel were found now, all those weeks of work and ingenuity would have been in vain.

Suddenly they heard his voice. "Just putting the shoring in. You can fill-in, in about five minutes."

Calm, unruffled, he was down there repairing the damage. When he got out, was carried away hidden in the horse, there were minutes left before roll-call. If he had missed it, the game would have been up.

By the time they had done forty feet, it was obvious they would never finish a hundred and twenty. The rate grew slower each day, with the excavator having to wriggle, using only toes and fingers, backwards and forwards in his tunnel, dragging a pitiful few ounces of sand. The war would be over, the world come to an end, time to a stop, before they finished their tunnel.

They thought about this and hit upon a complicated plan. They would improvise a toboggan in the tunnel, to bring back sand from the face to the shaft. A second man would be needed to operate this.

Could the vaulters carry a horse with two men inside?

Just.

In that case, they would be unable to carry away sand: the load would be too great.

John and Peter thought this out too. There had to be an answer —the scheme mustn't founder now.

There was an answer. The two of them would be carried out to the trap with no less than thirty-six empty bags. While one worked at the far end of the tunnel (which would have to be widened into a chamber to make this possible) the other would drag back the sand on the toboggan and fill up the thirty-six bags inside the vertical shaft. When this was done he would stack the bags there and they would go back in the horse. Without sand. Later in the evening the horse would be taken out again, with only one man inside: he would bring back twelve of the bags. The next afternoon, twelve more bags would be brought back, and again in the evening.

It meant that actual digging and bag-filling took place only every second day. There was no alternative.

Meanwhile, helped by the Escape Committee, they were assembling civilian clothes and forged documents. Most of the clothes were in fact ingeniously recut service jackets and trousers, with new buttons. Summer was passing by and they were anxious to make their exit before winter. But a new problem arose as rainy weather arrived: the vaulters would not be able to go on vaulting—however mad, however English, they might be deemed to be—right through a rainstorm. The stupidest goon would become suspicious. By the same token, they would be unable to leave their precious horse with its padded top out in the rain while they ran for shelter: that would be just as suspicious.

And if they took away the horse—or the guards took away the horse while work was going on below?

No digging, or vaulting, would be done if there was likelihood of rain.

Inch by inch they progressed. It was agreed that John and Peter and a third man, Philip, would make the escape together. Probably all that the other dedicated helpers, the vaulters, the assemblers of clothing and money and documents, would get out of it would be the satisfaction of having helped in a successful escape. If it were successful. There was a chance the tunnel would not be discovered after the first break-out, in which case it should be possible for others to use it later.

On 28 October, the three made their escape. They took out the last load of sand in the afternoon and Philip and Peter left John alone in the shaft. Someone impersonated John at roll-call and when it was over they prepared to go back. It was the first time they had ever vaulted after evening roll-call and everyone was jumpy. This time, despite the fact that John was already down the hole, the horse would have to take three passengers: Peter, Philip and a man to replace the trap after they had gone.

Somehow they made it, with vaulters struggling and stumbling and two men inside the horse standing on its wooden frame, holding a third by his elbows and knees. They got to the spot, carefully opened the trap. Peter and Philip, with muffled farewell to the vaulters, slipped down.

They struggled along the tunnel, dragging and pushing their kitbags of clothing. Roll-call had been at a quarter to four: exactly at six, as arranged, they broke through to the open air and heard the bedlam of the "diversion" which their friends were staging inside the wire. Trumpets were being blown, men were singing and yelling, thumping the walls of the hut. The noise was indescribable.

" 'The silly bastards will get a bullet in there if they're not careful,' John whispered.

" 'Go on! Go now!' Peter said. He was scared. It was too light.

"Quickly John hoisted his kitbag out of the tunnel and rolled it towards the ditch. He squeezed himself out of the hole and Peter saw his legs disappear from view.

"Peter stuck his head out of the tunnel and looked towards the camp. It was brilliantly floodlit. He had not realized how brilliantly it was lit. But the raised sentry-boxes were in darkness and he could not see whether the guards were looking in his direction or not. He could not see the guards outside the wire. He lifted out his kitbag and pushed it towards the ditch, wriggling himself out of the hole and rolling full-length on the ground towards the ditch. He expected every minute to hear the crack of a rifle and feel the tearing impact of its bullet in his flesh. He gained the ditch and lay listening. The diversion in the huts had reached a new crescendo of noise.

"He picked up his kitbag and ran blindly towards the pine forest on the other side of the road, where John was waiting for him."

And so the fantastic scheme was carried out. There were trials ahead, but John and Peter made their way back to England via the Baltic port of Stettin, and Philip, who preferred to travel alone, got back via Danzig.

How were they greeted?

They arrived with no English money and were told by the army intelligence officer at the midlands aerodrome where they landed from Sweden that they *should* have been given English money. There was no machinery for giving them English money here. After all, there *was* a war on——

"There was a short silence. The intelligence captain spoke.

" 'Do you have a cheque book?' "

" 'Don't be bloody silly—we've just come from a prison camp!'

"The captain turned to the major; he had solved the problem. 'I think we can trust them, sir. After all, they *are* officers.' "

205

Chapter 21

HEINRICH HARRER CLIMBS THE
HIMALAYAS INTO TIBET

Dehra Dun is an attractive little town—hardly the sort of place one would wish to escape from. It sits lightly in the Himalayan foothills at the top end of what used to be "United Provinces", that "U.P." which has ever been the heart of India, and in which so much of her history has taken place. The initials have been retained in the newer, post-independence title of "Uttar Pradesh".

The character of Dehra Dun has altered little since the years when it was known with affection by the old Indian Army as a place one was lucky to be sent to: where one trained, and worked, and played, in cool and pleasing surroundings, overlooked by the beauty and the might of the Himalayas. The hill station, or holiday resort, of Mussoorie was a little farther up, at an altitude of seven thousand feet, and twenty miles away, up a winding, frightening, road which one ascended according to one's finances and one's courage, either by taxi or by rattling, string-tied bus, with as many cheerful Indians on the roof as inside.

Mussoorie and Dehra Dun are still there. They are much the same, with an Indian National Defence Academy providing a military fabric to life, and the Himalayas, smiling or stormy, in the sky behind.

But in 1943, to a young Austrian interned there, Dehra presented a less pleasing aspect. Heinrich Harrer was a skier who had been a member of the Austrian Olympic Team in 1936, a mountaineer who had been with the first party to climb the north wall of the Eiger. Nothing seemed to daunt him: at one stage of his short career, he had fallen 170 feet and lived to tell the tale, to climb the same mountain again.

It was the summer of 1939 that brought nearer the realization of his dream—the dream of every mountaineer. Heinrich Harrer was invited, at four days' notice, to join a German Himalayan expedition. The plan was to reconnoitre the 25,000-foot Nanga Parbat. The second stage would be to return in 1940 and climb it, up the route they had reconnoitred and mapped.

To some of us there is little glamour in the ascent of mountains —particularly now, a generation later, when Everest herself has been conquered. The conventional picture of a rigidly disciplined band of Teutons making earnest, slippery progress up one of Everest's little sisters is less than gripping. But the climb that Harrer eventually did make, in place of Nanga Parbat, is one that grips the most sluggish imagination.

Plenty of people have climbed the Himalayas. Very few have climbed them with an army and police force at their heels.

In 1939, the recce of Nanga Parbat was successfully concluded, and the little team—Lutz Chicken, Hans Lobenhoffer, Heinrich Harrer and their leader, Peter Aufschnaiter—was waiting at Karachi for a ship to take them back to Europe. Had the freighter on which they booked passage not been late, we would have no story to tell. But it was late indeed, and long before it arrived Harrer and his companions had loaded themselves into an old car to escape internment as enemy aliens.

The attempt failed, owing to what Harrer with an unwitting compliment describes as "The Secret Police". The ponderous, creaking, frequently ineffective, apparatus of Indian "internal security" had got into gear. Someone, late in the day, had decided that a team of young aliens with a special knowledge of Indian geography must not be allowed to get back to Germany. They were—miraculously—apprehended after a few hundred miles in their crumbling car and brought back to Karachi. Here they were allowed to go more or less where they pleased, do what they wished, while reporting at regular intervals to the police. War, though imminent, had not been declared.

But two days later and five minutes after it had been, a score of puzzled Indian soldiers clumped into the restaurant where they were all sitting, arrested them, and loaded them up in a truck.

They were taken, protesting, to a hutted compound. This turned out to be only a transit camp: within a fortnight they were transferred again to a real place of internment, near Bombay. A little later they were loaded up and taken towards Deolali, one of the bleaker training areas of India, the grim "Doolally" of the British soldier, where a new camp had been set up. It was while they were travelling in convoy along the dusty road that leads there from Bombay that he and Lobenhoffer made a first attempt to escape. The convoy was crawling through a dust storm, and this gave them a chance to hop out. They made hurried preparation to do so, agreed they would lie low in a ditch and then make a way overland to Portuguese territory.

But the unfortunate Lobenhoffer was carrying their heavy rucksack, and as he jumped from the back of the lorry there was an appalling clatter of mess tins, knives, forks, enamel cups. The alarm went out, the convoy halted in a cloud of dust, a scream of brakes, and within minutes the two fugitives had been rounded up and the convoy was on its way again to Deolali.

This is hardly an escape—but it was a first practice leap of several that were ahead of Harrer, from each of which he would pick up a bit more information: so that when, in 1944, he embarked on his final attempt, he knew as much about the problems of escaping from British captivity in India as any man living.

By this time they had been moved to Dehra Dun, which as we have seen is up near the top of the sub-continent, hard by the Himalayas. It was here that an audacious scheme came to Harrer for breaking out of this biggest, most heavily-guarded camp in all India. What more attractive and reasonable, to a

208

hardened mountaineer, than to escape into the Himalayas and thence into neutral Tibet?

And from Tibet? Well, the final objective would probably be the Japanese lines in China or Burma.

Fortunately for Harrer, who knew nothing of the Japanese, he got to Tibet and stayed there.

But first he set about collecting useful items for the expedition: cutters and gloves, to get him through seven rows of barbed-wire fencing; then maps, cooking and mountaineering equipment; and, as important as anything, money. His companions helped him as best they could with these items, on the understanding that his escape would be his own, and his alone. A man stood a better chance alone. They would try to follow later.

He began to spend evenings and as much of the day as possible in learning Hindustani, Tibetan and Japanese in the prison library. He took regular and violent exercise to make himself fit, make his body hard as granite for the test to which he would soon be putting it.

The question of money remained pressing. No man could expect to take much in the way of provisions, least of all from an internment camp: he would have to buy these and perhaps also the services of guides and a porter. Day after day he counted up his pitiful savings, and postponed the escape.

It was then that he heard about General Marchese.

Forty Italian generals were housed in a special compound of the Dehra camp; it was a comparatively easy matter for Harrer to climb into this compound and introduce himself to General Marchese. The general was a pleasant, fit-looking man of forty, who had let it be circulated through the camp grape-vine that he not only was willing to escape, but, having the pay of a British general, would have sufficient money to bribe and buy a way to the north—or any other direction decided on—for one or more companions.

They conversed painfully in French and agreed to escape together.

For many weeks Harrer crept back each night to discuss the details. At last, in May, 1943, having assembled money, a compass, provisions and even a small tent, they were ready.

After much alarm and delay, being nearly caught in the

attempt, they found themselves at dead of night outside the wire, gasping from their exertions, with all guards firing wildly into the night. Heavy laden, they stumbled off into the jungle.

A few miles farther on they lay down, exhausted, to sleep, but after an hour they were on their feet again. They had planned to move only by night, and when dawn broke their first day of freedom was spent eating and sleeping in the dried-out bed of a river. They were hot, tired and thirsty, but full of a sudden exhilaration, a sense of freedom. Neither had realized till today how it felt to be free after years of captivity.

Day after day they slept, and night after night they marched on, by map and compass. They had by now made themselves passably into Indians. For the little Italian this was not too difficult, but for a blonde and blue-eyed Austrian the disguise presented problems. They darkened their skins with a mixture of permanganate, brown paint and grease—all carefully thought out behind the barbed wire at Dehra—and then Harrer succeeded in dyeing his hair and beard a lustrous black.

Almost immediately it started to fall out in handfuls, but there was no time to consider this. Better bald and free.

From now on, if they encountered anyone, they were on pilgrimage to the sacred Ganges. And among India's babel of dialects they stood a fair chance of convincing an interrogator that they hailed from some distant part.

They still moved only at night, using the home-made maps and their compass, up the Jumna valley, then up its tributary, the Aglar, towards the Ganges. Their habit was to prepare to move in late afternoon and set out the moment the sun had fallen—for there is little twilight in the tropics; darkness rushes in at once.

But on one occasion they were over-eager. They set forth, heavy packs on their backs, before the sun had vanished. They marched on slowly, still feeling its warmth, until suddenly there was a shout in front, and they instinctively flung themselves to the ground.

A group of peasants were planting rice in the muddied water of a paddy, and these now stared at them in amazement. The two travellers might well be Indians from some other part—Persians, perhaps—but how strange their clothes, how vast and cumbersome the loads they carried on their backs. Certainly they were not Europeans: no one ever saw a European carrying a load.

As calmly as they could, the two fugitives got to their feet and marched rapidly on. The peasants watched them vanish, then got back to their planting.

After this incident they gained greater confidence and allowed themselves to meet Indians frequently, even daring to bargain with them over supplies.

On their twelfth day out of captivity, they reached the Ganges. But they were twelve days which had utterly exhausted Harrer and very nearly killed the general. The Italian had lost a stone or more, his eyes bulged black and blood-shot in a thin, dyed face, and he staggered when he moved. But he was game, and they carried on, still cheerful, knowing each step took them nearer safety.

They had reached the well-worn Pilgrims' Road up the Ganges, the path which winds along the river bank towards its source, and would take them, if strength lasted, right into the Himalayas. And the route, being well-worn, was dotted with little booths which sold tea and provisions. After having been chased from the first—he was a thief, a filthy thief, a *badmash,* and this was music to Harrer's ears, for it proved his disguise effective—he succeeded in buying, at the second, forty pounds of sugar, meal and onions. No doubt the shopkeeper cared little who would consume this quantity, as long as he was paid, but Harrer explained carefully in a laboured Hindustani that he was leader of a party of ten devout and hungry pilgrims. The man, whether or not he understood or believed, shrugged shoulders and smiled. No one came outside to count.

There were frightening, sickening, moments, as when a party of Indians decided the two must indeed be fugitives and started to blackmail them: there was a British officer down the road, with a party of soldiers, and he was paying good money for information about escaped prisoners. Harrer brandished aspirins, assured them he was a doctor, bluffed a way through.

Gradually, now, they were ascending from the green valleys to bare brown mountain, with the snows, white and gleaming, in front. At a height of some seven thousand feet they decided to risk a fire and cook a little porridge, their first hot food for a fortnight.

Refreshed, they went on, only to find themselves at midnight confronted by a wide stream, a rushing, icy, tributary of the Ganges, where the Pilgrims' Road seemed to end. They splashed about for hours in the dark, trying to find a way over, then decided to sleep for an hour or two and watch at daybreak to see if anyone else came to it. It was hardly possible, after all, that a Pilgrims' Road would end suddenly in the middle of nowhere.

They were right; the road carried on, on the other bank. To their amazement they saw from their hiding place a large band of pilgrims come to the river bank, disappear from view behind a grove of trees, and reappear a minute later on the far bank.

Weak with exhaustion, Marchese almost delirious, they wondered for a moment whether magic had played its part, whether the waters had miraculously parted to let the faithful through.

Then they saw what had happened. The river was much lower than it had been the evening before, and it was quite possible, now, to ford it. Obviously, fed by mountain snows, it reached its highest level in the evening, after the longest spell of sunlight, and dropped to a shallow stream in the morning.

They crossed and rested again on the farther bank.

It was here that disaster struck. An Indian came up, looked carefully at them and went away. A minute later another appeared, a distinguished-looking man with a small party of soldiers.

"Could I," he said in English, "have your passes?"

"*Malum nahin*," said Harrer in Hindustani. "*Hum Kashmiri hain*. I am a Kashmiri."

"*Bilkul thik*," said the other, also in Hindustani. "There are two other Kashmiris staying in that house over there. You must come and meet them."

The game seemed up. Harrer, with heart pounding, turned to Marchese and spoke in French, "*Qu'est-ce qu'on fait maintenant?*"

"*Eh bien*," said the Indian, also in French. "Please open your packs."

It was an almost unbelievable stroke of ill luck. They had

been apprehended by an Indian forestry official who spoke English, French and Hindustani, and, as Harrer now discovered, fluent German. He had come up to the hills to investigate flooding which was the worst for a hundred years. He apologized for doing his duty, but he had been warned that the two of them might be in the area.

They had been at liberty for eighteen days. Their captor did his best to ease the pangs of loss of freedom; let them stay with him in his stilted bungalow, well fed and only reminded of their captivity at night, when he apologetically shoved his bed up against their door to block any attempt at escape.

The window, high above ground, was too high for a man to jump from: of this, the Indian was certain.

Marchese was too weak to consider any further escape, but he generously handed over all his money and wished his companion luck. Then he acted both parts in a little tableau which enabled the Austrian to escape—from the window. A loud and acrimonious quarrel struck up in the prisoners' room, a high voice and a low, shouting abuse in which the names "Harrer" and "Marchese" figured often.

Harrer jumped and ran, and as the bungalow vanished behind him in the darkness, could hear his name being shouted furiously by Marchese, and the General being abused in return, till the sound was swallowed up in the night.

But still bad luck dogged him. With an icy Himalayan wind roaring past, he realized suddenly that the map he had copied was inaccurate in this area. Baffled and angry, he wandered about trying to get his bearings, then hid himself and went to sleep.

The next evening he set off again and within minutes entered a village not shown on the map. Here, as fate would have it, were his pursuers. He was arrested again.

That day he was offered the Tibetan staple diet of *tsampa* and butter-tea. It made him ill instantly. Had he known that he would live on that and little else for the next seven years, one wonders whether he might not have abandoned his plans.

After a total of thirty-eight days' freedom, he was back in Dehra Dun, but already with plans well advanced for an escape next year. On the way south under escort he had made friends with an Indian who not only undertook to look after his maps, compass and other essentials, but agreed to come back and meet him at this exact spot the following May.

Sentenced to twenty-eight days' solitary confinement by an apologetic British C.O., Harrer settled down to work out the details of what he knew must be a final attempt. This time nothing could go wrong: one must cater for everything, even the million-to-one chance of a polyglot Indian on an unaccustomed visit to the Himalayas.

Marchese was back in the camp, but though he wished Harrer every luck, he refused to try again. This time Harrer decided on a mass escape with a number of other internees. Seven men now disguised themselves as a working party of five Indians under two British officers: Harrer, with shaven head and dyed skin, was the humblest labourer.

The perimeter fence was always in need of repair and this the strange little group proceeded to do, with more gusto than skill, armed with a stolen coil of wire, a pot of tar, a few brushes, and a precious ladder which had been "won" during a small outbreak of fire in the compound. There was much waving of swagger-canes and blueprints.

By bluff and bravado, they found themselves outside the main gate just as the Camp Sergeant-Major cycled past. He glanced at them with some interest, then wobbled off into the distance. The party received a smart salute from the sentry and followed the C.S.M. for a few hundred yards. Then they turned off into the jungle.

Once there, they shed uniforms and split up, each man going his own way. Harrer set out along the route he had followed with Marchese; and now, familiar with it and unencumbered by a companion, he covered in the first night what had taken four days the year before. But the others moved fast as well; a little later he literally stumbled over four men resting in the roadway, and found them to be Peter Aufschnaiter and another three. They spent an hour together, and Harrer pressed on alone.

A week more and he reached the village where he had asked his Indian friend to meet him. Suddenly his spirits sank. What chance—if one really thought about it—was there that a man would risk his own freedom, perhaps his life, in helping another escape?

And even if he were so foolish—would he be likely to wait through the entire month of May, as he had promised, miles from his own home, awaiting his friend's arrival?

Harrer came to the house. The moon was shining full on the door and he stood and watched it for some time. Then he whistled, called the man's name.

There was no answer.

He called again.

There was silence, and then, to his unbelieving delight, the door was flung open and a man rushed out, threw himself on the ground and kissed his feet.

A minute later Harrer had been reunited with his kit, and his friend was preparing a large meal.

He slept through the next day in a nearby wood. Then, as evening fell, his friend came out to say farewell and give him a present of a blanket.

After ten more days along a route he now knew well, days in which he encountered apes, leopards and bears and was often frightened, he found himself in the village of Nelang. This, he realized with sinking heart, was where he had been recaptured the previous year.

He entered cautiously. But to his delight there was no party of gaolers, only the four fellow-prisoners he had left farther back. They had caught up while he spent a day and a night with his Indian friend.

This time Harrer teamed up with Aufschnaiter and another man called Kopp, and a few days later the three of them found themselves on the Tibetan frontier.

It was icy, bitterly cold—though May was half gone—and their rations had almost run out. They had a frugal last meal in India, cakes made of flour and water, baked on hot stones, while they cringed against the wind, behind a stone wall.

A few more gasping, high-altitude minutes and they were at the top of the Tsangchokla Pass, 17,200 feet above sea level, and over the frontier.

It was 17 May, 1944—and they were free.

How they were received, how they established themselves in this strange mountain land, is another story altogether, told excitingly in Harrer's book, *Seven Years in Tibet*. Kopp soon left them for asylum in Nepal, but the other two, Harrer and Aufschnaiter, stayed on, living as Tibetans. The war ended a year after they had crossed the border, but it made no difference: by this time, the two had become a part of this wild, seductive land and had no intention of leaving. Harrer, trusted and loved by the people, had become tutor to their Dalai Lama.

Only the Chinese hordes, bursting into Tibet in 1950, forced them to leave, and this was the saddest moment of both their lives.

Their escape had brought them not only freedom, but a new philosophy and way of life.

It left them sadness.

Chapter 22

OTTO SKORZENY
RESCUES MUSSOLINI

TWELVE of them hung to the fuselage of the tiny plane as he raced the engine. The noise mounted to a whine and a scream and a roar, then a terrifying thunder, and the slipstream seized a cap from one of the gasping carabinieri, hurled it in the air. Still he refused to drop his hand in the prearranged signal, and it seemed as if the *Fieseler-Storch* would shake itself to bits, dump its three crowded occupants in a sweaty, frightened heap on the rocky plateau.

But Gerlach was determined to get the last ounce of power from the little engine, get it to maximum revs before giving the order to pull away chocks, let go. With an absurdly short cleared space, a rocky, fifty-metre ribbon on the scalp of a mountain, where he'd only just managed to put it down, he was expected to take off again—and with two passengers. It was as near suicide as he, Gerlach, had ever been.

But the order came from the *Fuehrer*.

The rev-counter had reached a maximum, refused to budge.

217

He dropped his hand.

The *Fieseler-Storch* shot forward as if from a gun, hit a boulder with the port leg of its undercarriage and nearly capsized. Sweat trickling down over his uniform collar, he kicked the rudder, first this way, then that, touching each brake with his heel, trying desperately to keep straight without sufficient airspeed over fin and rudder to make controls operative.

The ravine was just ahead, fifteen metres off. Gently, tentatively, he eased the stick back and the aircraft wallowed into the air—the height of a small dog, perhaps—then dropped sickeningly back, with a bump.

They were on it, now, there was nothing to be done but give another gentle pull on the stick to clear the boulders at the edge, then ram it forward and dive, get airspeed as they plunged into the ravine, rather than stall and drop like a sack of cement to the rocks below.

He did and they plunged. There was a gasp of terror from the seat beside him, another from the one behind.

There was a scream from the watchers as the little long-legged stork vanished into the abyss. The sound of it went completely for a moment and two *carabinieri* and a German soldier started running towards the edge.

Seconds went by and then, to the amazement of all, the relief of most, the *Storch* reappeared at the farther side, clawing its way upward.

Clear of the rock walls, it altered course south-west, headed for the Avezzano Valley.

This had been the last, most difficult, move in a fantastic rescue operation, a detailed and complex plot which had begun six weeks before, and which, in the long term, failed. Benito Mussolini, fallen idol, sick and in disgrace, had been saved—for the moment—from the vengeance of the enemy and his own people. It made little difference which—for both sides had separate and unpleasant plans for him.

Before looking at this extraordinary tale more closely, from Mussolini's arrest by his king, to his death; before we allow ourselves the luxury of knowing it-couldn't-happen-here, we may stop for a moment and consider just what might have happened, had things been different. A fable perhaps. Or a cautionary tale.

Our tale begins, like Mussolini's, in 1943. That, of course, was the year when the second German attempt at invasion of Britain succeeded: a lightning pincer movement from Calais and Cherbourg after the heaviest aerial bombardment the world had ever known. No invasion, however brilliantly planned and conducted, is a success till the enemy has surrendered, but this, by July, seemed tragically inevitable. Loud talk of fighting the enemy on the beaches, never surrendering, was no longer heard, since the illness of Winston Churchill. There was a German Army H.Q. at Canterbury, another at Southampton, and a pair of airborne divisions settled on the coast of Suffolk. For the moment, General Rommel from his Rear H.Q. at Hastings seemed willing to bide his time. Germans and Englishmen were dug in facing each other; both sides were putting out patrols, little else was happening. The Americans, who had taken little part in resisting the invasion —for their training areas were far from the zone and the whole thing had been over inside two days—were now regrouped north of London.

A week after the invasion, Churchill was placed under arrest, first at his great family home of Bleinheim, then, when it seemed he might escape, to the Isle of Man, and thence to the remote highlands of Scotland. There was still a very faint mumbling of defiance, but the spirit of Britain seemed to have gone. War against Germany had been a mad thing, a wicked thing, and there was hardly a man in public affairs who could not point to having at least hinted at that, years before. Germans were our kith, our kin, blood brothers: our Royal Family was German, and the Germans were our friends.

Churchill—"Winston S."—God, how American could you get?—had still commanded some small allegiance, particularly among older people, but the south-coast debacle had sadly coincided, for him, with a severe bout of illness. Bronchitis had turned to pneumonia and he had made a gallant, but far from complete, recovery. He was seldom seen—and then he was almost unrecognizable, for he had lost a great deal of weight and was suddenly a foolish little pixie of a man—and he never broadcast. The famous voice—and how boastful, how stupid it had been! —was still.

Under arrest for his own good, he was forgotten.

219

The morning of 26 July, the day after Churchill's arrest, a young Paratroop Captain in the United States Army was ordered to Washington from the course he had been attending at Fort Worth.

After a long, nervous wait in an ante-room at the White House, he was finally ushered into the President's study. Franklin Roosevelt, face grey and taut, was seated behind his desk. Five young officers stood awkwardly about him, and Stewart marched over, saluted.

There was scuffling; the officers and a White House aide found chairs. A Colonel remained standing at the President's side.

"Good," said the President. "Now I'd like you gentlemen to come up, one at a time, and sit here. The rest of you, please, smoke, talk, do as you please, till your turn comes."

The Colonel spoke. "Lieutenant Wheeler——"

A tall, red-haired youth unwound himself from a chair and went to the President's desk. The Colonel had a thick file—six thick files—and this one must have contained the whole of Wheeler's career, if not his life. The three of them, President, Colonel and Lieutenant, talked in low voices for about five minutes.

Lieutenant Wheeler returned to his desk and it was Stewart's turn. He marched up to the desk again, saluted.

"Sit down, Captain Stewart."

"I see, Captain," said the Colonel, "you were a Rhodes Scholar in 1937——"

The interview went on, minute by minute, tracing Greg Stewart's career to the Philippines in '41, on to the training of paratroops in northern England. His views were solicited on everything he had done. Then he was ordered, courteously, back to his chair.

The six interviews over, Roosevelt, helped by the Colonel, got to his feet and walked slowly, on his cane, across the room. The officers got to their feet and he chatted brightly, inconsequentially, with them all.

Suddenly, the other five were dismissed.

The President stood silent in the exact centre of the big room and Greg Stewart could feel his eyes. Then he spoke. "A job for you, Captain."

"Yes, sir."

"The British have betrayed Churchill. And with him, you and me."

"Yes, sir."

"Winston Churchill represents resistance against Germany, he represents an Anglo-American alliance. And that, Captain Stewart, has become very, very, unfashionable in Britain. But Churchill is going to be rescued, to fight another day——"

Half an hour later, Stewart was two miles away down Pennsylvania Avenue, discussing the details of his assignment with two Generals, while a nervous Secretary of State stood behind.

He stayed a week in Washington, studying O.S.S. reports. No sooner had these shown Churchill to be at Blenheim than he was reported to have been taken away at night, to the coast of North Wales, and there loaded on a destroyer. It was believed he was now in the Isle of Man.

This was correct. Churchill stayed there for exactly two weeks. At the end of the first, he was forwarded a telegram from General Marshall, wishing him speedy recovery and assuring him the war, in God's good time, would be won. It made no mention of his imprisonment, even of his resignation.

An hour before dawn on 27 August, Churchill was taken from his island prison, put on another destroyer and taken up the west coast of Britain, to the Isle of Arran, off southern Scotland. His life here became still more secluded, he was denied access to newspapers and to the radio, and thus he did not learn of Britain's surrender to the Germans on 3 September.

An American spotter plane, an L1, was seen on the 4th.

The next day he was moved again, very early in the morning, to the mainland, and thence in a military ambulance—a long, hideously bumpy journey, over country roads—into the Perthshire hills, near Crianlarich. Here, in a mist-shrouded hotel near the top of a mountain, he was at last made comfortable. Two doctors were sent in to attend him, he was given a radio and a large, comfortable room. A more skilled chef than the little hotel boasted was sent up from London, and with him came wine, cigars and books.

It was from the radio in his room that Winston Churchill learnt

221

the surrender terms: among them, an agreement to hand him over to the Germans.

On the afternoon of Sunday, 12 September—a perfect day, with only a few white puffs of cloud in the sky—twelve gliders towed by C47 Dakotas circled to gain height above an American-held airfield in the border country. Greg Stewart was in the leading glider. Still climbing behind their tow-craft, the twelve headed in line astern for the Perthshire hills.

It was a minute to two in the afternoon when Stewart saw, through a gap in the clouds, the roof of the hotel. It was a mile in front, a thousand feet below.

He waited as it grew nearer. It vanished exasperatingly into cloud, then reappeared.

He gave the order to slip tow-ropes. A jerk, and his glider was floating silent, helpless in the thin air, as others slipped tow-ropes and joined it, and the Daks banked hard, wheeled away to the south.

And here we may leave our fable. Almost every detail, if we accept that the rescued man and his rescuers have been altered in name and nationality, and a hotel prison in the Appenines has been moved to the Scottish highlands, is correct. For it was not Greg Stewart, but a young Waffen S.S. Captain, Otto Skorzeny, who was summoned with five others to meet his country's leader.

When Skorzeny's airborne force had taken the hotel—he himself destroyed its army radio-transmitter—the surrender of Mussolini was accepted over a glass of red wine. The erstwhile dictator recovered a little of his dignity when the hotel staff lined up to be thanked for their services, but he was still shabby and pale when he was loaded into the tiny *Fieseler-Storch*. This, as part of the plan, had landed in the wake of the gliders. Young Captain Gerlach was unhappy at the prospect of taking off in so short a run with a passenger. He was appalled when Skorzeny announced that he, too, would be coming, for if Mussolini were killed in the take-off there would be nothing for Otto Skorzeny but to blow out his own brains: he might as well get killed with the other two. An astonishing piece of reasoning, but Gerlach, assured that all orders came from the *Fuehrer*, got in after the other two, switched on and started up.

As we have seen, he made it: the culmination of perhaps the most dramatic rescue operation in the war. Mussolini, when the *Storch* landed at a German-held aerodrome, was loaded, still with Skorzeny, into a Heinkel and flown on to Vienna.

The next day, Monday, 13 September, he was flown to Munich. His wife Rachele met him at the airport, was horrified at his appearance, but impressed by his cheerfulness. He was permitted a mere two days with her before being flown to East Prussia, to Hitler's Headquarters (where Skorzeny had been chosen and briefed, rather less than two months previously). His first enthusiasm for taking charge in Italy, re-establishing himself as the Duce, had began to wane, but Hitler gave orders that he must return, and on 27 September he did so, the puppet ruler of a shrinking, hostile country.

Eighteen months later, Nemesis caught up. It was 27 April, 1945, and the defeated Germans had abandoned him, when he was captured and shot. His body, with that of his mistress Claretta Petacci and several others, was hung up by the heels in the Piazzale Loreto of Milan. There was a bloody pile of other bodies underneath, for whom there had been no convenient beam, and the crowd gathered to stare, and to spit and to curse. Men poked the swinging bodies with sticks, a woman fired half a dozen shots into Mussolini's.

But, of course, this was Italy.

It could never happen here.

Chapter 23

THE MIDGET SUBMARINES
AND THE *TIRPITZ*

THE story of the audacious raid by midget submarines on the German battleship *Tirpitz* is an epic of human courage—and also a multiple escape story; a whole series of escapes from what must have seemed certain death. Six midget subs were involved and one returned; but the casualty list was not as long as these figures would suggest.

The Germans in occupying Norway derived many strategic advantages. For one thing, they were able to protect the capital ships of their navy, when these were not actually raiding allied shipping, by hiding them far up inside the long narrow fiords which are such a feature of the Norwegian coastline. No ordinary vessel could penetrate to their anchorages, through anti-submarine nets, torpedo "cages", and the fire of batteries on shore. The German ships could be photographed from high altitude by reconnaissance aircraft, but they were out of range of R.A.F. heavy bombers. They were in fact as safe as any ship can be, once launched. And yet the damage these fast and powerful warships could do among allied convoys was enormous. The Royal Navy found itself contemplating the prospect of a midget submarine—something able to penetrate these German defences, get right up to the ships.

The first midget was launched in March, 1942, and named x3. She handled well in her trials, and soon another experimental one slipped unnoticed into the waters of an English river.

Well satisfied, the Admiralty put through an order for six operational midgets—x5, x6, x7, x8, x9, x10. Meanwhile they ordered an intensive training programme for potential crews, under the two young officers most experienced on x3 and x4, Lieutenant Donald Cameron and Lieutenant Godfrey Place.

There was much to learn, for the tiny craft were very different to anything else, above or below water. They were fifty feet long, a mere five-foot-six in diameter at the widest point, so no man could stand properly inside. They carried no torpedoes, no gun —only a pair of enormous H.E. charges, weighing two tons each, and slung over the little hull like a saddle. The operational crew would consist of four men. Such a craft was intended to creep up to its target underwater, slip underneath it and place the two charges on the sea bed. These would be detonated later, by time-clock. So large a quantity of H.E.—equivalent to a full torpedo salvo from a conventional submarine, thirty times its size—would be sufficient to cripple and probably sink any warship, for the bottom of a ship is its weakest point.

As for the subs themselves, there was the minimum of comfort for a crew: for this reason, as well as the diminutive size which made them less than seaworthy on the surface in bad weather, they would have to be towed to any scene of operations, and with a "passage crew". At the agreed start-point for the actual operation, the "passage crew", stiff, aching, exhausted, would be relieved by "operations crew".

There were casualties as well as headaches during training off the north-west coast of Scotland. Loch Cairnbawm had been designated "Port HHZ", advanced base for "x-craft", and long hours each day were spent in the little vessels, practising navigation as well as the problems of slipping through booms and submarine nets, cutting the close mesh of torpedo netting. A number of men and officers were killed during these manoeuvres.

The first three operational craft were delivered early in 1943 and it was planned to attack German warships in the fiords that spring. Then it was decided to postpone the attempt until autumn when all six craft would be available and more training would have been completed.

The Soviet Union, while loudly demanding a "Second Front", had been doing its best to make an operation of the sort envisaged off Norway quite impossible. Up-to-the-minute aerial reconnaissance was essential and for this the short-range P.R. Spitfires would have to use a Russian aerodrome. Their photos could then be flown to England by Catalina flying-boat. After months of obstruction, the Russians gave permission for one Spitfire flight to operate from Vaenga field. At this point they impounded the carrier-pigeons which Catalinas carried, "because it is illegal to import livestock into the U.S.S.R.".

But eventually, and despite the Kremlin, the expedition was ready to set off. The six midgets would be towed a thousand miles behind conventional subs to a rendezvous off the Norwegian coast, and from here x5, x6, x7 would attack the great battleship *Tirpitz*; x8 the pocket-battleship *Lutzow*; and x9, x10, the battle-cruiser *Scharnhorst*. They were all in small fiords opening off the big Lange Fiord—and the *Tirpitz*, with which we are concerned here, was in the little Kaa Fiord. The journey to rendezvous would take eight days.

They set sail on 12 September.

For the first three days everything went well. Then the weather got up, and one by one x7, x8 and x9 parted their tows. X7 was quickly hooked up again, but x8 fell far behind and was nearly lost, being only recovered the following day. Because of injuries she had sustained after jettisoning and destroying her charges —though these exploded three miles away—she was scuttled.

X9 and her passage crew were lost. Probably the heavy tow-rope parted near the towing *Syrtis* and dragged her to the bottom.

So only four out of six arrived at the rendezvous off Norway. As each crew had been elaborately briefed on its own target, it was essential these be adhered to: x5, x6 and x7 would still attack the *Tirpitz*, x10 the *Scharnhorst*. The *Lutzow* would be in luck.

Each would act independently of the others: x5 under Henty-Creer, x6 under Cameron, x7 under Place and x10 under Hudspeth slipped tow fifty miles out at sea and set off individually. The big subs prepared to wait and retrieve them, three or four days later—though there can have been few on board big subs or little who really believed this.

The big subs waited there four days, saw nothing. It began to look as if the midgets had failed.

But on the eighth day *Stubborn* sighted x10 and took her in tow. She was the only x-craft to return from the operation.

Lieutenant Hudspeth and his crew were taken on board. What had happened? Where were the other three?

Hudspeth's story threw little light on the fate of the others. X10 had got through the minefield at the mouth of the Alten Fiord but compasses and periscope had suddenly failed and she limped a few miles towards the Kaa Fiord before having to abandon the attempt, blind and directionless. It had taken Hudspeth a week to get back to the open sea. He had heard two very big explosions at about 0800 on the 22nd, and he hoped the others might have achieved their object.

They had. The *Tirpitz* was crippled, and it would be many months before she was able to put to sea.

Six men and all three midget subs attacking her had been lost—but it was months before the full story came out.

All three, x5, x6, x7, had managed to cross the minefield at the mouth of Alten Fiord, surfacing and sliding over the top. Place, commanding x7, had only recently married, and in the darkness—it was midnight—he shouted and waved at Henty-Creer, commanding x5, who had been his best man. Once over the field, they descended to periscope depth with a slight moon showing a jagged silhouette of land on either side. The R.A.F. and Admiralty had at last been able to produce charts and photographs, and armed with these all three captains felt reasonably confident of reaching target. Returning would be another matter.

Dawn came, then morning, then noon. They dived deep every time they saw an aircraft. Cameron's x6 had developed a faulty periscope, but by surfacing frequently for a second or two he managed to get to his "waiting position" among a group of tiny islands at the mouth of Kaa Fiord. Place's x7—though they were not aware of each other's presence—was already here. It was evening of the 21st.

Place and x7 got under way long before dawn: an hour later Cameron followed in x6. There was a boom at the entrance to Kaa Fiord which Cameron negotiated successfuly, despite his fogged periscope, by going through the narrow gap left for German shipping. A moment later—it was 5 a.m.—he came in sight of his huge target. *Tirpitz* was facing him and a mile away, a magnificent ship with towering superstructure that made her seem nearer than she was. In between were two tankers and a number of destroyers. He knew the battleship would be inside its own "box" of anti-torpedo nets, which he would have to enter, but, with a useless periscope, his first and most difficult obstacle would be other shipping. He dived to sixty feet, carried on by dead reckoning.

He came up again, inches from a destroyer. Miraculously, x6 was unnoticed, and he blundered towards the shore, inching round towards the *Tirpitz*.

He was lucky. A small supply ship was heading towards the battleship, and a gate was opened in the "box" for her to slip through. Cameron followed. The enclosure was much bigger than the ship it contained—even a ship as big as the *Tirpitz*—and while still inside it Cameron found himself aground. His frantic struggles—stopping, going forward, then back, then repeating it, again and again—got him free and flung him suddenly to the surface.

At this point he was noticed from the deck of the *Tirpitz* and the alarm was sounded. Cameron, without knowing this, submerged and headed, blind, for his target.

Place meanwhile was having almost incredibly bad luck with nets. Shortly after getting through the gap in the boom he was tangled in an empty "box" whose occupant was out at sea. It took an hour to get clear. A little later he was helplessly trapped in the "box" around the *Tirpitz*.

Another struggle and he broke free. Like Cameron in x6 he came to the surface as a result of the exertion, but unlike Cameron he was not seen. Miraculously, or so it seemed to Godfrey Place, he had come up inside the box with his target thirty yards away. X7 dived, struck the hull of the battleship twenty feet below the waterline, slithered underneath.

Carefully, Place released his port charge—two tons of HE.—

directly underneath what he reckoned would be a forward turret.
Then he motored slowly back along the ship's keel and dropped
his starboard charge underneath what he estimated would be a
rear turret.

Cameron in x6 had dropped both charges together, alongside
the battleship. He had surfaced, for he was blind at periscope
depth, had calmly selected the point, right under the ship's great
flaring bow, where he would like to place them. No one saw him,
though he had of course been sighted earlier.

Now, both charges away and his craft unseaworthy, Cameron
and his crew opened vents and let water rush in. As she began
to sink, the four of them scrambled out of the two hatches and
stepped into a convenient boat roped to the *Tirpitz*'s side.

A little later they were on board the battleship, being treated
with every courtesy, drinking coffee with schnapps. But it was
an unpleasant sensation, knowing that at least four tons of
amatol would explode right underneath in a few minutes' time.

Meanwhile Place was having difficulty with his compass and
had lost all idea of which direction he was pointing. A minute
after laying his charges he was stuck again in the net. More
manoeuvring and x7 escaped yet again—noting that the time
was exactly 0740.

He surfaced for a moment and was fired on by light automatic
weapons from the battleship: he was too close for them to bring
heavy guns to bear. Diving, he waited a minute before surfacing
farther out to get his bearings—but once again he was trapped
in a net.

Cursing, the crew went through the same old manoeuvres,
knowing the compressed air which made them possible was
running out. And—more alarmingly—so was the time before
the first charges went off.

X8, as we have seen, had jettisoned charges in the course
of her passage towards rendezvous, and sustained such injuries
when they detonated three miles away that she had to be
scuttled. What would happen to x7—with at least two charges
going up in minutes, perhaps seconds, and a hundred yards away?
Once again, the crew of x7 faced what seemed certain disaster.

The grim dilemma was soon resolved. At twelve minutes past
eight a first charge—it might have been either Place's or

Cameron's—went off, and the explosion detonated the other three. X7 was catapulted from the net where it had seemed she would stay forever, popping out of the water like a jumping porpoise, but badly damaged. Place just managed to dive her before the gunfire opened up again.

He found the sub would not respond to controls and water was pouring in. She would have to be scuttled.

They wobbled to the surface and he climbed out of the hatch, crawled a little way along the casing of the sub and took off his white sweater. He waved it. The firing which had begun, stopped abruptly.

Suddenly x7 began to sink. Water started pouring in through the open hatch, and before she disappeared it was slammed shut from inside.

There was a convenient battle-practice target floating a few feet away and—much as Cameron and his crew had done with the dinghy—Place hurled himself at it and managed to get aboard. A minute later he, too, had been taken aboard the *Tirpitz,* now badly damaged, heavily listing, and completely out of action.

It was at this point that her gunners saw yet a third submarine a quarter of a mile away and approaching. Panic mounted, for this little beast might well deliver the *coup de grâce.* Every gun still capable of firing opened up on Henty-Creer's x5 and she sank. Destroyers finished her off with depth charges.

The five captured submariners, Cameron and the three other members of x6's crew, plus Place, were below at the time, could only guess at what was happening. But uppermost in Godfrey Place's mind was: what had happened to the crew of x7?

She was on the bottom, crippled: at this very moment the three men aboard her were preparing to use their Davis escape sets. First they would have to flood the craft; but while this was happening, the fumes from the batteries as they filled with salt water made them put on their Davis sets and start breathing oxygen while they waited for the flooding to be complete.

But oxygen at high pressure, as we now know, produces the terrible symptoms of "the bends" within a few minutes, and both Lieutenant Whittam and Artificer Whitley died, even before they could get out of their craft. Sub-Lieutenant Aitken survived to get out, and when he was retrieved on the surface made a complete and surprising recovery.

The *Tirpitz* had been such a killer that by the cruel logic of war the loss of five midget submarines and nine men was deemed a fair exchange: *Tirpitz* would have destroyed thousands of tons of allied shipping, and many more than nine lives, during the months she was to be out of action.

Godfrey Place and Donald Cameron were both awarded the Victoria Cross—but it was months before they knew the fact or their anxious relatives in Britain knew whether they were alive or dead. Within twenty-four hours of being picked up by the *Tirpitz* they and the other four survivors of the raid were on their way to prison camp in Germany.

It was the end of September, 1943: the war in Europe had some twenty months to run. Having escaped death more than once in the course of their mission, they were denied opportunity to make a final get-away from prison camp.

Donald Cameron, who had been in the merchant service before the war, transferred to the Royal Navy immediately after it. He and Godfrey Place continued maritime careers in the rather less exacting atmosphere of peacetime sailoring. It seems doubtful if any situation would ever befall them, one half so desperate, or hopeless—or triumphant—as what took place in the early hours of 22 September, 1943.

Chapter 24

"GENERAL" FERTIG
CARRIES ON

ONE American escape is of staggering importance: had Douglas MacArthur not got away from the Philippines in 1942, the war against Japan might well have been lost, before anyone got round to making a nuclear bomb.

But this is not about MacArthur's escape. It is about another, closely bound up with it; the escape of a middle-aged mining consultant who wanted to go on fighting.

Wendell Fertig escaped from the Japs—but he never left the Philippines. He dogged the enemy for three long years, harassing, immobilizing them with his own private army while he waited, with the Filipinos, for MacArthur to return, and "The Aid".

"The Aid" came at last, but after so many frustrations—for Fertig—that it had come to seem as if the glittering general back in Australia was fighting a different war. Perhaps Fertig should have made more of an effort to get to Australia himself, for he, too, had been ordered there. He had tried, without enthusiasm, to obey the order, but rescue planes crashed, rendezvous were missed, and it seemed as if some power to shape men's destinies were determined to keep the temporary, middle-aged lieutenant-colonel in the islands he knew so well.

MacArthur's escape, like Napoleon's from Elba, was of colossal importance—but judged at this late date, purely as an escape and set against others of the genre, it is less than gripping. Like Napoleon's. Bonaparte left in comfort and dignity from Elba, and MacArthur, despite the breathless urgency with which he was awaited, left in equal, if not greater, comfort, with baggage, family and Filipino *amah,* in a Navy PT boat which could well have been molested but was not. It is not to denigrate the brilliant MacArthur that, almost by the spin of a coin, I have settled, in this book, for Napoleon.

But while Douglas MacArthur sped south to Australia, a gaunt citizen-soldier in the U.S. Army Engineers, one-time mining consultant from Manila, prepared to stay behind on the island of Mindanao and await his chief's return. His wife and daughters were out of harm's way, he knew the country and the people, he could look after himself—and he would stay.

But the decision to fight—this did not harden in his mind until 4 July, 1942, after he had been in hiding for two months. The hiding had not been arduous: he had quietly farmed for himself, planting corn, tobacco and beans in a jungle clearing. As yet, he had little need of home-grown produce: the Americans had left dumps of food and he had been able to provide himself with a fair supply. Wendell Fertig's agriculture was a therapy. While he scratched with home-made hoe, he thought, and planned. He worked slowly, carefully, and the crops, in that unbelievably fertile climate, seemed to spring from the ground.

Like dragon's teeth.

But on 4 July, 1942, he had taken time off from agriculture to find hiding place above the main road leading to the port of Iligan. Here, the Japanese had announced, they would hold a parade, and Fertig resolved to see it.

As he lay there, hidden above the road, it passed below.

First came a truck, moving very slowly, one man by himself sitting upright in the back. Behind, shuffling and stumbling along, now and then falling, being dragged up by their fellows, were hundreds of American soldiers. Some were barefoot, all were ragged. The Jap guards who marched alongside had tied the prisoners' hands together with telephone wire, each man to his neighbour, so that if one fell he dragged others with him.

And in front, in quiet dignity, sat their Commanding Officer, Brigadier-General Fort. The Japs had put him there as a figure of fun, something for the Filipinos to jeer at, but there was a sudden hush among the audience on both sides of the road as the gaunt figure passed by on its tumbril. The parade was not having the desired effect. Jap guards, sensing that something was wrong, began to stab more viciously at the legs and buttocks of prisoners with their bayonets, keeping them moving, keeping them up with the gaunt, strangely dignified figure in front, trundling down the road like an effigy in a New Orleans Mardi Gras—or, more exactly, a skeleton at some pagan funeral.

A soldier fell and was unable to get back on his feet. The men on either side struggled to raise him, but he flopped down again. Suddenly three Jap guards rushed the column, clubbed them aside, hacked through wires and dragged the man away. They raised him to the vertical and frog-marched him off the road, towards a clump of banana plants.

While Fertig watched in horror, two of the Japanese held the man up by his armpits and the third, taking careful aim, lunged with his bayonet.

There was a terrifying, astonishing, scream which echoed up to Fertig's hide-out as the steel went in. The Jap kicked the man's stomach with his boot, withdrew the crimson blade, and the American fell to the ground. The three of them bayoneted him, again and again, till the twitching was over. Then they kicked the body into the undergrowth and broke into a trot to catch up with the parade.

This, to Wendell Fertig, was the moment of decision. As he got up, he knew he must fight, and fight now. All that mattered was to kill Japs.

Already, though he had done little more, so far, than escape from imminent capture, he was much in the minds of the Japanese command. Their military intelligence told them, correctly, that he was the senior U.S. officer at large and a potentially dangerous one because of his wide knowledge and his standing among the Filipino people. The local garrison commander had already sent him a letter which for its ineptitude and comic phraseology ranks beside the one MacArthur himself received before his departure: "Do you feel duty to flow your blood while you have no master to serve for? You should not be so fooly as to flow your blood standing for America, when you comrades accepting Japan heartful advice are surrender. It is necessary to flow your blood on behalf of Philippines now? I believe God did not teach you to perform such a funny duty——"

God might not have. But the Japs themselves, bayoneting helpless men who were "accepting Japan heartful advice" to surrender, these had done so.

As he wrote in his diary, the moving document which he managed to keep from the Japs throughout three years in which he alternated as fugitive and pursuer, "I do not envision failure; it is obvious that the odds are against us and we will not consistently win, but if we are to win only part of the time and gain a little each time, in the end we will be successful——"

But in the beginning there were many obstacles, many enemies. One of these, who yet helped him get his "United States Force in the Philippines" under way, was a Filipino police lieutenant. Luis Morgan hated all white men, not least Wendell Fertig, and he was working hard to establish his own supremacy in the islands. With luck and ruthlessness he might easily become a man of power, a virtual ruler of the Philippines, before either the Japanese or the Americans were the ultimate victors: it made no difference to the young, handsome and arrogant Morgan. So far, he had deserted from the American forces to which he was attached, believing them the losing side. He had established a "Guerilla H.Q.", surrounded himself with men—and adoring women—who awaited his next move.

Fertig was not surprised when an emissary came from Morgan, asking him, as senior American officer in the islands, to take charge. Knowing the man as he did, he had no doubt that this was an expedient to win over waverers with the real, if sadly tarnished, lustre of an American rank. Equally, Fertig knew that Morgan would try to eliminate him, have him killed, when his usefulness was over.

He kept the Filipino waiting. Then he accepted—and took command immediately. A day later, thanks to the skill of a local silversmith, Wendell Fertig wore the stars of a Brigadier-General in the United States Army.

MacArthur, when he learnt of this, seems to have bridled. But MacArthur knew less than Fertig about Filipinos. If an American, at this stage, were to command the Philippines, he must do it from the top. And furthermore, his staff—these were as important as his own insignia, and for the same reason—must be suitably senior. Almost before he knew what was happening to him, Luis Morgan found himself Chief-of-Staff and a Colonel. Other men, American and Filipino, who had rallied to Fertig, were suitably promoted.

But generals, unlike dragon's teeth, do not grow up through the ground. This one had to have a pedigree. It was simple: he had been sent from Australia, he was the first instalment of "The Aid".

The word spread by runner, by drum, by rumour, by the garbled misquotation of "Brigadier-General Fertig's Orders of the Day". These, written in pencil on the back of an old army form with an impressive and meaningless "list of addressees" (there was but one copy), were suitably displayed on a suitable board on a tree. Their import was carried by word of mouth over Mindanao.

The new H.Q. of the "USFIP" would be the province of Misamis Occidental. Here, as yet, there were few Japs, and an army could be raised and trained in comparative peace. Fertig and another American, the faithful "Colonel" Hedges, now sailed across the bay from their hiding place to this new area, sailed with some dignity in a native outrigger, followed by others, bearing more than two hundred men, the advance force of a future army, a force which was stuffed like sardines into the vessels of its navy, spilling over the gunwales.

They landed at the little port of Tangub, where the whole population was there to greet them, bravely singing a cheerful American song for their new American General, even though he failed to recognize the words. "Some—Wheah—Over Rainbow——" came the refrain, a message of hope.

To Fertig's delight, the telegraph system of the province was still intact, operators at their posts. To the unspeakable joy of Hedges, who had, in what now seemed an earlier incarnation, been in charge of a motor pool, this pool was found to have been hidden from the Japs and to be intact. There was little fuel, but Fertig decreed that sugar be made into alcohol and the motors made operational.

Aided by the telegraph, recruiting quickened each day. At the same time the Japs, believing reinforcements to have been smuggled into Mindanao, made plans to get Fertig, dead or alive.

A few weeks later, as Filipinos and Americans—and Japanese —converged on the new H.Q., a radio transmitter came into being. It was perhaps the strangest ever constructed, for it followed exactly the schematic diagram provided by the International Correspondence School course in radio servicing, with its neat right-angles and its wide-open, easy-to-follow layout of components. In order to find space for such a distribution of parts and wiring, three walls of a wooden hut had to be used, with condensers, chokes and potentiometers nailed carefully on them, and yards of telephone wire between.

It worked, and someone was able to work it, though weeks went by before contacts were established. Fertig during his three years was to help many men and women escape, and the first party, which left now under his auspices, went in a small boat under a man called Charlie Smith. Smith took with him the information, for MacArthur's benefit, that the home-made transmitter had a call-sign, "MSF", the easy-to-remember series "Mindanao-Smith-Fertig". It was of course possible that the call-sign would never be heard.

In fact, it was heard often: but contact with it was impossible. The bamboo tuning-coil unravelled and spread the signal across all wavebands, so that operators in other lands either tried unsuccessfully to follow the unfamiliar signal across the tuning dial as it receded, or cursed the interference.

By the time Charlie Smith reached Australia, Fertig, despairing of contact, had forgotten about the call-sign. There was so much to do: collating information which came from all over the Philippines, from every bar-girl, every market trader; speeding up the manufacture of motor fuel as well as the rifle ammunition from conveniently-calibred curtain rods which abounded but had to be cut into lengths and sharpened; the training, the planning, the local government, all of it dumped into his lap. To add dignity to his unexpected rôle as Governor, Fertig grew a beard.

Casually one day the radio operator remarked that he had heard a persistent signal, "KSF to MSF, KSF to MSF". Fertig shrugged his shoulders.

Then he remembered: Mindanao-Smith-Fertig! Frantically, they pounded out a reply, again and again, and after a long delay it was acknowledged. Contact, though hesitantly, suspiciously and in an incredibly roundabout way, had been established with H.Q. in Australia. Fertig had no current codes available, so an ingenious one was improvised using names and addresses of next-of-kin in a double transposition.

Fertig knew that information about his organization, its aims, would have been handed over by Charlie Smith. But it was obvious from the tone of messages coming in that the organization was viewed with suspicion, if not outright hostility. What right had a temporary lieutenant-colonel to set himself up with general's rank?

Fertig had not cared about his own, but he was anxious that the ranks he awarded men in the field—who were fighting bravely, desperately, on MacArthur's behalf—should stick when "The Aid" came. His requests to this end were brushed aside, and he was referred to, curtly, as "Lt.-Col. Fertig" commanding only a piece of Mindanao, the "10th Military District".

But the information he was sending was valuable and hearts softened. A submarine arrived off Mindanao, to the hysterical joy of the inhabitants, and brought four tons of ammunition which seemed like manna and worked out at a few bullets per man. The radios which arrived with it were earmarked for "coast-watching": they would not be used for intercom within Fertig's army.

There was an autographed photo of MacArthur.

By now, Fertig had the hang of things. He wrote: "Your autographed picture is worth a million pesos in convincing the few remaining sceptics. Could you send my wife a duplicate? Mine will never reach home, for everyone insists on seeing it and touching it. The 10th Military District and Staff thanks you for the quantity of supplies. God grant that they continue to arrive——"

But, cynical though he had become, Fertig was beginning to

realize that MacArthur was but a small cog in a machine which stretched from Europe to Alaska, a war machine which had more pressing duties than the comfort and encouragement of the Philippines. Each thing in its turn.

The months lengthened into years, the quantity of information radioed to Australia grew daily. To his annoyance, Fertig had been ordered not to harass the Japanese, lest they lose patience and drive him out. He explained that occasional—and, of course, quite unauthorized—sorties did sneak out and kill a few hundred Japs.

A steady submarine traffic built up, and subs returned to Australia with men, women and children which Fertig's command had sheltered and in many cases saved from death. From time to time he was forced to flee, to escape from an exasperated Japanese Army which launched more than one major attack against him, supported by sea and air, and of magnitude sufficient to knock out a Singapore or a Pearl Harbour. He managed to go on sending back information.

Thanks partly to this information, thanks partly to the "island-hopping" strategy by which MacArthur left Japanese garrisons stranded all over the South-west Pacific, the invasion of the Phillippines began in late 1944 and continued, in January, 1945, with one of the biggest amphibious operations of the war, that against Luzon. Mindanao, where Wendell Fertig had been tying up 150,000 Japanese, was left to the end.

When the fighting was over, Lieutenant-Colonel Fertig, still, and forever, unpromoted, retired to civilian life.

It was 1956 before he returned from the States, on a business trip. With his wife, he was leaning over the ship's rail as they approached the jetty, wondering idly what was written on a huge banner just too far off to be legible.

Then they made it out. "Welcome the Indomitable Patriot Who Have Lessened Human Suffering on Mindanao."

And Wendell and Mary Fertig, shy and a little incredulous, stepped ashore into the most heartfelt reception the islands have ever given any man.

Chapter 25

THE *AMETHYST*

IWAS in Australia at the time, a radio announcer. And though
the announcement was made not by me but by one of my
colleagues, I shall never forget how I, and the whole country,
thrilled to the news. In a post-war world, starved of heroes, a
world suddenly and bewilderingly divided into Commos and
the rest, the courageous dash of H.M.S. *Amethyst* down the
Yangtse was as thrilling and heartening a piece of news as one
had heard for years. There were overtones of Dunkirk, of course,
the outnumbered, out-gunned British making an escape to fight
again another day, but there was more to it than that. One could
thrill to the picture of the little frigate, all by herself, belting
down the river, foam from her huge bow-wave washing both
banks, all guns firing. This was an Escape, with a capital "E".

China at this time was split in two, with the advancing
Communists along one bank of the Yangtse, the retreating
Nationalists—the Kuomintang—on the other. Britain still had
diplomatic representation with the crumbling Nationalist

Government in Nanking, two hundred miles up the river from Shanghai on the coast. A small warship was maintained there to "safeguard" the Embassy staff and other nationals who might be in need of it.

This is no place for a political commentary, but one may pause for a moment to consider how we, whatever the party in power, would feel if a Chinese gunboat were anchored off the Houses of Parliament, to ensure the safety of Chinese *restaurateurs*: the parellel is more exact than it seems.

But *Amethyst* was, as John Kerans puts it, in his own tale of the adventure, "on her lawful occasions". On 20 April, 1949, she was on her way to relieve the destroyer *Consort* in this peaceful and time-hallowed rôle of guardship.

Fifty miles short of Nanking, she was attacked without warning by a Communist battery on the north bank. Within minutes, twenty-three of her crew were dead or dying and another thirty-one wounded. She was badly damaged, stuck on a sandbank.

The urgent signal from *Amethyst* was received at the British Embassy in Nanking, just as *Consort* was preparing to be relieved and move downstream to the coast. There was nothing for it but to get her off immediately, rush her to the stricken *Amethyst* and see if she could tow her clear of the mudbank and get her up to Nanking where her wounded could be put in hospital. In the meantime, the British Ambassador, Sir Ralph Stevenson, sent a strongly-worded message to Mao Tse-tung.

There was no reply. *Consort* set off.

A few hours later she too had met crippling fire from the shore. Unable to turn round or make fast to *Amethyst*, she had sailed on past her, heading for the open sea.

The situation was serious indeed. The Ambassador sent his Assistant Naval Attaché, Commander John Kerans, to investigate. The Chinese Nationalists had reported a few survivors reaching their side of the river and being taken to hospital in Chingkiang, the nearest town. Kerans set off at speed for Chingkiang, in a jeep.

When he got there, he learnt that *Amethyst* had succeeded in getting off the mudbank under command of her Number One, her captain having been mortally wounded. They had hurled everything portable overboard and with engines racing had broken free. Now she was anchored a little way out from the shore—and so far there had been no renewal of the Communist attack.

Kerans eventually reached the shore opposite her and tried to board her from a Chinese sampan. He failed, because she was changing position constantly with the current, and he failed also to make contact with messages flashed through the darkness from his torch. After a bit he returned to Chingkiang, telephoned the Embassy and suggested he try to get out again and this time, if he succeeded, take over command and try to get the ship upstream to Nanking.

The Embassy agreed.

Kerans made it this time, with the help of a Nationalist assault craft, and was horrified at what he found. His first task was to get away a great many wounded, including the courageous Number One, Lieutenant Weston, and to bury seventeen bodies over the side.

The next step was to attempt the trip to Nanking. He called the survivors together, explained the situation.

But now, exasperatingly, a message came through from the Embassy: he would evacuate survivors promptly and sink the ship. The safety of his ship's company was to be his first consideration.

He countermanded his earlier orders, explained the new ones. A thick and appropriate fog descended over the Yangtse and in the midst of it, scarce able to see what they were doing, the crew set to work. They had just destroyed the code books when a new order came, postponing the evacuation and the sinking. Patiently, John Kerans sat and waited for the next lot.

Nothing came, and the hours lengthened into days. A few ships of the Nationalist Navy slunk past at night, heading for the sea. On one occasion the sky was bright with explosions, shore batteries opening up, the ships returning fire, and utter confusion reigning.

Suddenly, the idea occurred.

Surely, in bedlam like this, one might be able to get *Amethyst* out into midstream, head her for the sea, and escape? A thousand-to-one chance—but better than staying here.

It would take careful preparation, as well as suitable traffic on the river, and for days no traffic appeared. Then, without warning, they were hailed from the shore in Chinese. The Chinese steward, Sai-Tin, translated: "They want you, send boat and officer, sir——"

The ship's whaler was so badly damaged that it would be a perilous business attempting five hundred choppy yards of water in it; but it would be still more perilous to refuse. With so few officers surviving, Kerans decided to dress his strongest swimmer up as one. Grinning, Petty Officer Freeman set off in lieutenant's insignia.

He returned after an unpleasant interview with the local Communist commander. *Amethyst* was accused of opening fire and causing heavy Chinese casualties, and it was made clear that she would stay where she was until "full compensation" was paid and "guilt" admitted. Any more trouble from her and she would be sunk.

Days passed, with more visits, some less painful than others, between ship and shore. Then the visits stopped and four weeks crept by. The fuel oil, which was needed to keep *Amethyst*'s electrical and ventilating systems going, even when she stayed stationary, got lower and lower each day. Kerans noted this with dismay. Soon he would not have enough to move, safe conduct or no.

Without safe conduct. The idea came back.

Next came a demand that he come ashore and "solve by negotiation the responsibility that ought to be assumed by H.M. ships which have done the brutal acts on 20 April in invading the battle front of the China People's Liberation Army——"

Kerans went ashore, headed for the Communist H.Q. at Chingkiang.

He was ushered into it, and suddenly what seemed every flash-bulb in Asia exploded in his face. He was greeted courteously and the interview began on a friendly note, only to end in anger when Kerans was called upon to "admit guilt of British fleet". He would not—and pointed out that in any case he was hardly qualified to do so.

Very well, then. No admission, no safe conduct.

More meetings followed and on each visit Kerans took a new member of the crew, trying to put as many in the picture as possible, in case he were killed. No one was killed, but rations, as they dwindled, had to be cut to half, as was the electric power, so that for twelve hours out of every twenty-four there was no ventilation. As spring turned to summer and the weeks crept by, he was forced to cut power for two or three days at a time, with the crew gasping for lack of air. With little optimism, he asked the Communists to provide fuel oil.

Three weeks later a small supply came—with a "delivery charge" of £400.

On 30 July John Kerans decided the time had come to use his own initiative. Even after the delivery of fuel oil, his supply came to only thirty-nine tons; minimum to reach the sea was thirty-three. Now or never.

At half-past six that evening he ordered the engine room to get up steam, but as quietly as possible. An hour later he had a meeting in his cabin and told the delighted senior ratings that they would break out at 2200. In the meantime, screens would be prepared to alter the silhouette of the ship, white paint would be darkened as soon as dusk fell, brasswork would be coated in black grease, light clothing removed.

Dusk fell and the work of disguise was well advanced when the local vegetable contractor arrived in his sampan. While friendly delays were put in the way of his coming on board, screens were hastily removed, light clothing donned, in a frantic effort to make things seem normal. At last the little man was allowed up, bringing not only vegetables but heaven-sent (and hellishly-expensive) bottled beer. Beaming, pocketing his money, he descended his ladder and was lost to view; and a moment later, the screens were back in position. Kerans considered his plan in more detail. There were a hundred and fifty four miles of river ahead, and the first fourteen would be as perilous as any, for apart from the Chinese batteries which covered them they were completely uncharted.

Then, out of the darkness, luck came their way.

There was a familiar rumble, the steady thud of a marine engine, and a Chinese merchant ship came round the bend, fully lighted.

It was too good to be true. "Ring on main engines——"

They had been stationary for a hundred and one days.

Silently, in the darkness, anchor was slipped. "Slow ahead port——"

Hardly daring to believe his luck, Kerans turned round in mid-stream, got astern of the merchant ship as she chugged by, kept up with her. Soon they were steaming silently past the battery whose orders it was to cover them.

A flare burst high above and the Chinese ship acknowledged with blasts from her siren. Hastily, Kerans did the same, but the ruse failed and the night was hideous with the stutter of machine-guns. A shell burst off their starboard bow.

"Full ahead both engines!"

Faster, faster. The whole ship trembled and shook, her guns thudding into the shore positions.

Suddenly they were hard against the Chinese vessel; then with an inch to spare they shot past, both ships now in utter darkness and black camouflage smoke from *Amethyst* blanketing them both.

In another minute they were well past her—and to make the affair more memorable they could look back and see the merchant ship burst into flames, hit by her own batteries. *Amethyst,* too, had been hit, and the crew worked desperately, plugging holes, manning pumps.

They reached the dangerous King Yin boom, a line of sunken ships with only the narrowest gap through which a vessel could pass, marked by lighted buoys. Only one was visible. It was anybody's guess and Kerans left it to starboard.

Miraculously, they were clear. Now they had travelled two-thirds of their journey; a hundred miles had slipped by in the roar and confusion; they had left battery after battery firing hopelessly behind them, firing at each other, at their own ships, at the sky.

They had improvised a code, much like that used, elsewhere in this book, between the fugitive Wendell Fertig in Jap-occupied Mindanao and American H.Q. in Australia, a code utilizing details of next of kin. Telegraphist French, who had worked single-handed in his choking, airless wireless cabin for a hundred days, bashed out messages, progress reports. Kerans requested that *Concord,* now at the mouth of the Yangtse, support them with covering fire if necessary. "Can do," came the reply.

They got nearer to the menacing fort of Pao Shan, with the long white finger of a searchlight feeling the water, groping for them. Kerans ordered the engine-room, "Give everything you've got!" and the little frigate shuddered and went still faster.

They were in range of the searchlight now; they had been picked out, they were bathed, soaked, in light.

But no—they were underneath the beam. And ahead of them they could see dawn, and the sea. And freedom.

At 0529, with scarcely a drop of oil left in *Amethyst's* tanks, Kerans made out the shape of *Concord*. She grew larger, clearer, more distinct. Then, with a rush, they were past her, sailing triumphant into the open sea.

INDEX